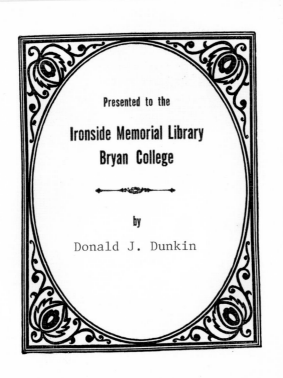

# Merry Widow

# MERRY WIDOW

*by Grace Nies Fletcher*

William Morrow and Company, Inc., New York    1970

# *Author's Note*

This book was designed neither as an autobiography nor as a travel guide, but rather as an invitation to laughter.

After a daily newspaper diet of riots, wars, and sudden death, I thought it might be amusing to tell about some of the gay, light-hearted, exciting people whom I had met on my last four trips around the world as a merry widow, free for the first time in my life to do exactly as I pleased. In short, the world was my oyster.

But a book, as it comes alive, has a way of thumbing its nose at its author, shouting like a small boy up to his ears in mischief, "Hey, Mom, look at me!"

There are so many kinds of laughter. He who has never known tragedy may explode with loud guffaws or the giggles of adolescence, but he cannot know the deep, quiet joy that comes with the conquest of sadness, or the relief of the discovery that laughter and tears are two sides of the same coin with which we pay our debt for the miracle of just being alive.

I have borrowed from some of my earlier books, therefore, happenings both ridiculous and tender that make clear how

I came to be a merry widow, to whom "a merry heart doeth good like a medicine." My thanks for permission to quote from my own books are due to the following: *In My Father's House*, McGraw-Hill Book Co., Inc.; *Preacher's Kids, No Marriage in Heaven, I Was Born Tomorrow, The Whole World's in His Hand, The Fabulous Flemings of Kathmandu*, and *The Bridge of Love*, all published by E. P. Dutton and Co., Inc.; and *What's Right With Our Young People* and *In Quest of the Least Coin*, published by William Morrow and Co. Thanks also to the magazines *Reader's Digest, Woman's Day*, and *The Christian Herald*. Where direct quotes are made, I have given credit at the bottom of the page, but frequently only the bones of an incident have been reassembled in order to explain how the skeleton later became full-fleshed and robust.

Most of all, my thanks go to my beloved Polly, with whom I island-hopped around the Pacific and whose wit and laughter are a joy forever.

GRACE NIES FLETCHER
*Sudbury, Massachusetts, 1969*

# Contents

# CHAPTER 1
# *Merry Widow*

It took me three lives to become a merry widow.

This title was thrust upon me involuntarily by a television MC in Baltimore who was introducing me as the author of my book, *What's Right With Our Young People?* He cast one dubious glance at my rimless spectacles, saw I was no Helen of Troy whose face had launched a thousand ships (I'd be lucky to launch a canoe), and reached for some valid reason why I should be sitting there in front of his cameras, anyway.

"This lady *looks* like a schoolteacher," he began, "but . . ."

"What's wrong with a schoolteacher?" I interrupted, bristling.

Too late he realized there might be some irate school marms in his TV audience and fumbled desperately. "She *looks* like a schoolteacher but she just got home from her fourth trip around the world in six years! She's . . . a merry widow!"

When you lose your entire family, when after thirty

years of a happy marriage your husband dies and your only son marries and moves three thousand miles away, you either panic, decay into self-pity, or are born again, an embryo growing, eventually emerging into an entirely new world.

Some of my best friends in the Orient cling to the belief that what we do in this life determines whether in the next we shall be born again as an elephant or mouse, as a flea or Buddhist saint. However that may be, instant transmigration *by choice* is to me no more miraculous than instant coffee; a change of personality can happen here and now to anyone, at sixteen or sixty. I know, because it happened to me. This is the light-hearted story of how I changed from a "Preacher's Kid" who could not dance, play cards, go to the theater, or even chew gum, to a gay, insouciant widow who, as I jetted from Occident to Orient, could (and did) pick up any man I wanted to and call him "friend," and put him down again if I found him uninteresting. Dates of birth and death are mere pinpoints in time. Where and when I was placed, squalling, in my economical, ecclesiastical, prune-box cradle is important only to me. One is born alone and dies alone and who else truly cares?

I had been too busy to count birthdays until after Jock and Rick had gone away. All my days up to then, I had been primarily daughter, wife, and mother . . . and loved it. Now I had no one to consider but myself. I realized, shocked to the bone, how little time I had left to do what *I* wanted!

So in 1960 I issued my own private Declaration of Independence and pasted it upon my dressing-table mirror. It went like this:

*From now on, I solemnly swear to*
1. *Refuse to be bored.* People en masse leave me cold; they take themselves too seriously, not a grin in a clubful. I will never listen again to "the minutes of the last meeting"

drooling on for aeons. Individual men and women I enjoy getting acquainted with; like onions, they have many layers you can peel off to find the real person. But that takes time and you can't strip inhibitions in a crowd. So I swear off women's guilds and indiscriminate cocktail parties.

2. *Do the things I like NOW!* For thirty-five years I played bridge because my husband (whom I adored) enjoyed it. Now he is gone I can say flatly, "I don't play." If I want to stay in bed till noon, eat oysters I know don't agree with me, I shall. Mine is the tummy ache. One thing is certain —I'm not going to stay home with a couple of cats and wait to die.

3. *Enjoy my grown-up kids the way they are and not try to make them over.* You can't anyway. If they've got faults, heck, I'm no angel. Warn them I shall never baby-sit for my grandchildren (if any) unless I want to.

4. *Go out with any new man who asks me.* I like men better than women; men are more transparent, you can see through them easier. But I don't want another husband. I'm still married to Jock, wherever he is. Besides, at my age, either candidates have pot bellies or you can imagine their dentures bubbling in a glass by the twin bed.

5. *Turn off the commercials on TV.* I'm sick of the advertisers' idea of "young love" that has girls ooze out of bottles of hair oil and owls offer you cigars. If that's love, I'm a chimpanzee. Or, as my mother used to call it, "cat and dog business."

6. *Remember the unimportance of THINGS.* If someone steals my car or a rabbit eats my delphinium, it can be replaced. It's even fun to *give* away now what you most cherish to those who can appreciate it, like my sixteenth-century Persian water color to a talented artist. After I'm gone, what will I get out of distributing my bits and pieces? Not hurting *people* is what matters, for these wounds hurt me as well as them.

7. *Study the dissonant "now" music and abstract art to see if it's the musician or the artist who is making a fool of himself or if it's me.* It's a great, wide, wonderful, crazy world and, good or bad, I want to be a part of it.

8. *Go to all the strange, mysterious places I have the cash to buy a ticket to.* I want to ride an elephant in India and go down the Nile on a barge like Cleopatra.

9. *Get acquainted with myself.* I might be a pretty nice person. How do I know?

But how to transfer resolve into action? How to shed old ties without giving offense? The New England Women's Press Association (they had once given me a gold medal for the best magazine story written that year by a New England writer. Query: what does one do with a gold medal? You can neither frame it, eat it, nor give it away) asked me to stop by Brandeis University to pick up their luncheon speaker, Mrs. Eleanor Roosevelt, because I knew her. She was a grand person; she even remembered that my son, Rick, had recently had a severe case of measles at the age of twenty-two and asked how was he and his spots. But club luncheons with chicken, canned peas, "headtables," as well as taxiing, were just what I wanted to get away from. I was fed to the teeth with lugging around Cub Scouts and Little Leaguers and wilting flowers from the church altar to sick parishioners. How did one shed one's dutiful skin to become a "what's that to me" merry widow? Why did I feel so strongly that I must, to stay sane? The new life would have to be exactly that, different, keep me looking ahead, not backward to the days I had loved.

It was Charles who sold me on the Orient, which I had never seen.

"What has happened is over, Susie," Charles told me firmly after Jock left me alone in our small white New England house, once so cozy, now an empty shell.

Charles and Miriam, his wife, had long been our closest friends. His keen mind and ability to put himself in the other fellow's place—he could tell you the most unpleasant facts in such a nice way that they changed into a challenge instead of a disaster—had taken him far above us financially. As counsel for one of the biggest banks in New York City, he flew as casually to Goa, London, or Hong Kong as I drove my little Falcon from my suburban home into Boston. He is so used to planes, I think he could go to sleep on a bar stool (he never drinks hard liquor) and wake up, fresh and ready to go, in Paris or Moscow. But he'd taken time from his busy world to drive his big Continental down to Jock's funeral, mostly to make sure that I was all right. He urged, "Come down to New York. Take an apartment."

"I must get farther away than New York," I told Charles. "Not from you, my friends. *From my old self.*"

"Why not go to India?" Charles suggested. "Miriam and I are going there next November. There's something about your first trip to the East . . . it's a sort of glory, a mystery of mind and culture that you can discover only once. The World Council of Churches is holding its Assembly in New Delhi. . . . Now hold everything. I know you're through being a Preacher's Kid. You just made that clear. But this should be exciting. The Russians want to join for the first time! Someone's sure to yell, 'What? Communists!' But I don't see that the political system under which you live need keep you away from loving God . . ."

"Using what for cash?" I countered, but an expectant glitter was already in my eye. I added recklessly, "While I'm that far, I might as well go on around the world. Sail down the Nile, hunt tigers in Nepal!"

"Sure thing," Charles agreed as if I'd said I'd run over to the children's zoo at Franklin Park near me. He kissed me and left.

One bright New England morning, I took the plane to New York and told my favorite editor who'd been obstetrician for four of my books that I wanted to spend a month in India. I wanted to ride an elephant, and to see how the Russians and the Archbishop of Canterbury got on together. What happened in New Delhi might be the first step in East and West cooperation that would hold off the Bomb. Having gone this far in dreaming, I added airily, "I might even interview the Dalai Lama of Tibet!"

"How much advance do you need on the new book?" was all my editor asked. So now I had a ticket! "A New England housewife visiting a Buddhist God-King—that's a good line, Grace."

(My parents, who grew up in Texas, had christened me "Grace-Susan." I'd kept the "Grace" professionally, but those who knew me best called me "Susie," as Dad and Charles had. But "Grace-Susan Nies Fletcher" sounded like a lady lecturer in a flower hat, heaven forbid!)

I was secretly a trifle timid about taking off all alone for the unknown East. How did one say in Japanese, "No, thank you, I don't want any raw fish"? If only I knew someone to go along, not to hold my hand, but just to be there. Someone who was already a merry widow? Then I thought of Polly. She'd been left alone, as I was, except for her lovable black and gold cocker spaniels. "Amigo and Chica are *people,*" Polly explained. "This is their home as well as mine." I knew Polly only slightly, but what I knew I liked. The "now" generation may have decided that senility begins at thirty, but actually one can lose his elasticity of mind at eighteen as well as eighty. If youth meant being independent, spicily witty, gaily, even stubbornly herself, Polly was it. So I called her up in New Mexico, without waiting for the night rates, to ask her to go with me across the Pacific.

"We can pick up any likely candidate in the jet or on the beach," I cajoled, trying out my blandishments for size, "since we're both beyond the whistle stage."

Polly sniffed. "*My* ankles are still good."

I bristled, "My hairdresser swears I haven't a gray hair!"

"You still come from Boston. It's a state of mind. Watch and Ward Society peeping through keyholes! 'Sacred cod,' my eye! Do they still keep it in the State House?"

"It's been there since 1700 something—but it doesn't smell because it's wooden."

"Of course. We were stationed once in Massachusetts."

Polly is Army with a capital A. She had grown up in both East and West, with the world as her backyard. As her lieutenant father had advanced in rank to become Commanding General of the Philippines, she'd lived her geography instead of looking at pink and blue blobs on a map. She'd shopped in Boston, New Orleans, Juarez, Dallas, as well as in Peking, Hong Kong, Tokyo, and Manila. She and her sister spent their early teens galloping on their ponies all over rugged Corregidor while the entire command looked out for them, saw they got home safely in time for tea. She also learned that a lady always carries two pairs of white gloves, one to wear and the other to keep in her handbag in order not to be caught short. Early she knew her own mind. At nineteen she married Chuck (a medical officer whom my Jock admired because the good doctor combined compassion with a delicious sense of humor) in the Episcopal Cathedral in Manila where her Papá gave her away. As time went on, with Papá with stars on his uniform collar, with Chuck a colonel in the Medical Corps, with Toby, her son, a colonel in the Air Corps, and with young Chuck, her grandson, preparing for West Point, Polly had, indeed, an impeccable army of her own. But, under all this weight of gold braid, she had remained unimpressed, yet ready for duty when needed. After the war when the Manila Cathedral, bombed by the Japanese, was being rebuilt, Polly, with no money to spare from raising three children, gave two blood transfusions. "I got fifty dollars for it, too! I wanted to send something of *me*, not what had been given to me!" The Orient to her meant nostalgia, romance, home.

As I waited on the phone for her answer (at a dollar a minute?) she murmured, "I haven't been back to Japan since Chuck was in command of St. Luke's Hospital in

Tokyo just after the surrender. Houses were so hard to find, we camped out for weeks in the Stock Exchange Building; we had to queue up for the john in the corridor."

"We could shop in Hong Kong," I tempted her.

That did it. Shopping to Polly is what a bottle is to an alcoholic; not just buying things, but getting her money's worth, is an exciting game she'd learned as an Army brat who had to make the most of a fixed income.

"I'll meet you in Los Angeles," Polly agreed. "But I won't spend a month in India . . . people starving all over the sidewalks and you can't do a thing about it . . . I don't think much of world missions, either; we've got enough hungry people in this country to feed. But I'll spend the November you're in New Delhi in Bangkok, meet you in Kathmandu. They say you can buy a Tibetan prayer wheel there for almost nothing."

Bangkok, Kathmandu—magic, wonderful names. . . .

"Why do you want a prayer wheel?"

"Oh, it might come in handy." Polly warmed to the hunt, promising, "We'll have fun. If you say *law* instead of *lawr* and *water-r* instead of *watah*, no one will know you come from Boston."

I threw back my head and laughed joyously as I hung up the receiver. To sniff high adventure, all one needed was a Polly.

We took off from Los Angeles with Toby, who as a test pilot had helped to get rid of the bugs in the Boeing 707 in which we were flying, kibitzing the takeoff, to be sure the pilot knew his business. Next stop was Tokyo. Polly and I looked in vain for the house to which she and Chuck had finally moved from the Stock Exchange; since the houses were numbered by the dates on which they were built, rather than their position on the street, and several million Japanese had been born and housed since the war, the address was too needle-in-the-haystack even for the taxi driver. Polly gave up and shopped happily for pearls (wholesale) for some fifty friends, sent them home in neat packages (ten dollars). So avid was she for proper shipping material that one morning she even accosted a strange man in the hotel elevator to demand, "Where did you get that nice box?"

"At my tailor's," admitted the startled stranger. Then he grinned admiringly at Polly. Was it really her ankles? "Just wait till I empty it. I'll send it to your room." The accompanying note said, "With the compliments of Australia."

All too soon the day came when Polly, true to her warning, packed her needlepoint and bright-colored wools for busy work and took a slow freighter to Bangkok while I flew on alone to India. I had to change planes at midnight in Bangkok. I never was so lonesome in my life, nor so lost. At that time, before the city became a favorite R and R for GIs from Vietnam, the small airport had no air conditioning or screens; you sat wilting on a hard bench in a temperature soaring around 110°, looked directly out at the planes landing on the tarmac, and swatted some six million mosquitoes all intent upon making a meal out of your hide. Miserably I watched the small Thai sentry with his gun, marching up and down the concrete. Here I was, alone at midnight, in a strange, hot country where I didn't speak a word of the language. I couldn't understand if that soldier out there said, "Advance!" or "Halt!" I could be swatted out like one of those mosquitoes and no one would ever know what had happened to me!

I was so homesick my teeth ached. Suddenly there was a great whoosh and an enormous Globemaster landed on the airfield. *It had the Stars and Stripes painted large upon its side!* I picked up my bag and began to run down the steps out toward that lovely plane from home. The little Thai guard ran up and pointed his bayonet at me, but I pushed it aside.

"That's *my* flag!" I yelled. "Get out of my way!"

He didn't dare shoot and he didn't dare not to, so he just

ran after me, jabbering, as I flew out to that plane. By the time I arrived, breathless, the ramp had been let down and was debouching tanks, guns, and other military whatnots, but the Navy boys in crisp white uniforms laughed at me and waved off the frantic guard.

"She's O.K. Just a nutty American," one explained to the Thai.

"Nice nutty?" I hoped.

"Sure!" He grinned.

As I chatted eagerly with a boy from Brooklyn and another from Oregon, I wasn't homesick any more. I *was* home.

Among the three hundred newspaper men and women reporting the Assembly at New Delhi for practically every country in the world, I was merely a comma. We newshounds all met together every morning at an ungodly 8 A.M. to be briefed upon what was happening among the godly that day. The morning when the Russian Orthodox group were to ask the World Council for membership, the pressroom was buzzing in so many excited languages, the Tower of Babel wasn't in it; in every seat someone was clamoring for the chance to ask the chairman a question. This tall, handsome presiding bishop from Ceylon, regal in his purple robe and red cummerbund (that's what it looked like to me, anyway, though I doubt that is its ecclesiastical name), looked out at the forest of waving hands.

"I feel like a mosquito in a nudist colony," he confessed. "I hardly know where to light!"

"On the Russians!" the Reuter correspondent beside me yelled.

The Russian delegation proved not to be mysterious at all, merely "funny peculiar" to Western eyes, in their long black robes, fabulous "holy" jewels, and Orthodox stovepipe hats. The youthful head of the group (now the Most Reverend Nikodim, Metropolitan of Leningrad and

Ladoga) had a bright red beard that stuck out aggressively as he marched up to the platform. There was an electric silence, but nobody yelled, "Reds!" Suddenly one man got to his feet, then another, till all the hundreds of delegates were standing to welcome these Christians from a new and powerful country. So that was that. They were in.

That night I had dinner at our hotel with two of the Russian priests, neither one of whom could speak any English, but the one with the long bright hair (who looked like Jesus) spoke German. Conversation was limited, however, since all I remembered from my college days was, *"Dies ist das Haus das Hans baute,"* and *"Deutschland über alles."* Neither seemed appropriate, so we beamed at each other while I admired the encolpion, a sort of medal that hung on a golden chain around one priest's neck; when he handed it to me to look closer, I saw the white stone in the center (jade?) was carved beautifully with the Virgin and Child. Circling this central work of art were emeralds as big as peas, another circle of rubies, and then one of diamonds about four times the size of my engagement ring. Hastily I handed the fabulous work of art back before something happened to it or I was tempted; whereupon the second priest unentwined a few feet of a rosary, stunning with huge topaz beads, and pushed it toward me to goggle at, explaining, *"Von der Ukraine."* If anyone had told me four months ago that I would be swapping diamonds and smiles with a couple of Russian priests at a dinner table in India, I would have sent for the little men in white. This was, however, the last steak dinner we had in New Delhi because the Hindus rioted when they heard the hotel was serving "those barbarian Christians" with holy beef, so we had to go back to rubber chicken and goat meat.

The Archbishop of Canterbury proved less gorgeously jeweled than the Russians, wearing merely a regal robe with a heavy silver cross, but his robe was of purple since he ranks only just below royalty in England. He swept through the lobby like a mighty purple wind, so that even when I got permission to speak with him from the colonel who guarded his privacy, I had to interview him "on the air," so to speak. I got more information fortunately from Jim, a young American who was writing Mr. Ramsey's biography. Mrs. Ramsey was a friendly little English woman dressed as quietly as a lady quail, who meekly followed in her husband's train. Or so I thought till one Sunday when I found out who was the boss in that family. We were coming out of the cathedral after service, where her husband had officiated in a dazzlingly bright golden outfit but in his stocking feet in deference to the Indian priests who always serve communion in their bare feet to show humility. The Indians kicking off their sandals seemed proper enough, but it was disconcerting to kneel at the communion rail looking down at the Archbishop's socks. Many of us were going on to the American Embassy for lunch, and as His Grace and his wife appeared at the church door, a dissonant brass band, sent in his honor by the President of India, burst uncongruously into "There'll Be a Hot Time in the Old Town Tonight." Mrs. Ramsey, raising her voice over the cymbals, called to her gorgeous husband in his royal purple robe, "Hurry up, Duckie! We'll be late!"

Jim was having a difficult time getting facts for Mr. Ramsey's biography: not only did he have to chase after His Grace from dawn to dusk, but since all the hotel rooms in New Delhi were filled with delegates, Jim had to sleep in a broom closet. I had, however, a room not only with bath but with a tiny balcony looking out at the lovely Indian lacework screen of the American Embassy. So when I got permission to have an audience with the Dalai Lama in Upper Dharamsala, an Indian town nestling among the Himalayas many miles north of the capital, I asked, "Jim, how would you like to keep my bed warm while I am gone? You may have to sleep in my sheets, as I don't want to alert the hotel that I'm to be away; they'd probably rent my room before I called 'Taxi!' But you could have a bath; I get clean towels every day."

"How'd you get permission to see His Serenity?" Jim demanded. "I hear that takes some doing."

"It's all in knowing the right people," I assured him lightly. "I've never seen a real live Buddha before."

"Nor," chuckled Jim, "has he met you! Sure, I'd love using your room."

So I packed my bag and Jim sneaked it out through the dining room to the taxi; but while I was picking up my gloves and handbag, the phone rang. "Mrs. Fletcher?" a strange voice asked with just a hint of accent. "Will you have dinner with me? I am to be your host next month at the hotel in Kathmandu." I explained that I was just running to make a train but he insisted, "In that case, I'd better go with you to the station. It's a little different from the Grand Central. I used to be a train man here myself."

The smiling Indian gentleman who arrived at my door smelled like a whole field of violets and had a lace-edged handkerchief peeping out of his coat pocket, but when we got to the station, complete with my sleeping bag, elegant with embroidered sheets, pillow cases, and a blanket which New Delhi friends had lent me because the sleeper would furnish only a hard bench, I was glad to have my violet-scented friend along. The racket was terrifying. Hundreds of families were keeping house here in the station; you had to step over babies, old men, young men with lady relatives in saris. By myself, I'd have turned and run; I would never have found the sleeping car with my name tacked up on the outside. But I reached my compartment safely where Anne, an English newspaper woman who was also going to interview His Serenity, was waiting. I thanked my flower friend heartily, locked our compartment door behind him, leaned back, and began to laugh.

"What's the joke?" asked Anne.

"I'm just thinking about my room boy's face at the Ashoka when he arrives next morning with my tea and finds a strange man in my bed!"

I wasn't doing so badly turning into a merry widow after all; I'd held the fabulous Russian encolpions in my hand; I had met the President of India, Nehru and his daughter Indira, when they visited the World Council, "Duckie," Jim, and my flower friend. But, as yet, no elephant.

Pathan Kot, where the Dalai Lama's jeep was to meet Anne and me, turned out to be the end of the railroad; it seemed as if we'd never get there. We'd brought our own water and sandwiches, for we didn't dare buy chapattis and fruit through the window for fear of getting "Delhi Belly," crippled by which we could hardly climb a Himalaya to the Heavenly Abode where the Indian government had perched His Serenity. It was noon the next day before we got wearily out onto the platform to look for his jeep . . . it wasn't there. Not even the ticket agent talked any English. We were standing on the platform, wondering what to do next, when we spied a bus. It was so crowded that people's arms were sticking out the windows; there were even people up on the roof, but . . .

"You going to Upper Dharamsala?" I yelled to the driver. When he shook his head blankly, I tried desperately, "Dalai Lama?" That worked. He shoved a couple of Indians and their luggage off the front seat and motioned for us to climb up beside him. I protested, "But they got here first!" The driver, waving his arms, exploded again into a fusillade of Hindi.

"He says they're going only to the next village and this is a through bus to Dharamsala," an educated voice translated through the window. So Anne and I climbed aboard. It didn't seem possible that this ramshackle, overcrowded bus could ever climb a mountain; but it tried. A thousand feet below on the right of the narrow road, already crumbling along the edges so that they'd put out a few tin cans to warn drivers, lay the valley full of jagged rocks, while ahead and miles up were the Himalayas. Every time another car passed us coming down, we scraped paint. The bus groaned, swayed, grumbled ahead; when finally it stopped, I ate a banana, trying to show how unconcerned I was; but the driver only sighed, got out, plucked a twig from a nearby tree, jiggled something in the engine, and we crept painfully on up.

"Oh my goodness, look at that crazy man coming down the road!" gasped Anne. "He hasn't got a thing on but ashes . . ."

"Quiet. He's a Hindu holy man," I told her.

"Well, we could do with a few prayers," shuddered Anne.

" 'This road isn't passable, not even jackassable,' " I quoted.

As we finally and gratefully drew up safely at the bus stop, we could see a long line of black-robed priests coming down the muddy main street of Upper Dharamsala, holding their skirts high to show skinny legs. "Something tells me this is the welcoming committee from His Serenity," I surmised. It was. The jeep, it seemed, had broken down and there were no spare parts available. The tiny Austin sent to the village to transport us to the Heavenly Abode farther up the mountain already had six monks sitting in it, but to squeeze us in, several monks sat on each other's laps, and I sat on Anne's.

One monk proved to be the court interpreter, who warned us, "His Serenity doesn't speak English. Every word has to go through his Secretary of State and then me, I speak."

"Good grief," I muttered to Anne, "how are we going to chat with a God-King who doesn't understand a word we say and everything has to be translated twice?"

For the first time, hungry, dirty, and sleepy, I got cold feet about the whole thing. The Dalai Lama was not only reverenced by millions of Buddhists as the reincarnation of Gautama Buddha, but was the rightful ruler of a mysterious country few seemed to go to except Lowell Thomas. And the Reds, of course, who'd grabbed his kingdom so that in 1959 he'd had reluctantly to flee over the snow to save his life. Then I recalled the recipe for not being scared of VIPs which my dad had taught me long ago.

"Just remember to ask yourself," Dad had advised, "how does he look in his nightshirt?"

Arthur Guiterman had commented along the same line:

> The tusks that clashed in mighty brawls
> Of mastodons are billiard balls.

> The sword of Charlemagne the Just
> Is ferric oxide known as rust.

> The grizzly bear whose potent hug
> Was feared by all, is now a rug.

> Great Caesar's bust is on the shelf,
> And I don't feel so well myself!*

Me either. But remembering Dad and the mastodons, I sat calmly in the royal antechamber of the Heavenly Abode, while the King's courtiers bustled around us anxiously, with grave faces, making sure we had folded properly (according to some Tibetan Hoyle) the white silk welcoming scarves they had provided for us to lay reverently over the hands of the God-King.

"What happens to them then?" I asked.

"Oh, he gives them back to welcome *you.*"

It was time to go. His Serenity had been meditating on

*"The Vanity of Earthly Greatness," in *Gaily the Troubadour.* E. P. Dutton & Co., Inc., New York, 1936. Reprinted by permission of Vida Lindo Guiterman.

a mountain peak for four days, but was now ready to see us, the Secretary of State explained portentously. A cute pug-faced puppy skittered against my legs. "The little dog of the Dalai Lama," we were told. "He also has five hundred children. Shoo, you!"

"But I thought monks didn't marry!"

"Orphans whose parents were lost or frozen during the Great Trek from Lhasa," the courtier explained coldly. "They are all under seven."

Children and dogs . . . The Dalai Lama must be nice.

He was twenty-seven, exactly the same age as my Rick. Under a colorful canopy, a faded remnant of former glory, he sat there quietly on a shabby divan as regally as if he had been on a golden throne in the Potala Palace in Lhasa with its hundreds of steps by which one climbed to majesty. The gold-colored paint his courtiers had hastily slapped upon the walls of the Heavenly Abode was already peeling off to show the original blue underneath. But this tall, grave young man in his maroon robe with the white at his throat, patiently regarding me, who had impulsively come nine thousand miles to see him, with wise calm brown eyes behind his glasses, was regal without even trying. This God-King with his beautifully molded head, his high, untroubled forehead, his sureness and aura of inner peace, needed no dragons or thrones; his kingliness shone from inside—his jewels were invisible but eternal.*

Democrat that I am, I felt like dropping to my knees. I quavered, "Your Serenity, do you think that the strength of the spirit will ever win out over guns and napalm bombs? Bring peace to the world?"

"Most certainly. As man learns the futility of force, that no one wins but everyone loses. But this wisdom will take a long time in coming, as the killing of Jesus and Gandhi

*The Whole World's in His Hand. E. P. Dutton & Co., Inc., New York, N.Y., 1962.

has shown. You can't force men of ill will into peace. You must win them. What we have to try to do is to try to change the focus of men's minds."*

"But is there time for that? Before the Big Bomb wipes us all out?"

"Time is in the hand of Buddha," he shot back in my own tongue.

"So you *do* speak English!" I cried, delighted.

"A leetle." He smiled, but dropped back into easier Tibetan. "Buddha is everywhere. His Light sifts down, broken by the clouding sins of men, to many people in many ways. We must focus this Light upon world problems. You are a mother?"

"Yes, I have a son."

"Ah, then you know that love must be practical, homely as bread. I have my five hundred children here on this mountain to feed and shelter . . . and love."

"Do you ever expect to go back to your kingdom, to Lhasa?"

His voice rose fiercely, passionately. "Certainly I will go back! I and my people! I teach my children here our ways, our songs and history. *They must never forget that they are Tibetan!*"

A lump rose in my throat. What could a few thousand hungry, homeless, homesick people do against the endless hordes of Red China? But these Tibetans trusted in the Light—like the Israelites who had had the cloud that went before them by day, and at night the Pillar of Fire. I said softly, "I am an American and an Episcopalian, but I, too, believe in the Light." I asked Gautama Buddha: "Would you—will you give me your blessing?"

He rose majestically from his shabby throne, came toward me to hold the white welcoming scarf across my lifted hands, and murmured in Tibetan. I do not know what he said, but to me the words were a benediction.

*Ibid.

Tears came to my eyes as I backed out of the Serene Presence to whom losing his throne, poverty, were mere accidents of this life, negligible in eternity.

"How could you, a Christian, ask for a Buddhist's blessing?" an angry letter demanded when I told part of this story in my later book, *The Whole World's in His Hand.*

I wrote back, "Because he is a good man who loves dogs and children, who talks with God on a mountain. As Moses did."

I wanted a memento of this strange day in the Himalayas. As I walked back to the Dak bungalow where Anne and I were staying, I saw a skinny little Indian who looked as if he hadn't eaten for days, lying on his cot that had only a webbing of rope, no mattress or blankets. But beside him was a case displaying beautiful intricate silver ornaments, while on top of the case was a little pile of powdery, gray-looking silver.

"How much would you charge to make me one of these?" I held up a Hindu marriage ornament to lie on a woman's forehead, with the chain to go back through the part in her hair. A small child standing beside me, proud of his schoolboy English, translated, "He says it depends upon how much silver he uses."

I picked up between my thumb and finger what might be enough, dropped it into the jeweler's palm. He nodded and smiled, trusting me. Hours later I came back to claim my Hindu wedding jewelry. It was beautiful, a sort of encolpion of my own on a slender chain, its flowers enameled in red, gold, and blue, with a tiny heart hanging down in the middle of my forehead. I wear it around my neck with nostalgic pride.

I finally got my elephant ride in a howdah going up to the pink palace in Jaipur, but I was still so bemused by the beauty of the Taj Mahal which I had visited the day before that even an elephant was an anticlimax. The

*Ibid.

monument to a man's love for a beautiful woman, Momtaz, actually lives up to its billing. Small wonder that this marble palace of remembrance, with its insets of semiprecious stones, its delicately fretted screens, took 22,000 workmen seventeen years to build. After these many years, it still distills such a gentle essence of romance and remembered ecstacy that two of my American friends took one look and got engaged to be married!

But once in a howdah is plenty, I found; right there I gave up my idea of shooting tigers in the Nepalese Terai from elephant-back like the King of England. I'd be too seasick to aim my gun.

It was in Hawaii, on my way home alone to Boston, that I finally made it—became a certified merry widow! The adventure began with a green cotton bathing suit I'd bought in India to wear in the hotel pool. Apparently the manufacturer had never heard of sanforizing, for by the time I was ready to come out of the water, my suit had shrunk till it was practically a bikini. I was about to toss it into the wastepaper basket, but instead threw it into my suitcase. Honolulu was as ghastly humid as only it can be. From my hotel lanai, I looked longingly down at the swimmers disporting themselves in the long, cool pool. Oh well, nobody knows me here, I thought, and it's so beastly hot. And I reached for the green bikini. Down at the pool, however, I wasn't alone for very long. I'd barely swum the length of the water, stretched thankfully out to lie with my eyes closed, enjoying my new coolness, when a man's voice asked, "May I sit here beside you? You remind me of my wife."

"Well, that's a new line, anyway," I murmured, opening one eye. He was a distinguished-looking gentleman, if wet. He wore only bathing trunks and a straw sun hat.

"I really mean it! She died two years ago. Here!" He handed me his card; he must have carried it in his hat, for it was dry. The name was vaguely familiar, for I'd read it this morning in the newspaper; he was a VIP flown here to address some international lawyers' convention, I recalled hazily. "The dinner's an awful bore and probably I will be," he confessed engagingly. "But I should be able to get away by ten and we could have some fun. What number is your hotel room?"

I told him my room number but neglected to add that I wouldn't be there; I was checking out that afternoon to visit my cousins in Aiea. I have since regretted this evasion. How the mores of one's childhood do cloud one's adult common sense! Doubtless all the poor man wanted was as simple as he said—companionship. Now I'll never know.

CHAPTER 2

# I Become a
# Grasshopper in Spain

Merry widows do not, like Minerva, spring full-panoplied from the head of Zeus. They grow to independence through long years of baby bottles, adolescent pimples and emotional explosions, to the final shock of being left alone, kicking at circumstance, as blindly as any fetus. Only then, having shed their responsibilities to their family, can these ex-mothers pass out of the womb of time and custom to be born again *as themselves*. The manner in which this new life grows and develops depends upon the genes she carries over from her former incarnations.

As a child in a Methodist parsonage, I had been brought up on the rugged maxim: "Go to the ant, thou sluggard; consider her ways and be wise." From this it might seem that I enjoyed my third life as an emancipated merry widow better than my first incarnation when my brother, Ike, and I were all bound around with Puritan " don'ts." Quite the contrary. The springtime of our innocence was a happy one because the rules that governed it were so clearly defined; so long as you stayed within the guidelines you were safe. The children of today's chaos know no such security but have to manufacture their own rules and morals. A smug Victorian childhood is rather to be envied than sneered at.

My father's house had many more "dos" than "don'ts" and brimmed with laughter. Dad lived meticulously by the rigid rules of the Methodist Discipline; he never smoked tobacco, drank "liquor," played cards, or went to the theater. ("What *did* he do, then, Sue? Watch TV?" My grandnieces call me by my first name, in the modern manner. "There wasn't any TV then, darlings.") Beyond these rules, Dad's mind was free as a bird to light where it would, and we Preacher's Kids caught his liberal ideas by the tail. He held that feeding five thousand people with a small boy's lunch was no miracle at all, but perfectly normal. He took Ike and me out to watch a farmer harvesting a great field of wheat.

"The rain has watered the seed and the sun has warmed it, and now it is ready to be ground into flour so that you can go down to the corner grocery and buy a loaf of bread for five cents," Dad said. (Five-cent bread in those days was actually a "true fact," as the TV commercials advertise today, to my annoyance. What is an untrue fact?) "The only element added in order to feed five thousand from five small loaves and a couple of fishes is to speed up the *time.*"

Ike and I needed neither parables nor Einstein's formula $E=mc^2$ to understand the relativity of time. I was a hopeless tomboy, so Mother, sighing, bought me the same sturdy boy's shoes as Ike wore, black with little brass dinguses to hook the lace onto. When we were climbing trees or playing baseball, the hours flew, but it took aeons to cut and rake the parsonage lawn.

"Truth may be relative also," Dad went on dreamily. "What is sin for the Orthodox Jew may be permitted for Episcopalians; the Hindu drinks fruit juice instead of whiskey. What matters is the *reason* a man does what he does, if he is sincere . . . 'without wax,' the Romans called it. Even in those early days, crooked builders used to put wax in the cracks of pillars they were erecting because it was cheaper than substituting new, flawless ones."

Courtesy was as commonplace at our breakfast table as oatmeal, and as obligatory. Ike and I knew better than to spat until we were alone and could pull each other's hair in peace. Ike had a Buster Brown long haircut, which made it easier for me. But if Dad and Mother had ever quarreled in our hearing, our world would have been shattered. It was years before I realized that Dad's first name was not "Lovey."

Every night no matter how late he was getting home, sitting up perhaps with "some poor dying sinner" (Ike's phrase), Mother would be awake, waiting for him. She'd call downstairs when she heard the front door open, "That you, Lovey? You all right?" He would shrug off his weariness to call back in his rich tenor voice, "How could I be anything else? *Ich liebe dich.*" This was the phrase engraved on the back of the tiny gold cross set with infinitesimal pearls he had given her instead of an engagement ring. When I'd asked, "Why in German?" Dad had explained, "So it will be private to your mother and me."

To offset the stern Methodist ruling that we P.K.'s couldn't go to the theater, Dad used to read Shakespeare with Ike and me, and he sold his beloved *Life of John Wesley* to buy two season tickets to the Boston Symphony. Taking turns, we would sit behind the white-haired, haughty Beacon Street grandes dames with their necks tied up with black velvet ribbon to hide the wrinkles, and let the waves of glorious sound roll over us. Dad loved music with a passion; he used to weep at the sad bits and during the wild ride of the Valkyries, he'd mutter, "Go it, baby!" He could not read music, but he played the piano by ear and even composed anthems for the choir. When he hopped out of bed in the morning, his brisk tenor would waken us kids:

"The earth is the Lord's and the fullness thereof!"

"The world and they that dwell therein," Mother's high soprano would answer, adding, "Breakfast's getting cold and it's almost time for school!"

Ike and I would fall out of bed, chanting sleepily, "For He hath founded it upon the seas and established it upon the waters . . ."

We also sang, "I had a horse by the name of Napoleon all on account of his Boney-part," to the accompaniment of Ike's guitar. (Yes, children, we did have guitars even in those antediluvian days. You didn't invent the blues, only new words. We, too, used to wallow in happy gloom while we chanted, "Close the shutters, Willie's dead. Hope for him has fled.") Thus we flavored with nonsense our days in the parsonage which had so much to do with tears. People sick, in trouble, about to go to jail, or afraid to die rang our front doorbell, and likely stayed to dinner, so Mother's food bills were enormous. Tension in such a mental hospital could have been terrific. Laughter was the antidote. So we sang corny rhymes and played Flinch, which was permitted because the cards had no King, Queen, or Jack but only numbers. Ostriches with our heads in the sand? Perhaps. But it was nice, therapeutic sand.

I was sixteen and Ike thirteen before we were allowed to attend a stage play. It was, of all juvenile entertainment, *Macbeth*. We knew the bloody tale so well that when Macbeth paused on the stage for effect, Ike prompted him so loudly from the second balcony that the usher came running. "You kids shut up or git out!" How could we leave when Ike was Macbeth himself and I his lady? They were as real to us as our milkman and his wife.

. Most comforting of all, we kids had a Friend who was a powerful member of our family, who could do the impossible if He wanted to. Every morning at breakfast Dad would read briefly from the King James' Version; the verse I liked best was "underneath are the everlasting arms." When I was three, I thought God was a begonia plant. When I asked, "What does God look like?" Dad took me over to the dining-room window where the pink blossoms were flourishing gaily under the sun and Mother's watering. "Whatsoever things are lovely . . . that's God," Dad said. But that night I got a better idea. Because they couldn't afford a baby-sitter, Dad and Mother used to take me to choir practice on Wednesday nights. It was as dark as the inside of my mitten in the Sunday School room where they put two chairs together, seat to seat, to make a bed and laid me down, but I wasn't scared because I could hear the choir singing "Rock of Ages, cleft for me . . ." By the time they got to ". . . hiding in Thee," I was asleep. After rehearsal I'd only half wake up when they came to take me home. I'd feel the roughness of Dad's jacket under my cheek, his strong arms lifting me surely, gently, so I snuggled closer into his shoulder; and I knew what it meant, "underneath are the everlasting arms."*

In fact, I got so well acquainted with the Lord, I treated Him like another child. When I was too tired after climbing trees all day ("Susie, nice little girls don't do that!" "Well, I do!") I'd murmur, lying in my soft bed instead of on my knees, "Good night, Lord. Have a good sleep!" and slide into dreams. God didn't seem to mind. I don't think He wants us to go around all the time shouting, "Holy, Holy, Holy!" Of course, there's a time for worship and awe. But I hated the stern Big Eye on my Sunday School card which warned, "Thou, God, seest me." A God who didn't relax once in a while was only a policeman; at least

*Golden Moments of Religious Inspiration, edited by Ruth Elmquist. McGraw-Hill, New York, N.Y., 1954.

He might wink a little. I was to see the Eye of Buddha later, painted on a temple in Nepal, and get the same uneasy feeling of a prisoner being stared at through a peephole during his most intimate moments. Funny, a Buddhist and a Methodist a world apart would get the same screwy idea.

Actually, it was Mother who first introduced me to the "mysterious Orient," which she longed to visit but never would. She had a "thing" about people from far-off lands, and if there was a foreign student or a missionary from China, Japan, or India who landed in Boston and didn't eat at our table and sleep between her verbena-scented sheets, he must have been a Roman Catholic, who was even more alien to her insular Protestant culture. Usually the visitors left behind strange or sweet-smelling gifts, a red silk Indian scarf gilt at the edges, a ginger jar from China (it still stands on my living-room table, made into a lamp), a tiny piece of cool-feeling jade, or a small gold lacquered box from Japan. These whispered to me of adventure, of that far-off, impossible day "when I grow up and can do as I like." That such travel would cost a year of Dad's salary didn't occur to me. I was sure, however, I did not want to be a missionary; usually their long skirts draggled at the tail and they prayed too long at breakfast. For years the sweaty, sweetish smell of the cane-seated dining-room chair before which I knelt those mornings meant to me the magic incense of the Far East. I knew that some day I must go there. Meanwhile, all I could do about it was to try to write down my thoughts "without wax." My first verses were published when I was eight.

Many years later, looking through my manuscripts, pictures, the family diplomas (three of us graduated from Boston University: Dad, my son Rick, and I) to send to the university library, which was making a collection of my stuff for use by their students of "creative writing," I came upon a forgotten piece published in *A College Anthology for 1916–17*. The verses were hardly poetry, but a good mirror of the point of view of the "then" generation:

### God's World and Mine

They tell me heaven lies afar
Beyond the silent skies;
But I saw heaven yesterday
In Little Brother's eyes.

They say God is a fabric spun
On mind and fancy's facile loom;
But He and I talk face to face
Within my quiet room.

They tell me love is but a dream
Of passion, lips, and bursting flame;
But sun-kissed, in the white daylight,
Love, my Love came.*

By this time I had met Jock and fallen deeply in love. His baptismal name in the Anglican country church records of the island of Jersey was "Vivian." Two people brought up with more different backgrounds than he and I would be hard to find. Perhaps the far corners of the earth were again calling to me, for my first trip to England was to meet Jock's mother. To him, I suppose, I was roots in a new country.

Vivian had been educated in an English public school in Horsham, called Christ's Hospital, where the schoolboys proudly had worn dark-blue monk's coats, ecclesiastical white collars, gray moleskin trousers, and yellow stockings since the days of Edward the Confessor. After his father died, young Vivian (he was seventeen) had come to the States, graduated from Dartmouth College into the American Army, gone overseas from Boston with the 55th Coast Artillery Corps to fight in France. The

*The Poets of the Future, edited by Henry T. Schmittkind. The Stratford Co., Boston, Mass., 1918.

United States rewarded him with citizenship. After the war he adjusted again to civilian life by attending the first class of Harvard Business School, which was then huddled ignominiously in a basement in Cambridge instead of within its present ivied walls. "Vivian" had been changed hastily to "Jock" by his GI buddies from East and South Boston who could hardly countenance a girl's name in their lusty outfit. Especially for a man who had been promoted for bravery on the field of battle! So I called him "Jock," too.

And so England and America were married.

Jock never quite made the transition from the noblesse oblige of the English gentleman to the "dog-eat-dog" of American business, but his gentleness made him easy to live with. Our differences salted our days. It took a national depression to shatter our smug happiness, to teach us to "take what you want when you can get it; the opportunity may never come your way again"; to become sun-happy grasshoppers instead of ants.

One of Jock's Harvard professors was responsible for his being offered what was to us a fabulous salary to go out to Detroit to help build up the financial kingdom of which Henry Ford dreamed. Why go to Wall Street for financing? Let Wall Street come to you. By that time I was writing for the "slicks," *The Saturday Evening Post, McCall's, Ladies Home Journal, Scribner's, Century,* etc. We decided to save all of my not inconsiderable income, to invest this and as much of Jock's salary as we could spare in bank stock or in the company where he worked. So we rented a tiny apartment, squeezed the buffaloes on our nickels till they bellowed, experimented with peanut butter soup (it's horrible!), and hoarded like ants for the winter of our content.

"At the rate we're going, we'll soon have fifty thousand dollars!" Jock beamed. "On paper, anyway. When we're forty, we can retire, go around the world to pick out where we'd most like to live. I'd love to show you Jersey where I was born. It's a green little, sweet little island."

"Let's go!" Why not? We had as yet no children to worry about.

"Extra! Extra! All Michigan banks close!"

Till the newsboy yelled under our bedroom window one February morning, we had no inkling of disaster. Frozen into unbelieving statues, we stared at each other. Jock tied his tie meticulously, then rushed for the door to go to his office, forgetting breakfast. He came back at noon, with his tail feathers dragging. "It's my guess our company will have to fold up, so I'll have no job. Call me an investment man! If only I hadn't been such a fool as to buy into our company and that other stock with double liability!"

I swallowed, hard. Fifty thousand gone down the drain? It couldn't be possible! Not to mention all our scrimping wasted . . . I asked in a small voice, "How much would we have left?"

"Only our five-hundred-dollar government bond."

"Then let's spend every penny of that!"

"Oh, I say, darling, we have to eat . . ."

Jock's grim prediction came true. He looked so sick in body and mind, so defeated, that I was angry rather than depressed. I sniffed. "I'm sick of going to the ant, thou sluggard! Let's go grasshopper for a change. When I was in New York last week, selling an idea to *McCall's*, it was raining on Fifth Avenue, dirty newspapers blowing around my wet ankles. There was an ad in the window of the American Express showing a girl snowed under with almond blossoms and sun. So I went inside to ask where this was. 'Majorca,' he said. 'In the Balearics. I understand you can live there for a dollar and a half a day. May I sell you a ticket?'" I lifted my stubborn chin, the gift of my German peasant grandmother. "Now he can just sell us *two* tickets! Neither of us are morons. When we spend all our bond, we can come home and each get some kind of job. If it's only selling apples."

Mad, impossible, Jock kept muttering. Two weeks later we had stored our bits and pieces, were on the *Europa* sailing steerage to London, en route to Majorca. Grudging every penny, we landed in one of those grimy Russell Square cheap boardinghouses, full of broken linoleum and colonels' widows. It was a safari to the john, which sat in solitary glory on the landing, down two floors. Our bedroom had no heat unless you put a shilling in the slot; since the corridor windows were always wide-open to the chilly March wind and rain, you had, perforce, to run a marathon to the basement where they served breakfast. The teeny who waited upon us had adenoids and wrinkled stockings; I didn't know such runny-nosed waifs existed except on stage. She asked that first morning, "Will you 'ave heggs or 'addock?" She added sotto voce, "The 'addock's spiled."

We had heggs and then wished we hadn't. But our luck changed at Barcelona. The American Express courier who met us turned out to be a German who'd fought on the opposite side from Jock at the battle of Château-Thierry. They fought the battle all over again so happily at lunch that, instead of taking our tip, the courier tipped *us* with great juicy oranges when he put us aboard the "Pig Special" for Palma. The ship got its nickname from its chief cargo, enormous black Majorcan pigs fed on figs. Frequently the figs became fermented and the pigs staggered about below decks, but the resulting hams were considered great delicacies in Barcelona at Easter. Our stateroom above deck was a stenographer's dream, walled entirely with mirrors, which made Jock so embarrassed he turned out the light to undress.

I slipped out on deck early the next morning to watch the ship dock at Palma. The misty harbor was filled with opalescent light that ran a bright finger along the tops of

the surrounding hills, and the air was filled with the music
of church bells. When Jock came up behind me, I said
dreamily, "All those little white houses along shore, even
that big castle, are kneeling together, praying to that big
cathedral up on the hill in the center of town."

"Such a racket!" grumbled Jock, who hadn't yet had his
coffee. "When's breakfast in this joint?" But already he
looked better, alive again instead of defeated. Being a
grasshopper agreed with him.

We rode to the Grand Hotel in a horse-drawn covered
wagon with saints painted on its canvas sides. "Informations" (his title was on his cap) who met us at the door with
a shower of *"Buenos días!"* was a student of history. When
I handed him two letters to mail, I asked, surprised, why
the postage to the United States was less than that to
England, which was so much nearer to Palma.

"It is because the United States is a colony of Spain," he
explained grandly. "Did you never hear of Father Juni-
pero Serra who built the missions on the heathen coast of
California? He was born here. And so the postage is arranged."

"Oh," I said.

Informations motioned to a bellhop, so tiny he barely
topped our heavy bags, to lead us to our room. Informations warned, "Please be sure to lock your bedroom door
when you leave. Then hang the key on the hook on the
wall outside your door so the chambermaid can come in.
Things," he said darkly, "are not what they used to be."

We didn't dare even to smile until Jock and I were alone
in our bedroom full of soft air and the sound of bells. "It's
wonderful! Alice in the Looking Glass!" I flung myself into
Jock's arms and he kissed the back of my neck. He said
suddenly, "We've been grubbing around too long for
security in a world where there isn't any. We've been too
busy these past years to get acquainted. Hi, there, Mrs.
Fletcher!"

"I hope when we have children," I murmured, "and they do something crazy like this, we'll remember!"

Jock's face clouded, for we'd been married almost twelve years and the much-wanted son had not materialized. Partly, the doctor had explained, because we were both too busy at our careers, too intense to relax. "We'll remember," Jock agreed gently.

We were enchanted with Palma, but when we heard that one could live cheaper by the sea at Puerto Sóller, we moved there on an electric train with a tiny toy hoot. A sign on the wall warned solemnly that a passenger who emitted a two-peseta swear word might land in jail.

"That lets us out," I said cheerfully. "We didn't know even how to swear in Spanish. All I recall from high school is 'The little boy needs a napkin!'" I never saw a little boy use a napkin the whole four months we were in Sóller; usually he used the back of his hand.

But Puerto Sóller was perfect for relaxing. Small, white-washed houses were strung in an ivory necklace along the curving seashore and wound on up the hill. We found a room up over a restaurant where we could get bed and board for a dollar and a half apiece per day. The room, mostly filled with a big white feather bed, was very clean and had one wooden hook upon the wall to hang up Jock's hat. But our window was the door to the ancient Roman Empire.

"The proprietor says that lighthouse out there was built to get the triremes of Julius Caesar safely into the harbor!" Jock reported. "There are only three Irish tourists here—Quakers, no less." I didn't know there were Quakers in Ireland! But they'd surely come here to this peaceful island. The quiet outside was so deep you could imagine a ghostly Julius Caesar walking up and down the yellow sand. Clanking? No, that was the Toonerville Trolley which had brought us here from the station.

From early dawn, when the fishing fleet came home

from its nightly labors, to noon when a lone housewife mending her husband's net sat on a three-legged stool under our window as she hummed to herself, till dusk when we sat on the tiny patio in front of the restaurant, watching the enormous stars come out and hearing the lovesick youth on the village street behind us singing a *novia* to his ladylove . . . we were terribly busy doing nothing. Of a morning we would bestir ourselves to climb to the top of a tall cliff to look out from the ruins of a Moorish watchtower at the miles and miles of empty, unbelievably blue Mediterranean. The air was so still we could hear the sea sighing four hundred feet below us. Behind us, down beyond the orchards bursting with pale almond blossoms, a farmer was talking to his horse as they plowed.

"*Arri!* What a beautiful morning! Take care, my friend. Do you see that big stone? I will move him away. How silver the leaves of the olive trees, blowing in the wind! Be happy that you too belong here, with all such wealth. *Arri*, you slacker! Get up!"

"Let's never leave," Jock murmured, relaxed as a snail on a leaf. "By the way, those Irish Quakers at the hotel want us to join them on a trip to the monastery of Lluch. On top of Puig Major."

"Poo what?"

"The highest mountain in Majorca. They want to ride donkeys up to see the Black Virgin, as the old-time pilgrims did."

"Why be a pilgrim?" I was too sun-lazy to move a muscle.

"Oh, don't be a kill-joy. Ramon Llul, the patron saint of Majorca, founded a school of philosophy up there, which has now been turned into a school for choir boys. It's quite the place for honeymoon couples." He smiled at his bride. Naturally, I agreed to go.

When we got to the village square that morning in

Sóller, all the villagers were hanging out their windows waiting to see these crazy foreigners fall off their donkeys, which were milling around uneasily. I almost weakened. I hadn't ridden since I was a teen-ager in Texas on my grandfather's ranch and the harness on Felicity, my steed, was tied together with string. The saddle was wooden with a thin sheepskin thrown over it, and when I leaped astride and felt for the stirrups, there weren't any. The only thing I had to hold onto were the panniers filled with our lunch and overnight bags, hanging on either side of the beasts.

Julia, the wife of the eldest Quaker, had a donkey so woebegone and limp that she promptly slid off over its drooping head.

"You hurt, darlin'?" Her husband ran up, but she said bitterly, "No. But I'm all of a jelly, just. I feel like Mary going to Bethlehem." She looked at the steps ascending the terraces on the pilgrim path by which we were supposed to go up the mountain. "If she'd had to ride upstairs like that, Jesus would have been born on horseback!"

Actually, it was exciting to be a pilgrim, once you got used to a donkey climbing. The yellow stone steps went up and up between the olive trees, some of them a thousand years old. Since there is a tax on new olive trees in Majorca, the thrifty peasants merely graft new shoots onto the ancient twisted roots, generation after generation. The result is a forest of hobgoblins.

"*Arri!* Get going!" yelled the head groom, and his three boy helpers echoed him shrilly, urging the donkeys along up the steep ladder path. I looked down at the valley a thousand feet below, shuddered, and grabbed for a comforting pannier with one hand and for the string-patched bridle with the other. But the view was worth the risk; wave after wave of delicate orange blossoms foamed down to tiny white dollhouses in the village; beyond that shimmered the magnificent blue acres of the sea.

The wooden saddle was paralyzing my legs. "I'll walk like a hoop by the time we get there," I called to Jock on his discouraged-looking nag. "Hey, you have a horse! What's his name?"

"Rosinante," Jock yelled back. "He's a her!"

It was later in the afternoon when we finally arrived at the monastery on the top of Puig Major and hobbled stiffly across the paving stones to the little chapel where the choir boys were already singing vespers. Holding candles, they marched round and round, chanting like cherubs, before the Black Virgin of Lluch. She really was black with age, or perhaps with the good earth where some peasant had dug her up from under a bush. What did it matter whether she came from heaven or from Rome? The flickering lights, the silver sound of the boys' singing rose about her gentle face like incense. I dropped to my Methodist knees, for here, kneeling in this holy place, all men were brothers.

We were hungry enough from a day in the open to have eaten uncooked dried cod, but the monks served us a delicious dinner, lamb from their own flocks, young vegetables including tiny new potatoes from their garden. We pilgrims made up our own beds with handwoven linen sheets the priests gave us, but before Jock and I could climb into the tempting feather bed, a young monk rushed into our room. "Señor! Señora! Your passports and marriage license, please!"

Jock handed over our passports but explained our marriage license was back in the States; we hadn't known we'd need one.

"Unless you can prove you are husband and wife, each of you will have to sleep alone in the male and female dormitories," the monk insisted firmly.

It was too cold to sleep alone; I needed to warm my feet on Jock's back.

I dug into our one bag to hold up our two toothbrushes. "Here, look! Mr. and Mrs.!" I cried.

"Si, si, señora." The monk beamed and left us.

As we sank our aching bones gratefully into the soft feather bed, Jock groaned. "That bad?" I asked. "Try lying on your stomach."

"It isn't saddle sores," Jock murmured. "When I paid the good monk the three pesetas for our supper, I suddenly realized . . . we've spent all our cash except about a hundred pesetas, about twelve dollars. How are we going to pay our way home? Why on earth didn't we buy a round trip ticket on the *Europa?*"

"I'm pooped. Go to sleep. We'll worry tomorrow."

But even cheerful grasshoppers have to face facts when winter comes. We needed $200 and we needed it badly. "The Lord will provide," I'd been taught in my parsonage home, but sometimes, I'd found, you had to give Him a gentle shove. We wondered all the way back to Sóller (in a bus, thank heaven, for there was a road down the other side of the mountain as well as our rocky pilgrim path) whether we'd have to wash dishes for ten years at the restaurant, for our keep. I asked hopefully, "If we stowed away on a ship, would we be allowed to land in New York? After all, we are free American citizens!"

"Free to go to jail," Jock pointed out.

As we walked wearily into our bedroom at Puerto Sóller, a letter lay waiting for us, tossed upon our vast snowy bed. It was postmarked "Detroit" and the return address was that of a friend with whom I had worked on a youth hostel committee there. I ripped open the envelope.

Dear Susie,

I've been thinking of you all day with a queer feeling of urgency. When are you coming home? I have been asked to raise a million dollars for four women's colleges in the Orient. I wonder if you would like to help me as my publicity secretary? You'd write the advertising brochures, a pageant about girls in India, Japan, Korea and China. I would pay you fifty dollars a week. I know your husband hasn't been well, so I wonder if you could use a little advance?

Bless you, my dear.

The check that fell from my shaking hand was for $500. So the grasshoppers made it home, after all. Yet had our adventure been so foolish? We were both brown and healthy, Jock was rarin' to go to find a new job, and my head was already buzzing with ideas. Strange it should be the Orient I was to write about, where I'd never been but where I longed to go. Oh, well, sometime maybe . . .

As our ship drew away from the dock at Palma, the gay crowd on shore called out, *"Vaya con Dios. Buenos días, mis amigos!"* We called back in the lovely Majorcan subjunctive, *"Tenga!"* (May you have and hold these lovely days forever.)

"And the morning and the evening were the first day" of my creation. Perhaps, like the stars, I had already existed a billion unremembered years, had been burned up into gases which in turn had been transformed into the proper chemicals to make a wife. It was an intriguing possibility, being discarded stardust! But when we left Spain, I had not the slightest suspicion that, equally miraculous, the son Jock and I had yearned for at long last was on his way.

# CHAPTER 3

# The Cadillac Baby

With true grasshopper insouciance, I became aware of my second incarnation as a mother as well as a wife in a New York furniture store where I had gone to buy a new couch for our living room. Wistfully, I told the salesman that I wanted "something tough enough to stand a small boy and his dog." I did not mention that both existed only in my imagination. He led me to a nylon velvet-covered davenport. "You could drop an ice cream cone on that and it would wipe right off . . . Madam! Are you ill?" To my horror, I felt myself falling and then was wiped out like the ice cream cone.

"According to all old wives' tales, this should herald the coming of the dear little stranger," I scoffed to Jock that evening. He had been offered a job on Wall Street, and since my Oriental women's college job was finished, we'd moved to a house in New Jersey, where our Detroit apartment furniture looked like orphans. Glancing around, I murmured, "We need another chair . . ."

"What you need is a bunny test," Jock insisted. "Go to the clinic."

The bunny test was positive!

"You're pushing forty and this is your first baby. After thirteen years! We'd better find an obstetrician, fast," Jock pointed out, excited, thrilled and worried at the same time. We had, after Spain, no savings at all and Jock's depression salary was about a third of what he'd earned in Detroit. He went on firmly, "We may have a Ford income, but we need a Cadillac doctor with experience."

"I'll try Park Avenue, where the specialists are. Maybe we can pay on the installment plan. Even a VIP can be human," I told him hopefully.

I copied a list from the Medical Directory and started out to canvass Park Avenue obstetricians. The lobby of the first doctor's office I went into had a black-and-white marble floor, very impressive; and it seemed about a mile to the nurse's desk, so that you arrived feeling like a midget. The nurse's uniform was stiff with starch and her tone was stiffer. "You'd have to be referred by someone." She looked at my inexpensive summer seersucker suit. "Doctor [as if there were only one medical man in New York worth mentioning] charges a thousand dollars for an accouchement."

A fourth of Jock's salary! Then there'd be the hospital . . . Why was the nurse thumbing the Social Register?

"Is your address here?"

"No. Is yours?" I was so angry I began to tremble. "I suppose all the lower orders have litters? Doctor would have to earn his thousand dollars!"

I clanked out over the marble horror, glad I hadn't worn rubber heels. When I pulled out my list again on the sidewalk, my hand still shook, but I plodded on to the next address and the next. Not everyone demanded social and financial references so openly, but the devices and evasions of the nurses intent upon weeding out the indigent were myriad. The doctors in my home town in New England had been friends as well as medical men! I went in and out of five offices without a glimpse of "Doctor," although one nurse offered to send me the name of a younger obstetrician "who will do your job for you at a lesser price." But it wasn't only the price I was interested in; it was getting a competent usher-in for Rick. (I had named my first son "Richard" while I was still climbing trees.) Maybe Jock and I weren't rich, but we were both at least normally intelligent college graduates (I wore my Phi Beta Kappa key on my bracelet), wise enough to know that even a Ford baby needed experienced help when the mother was, well, let us say "mature."

It was dusk and I was exhausted physically and emotionally when I came to the address of the last specialist on my list, the head of a great women's hospital. There was probably small use in my applying to such a VIP, but since I was here I might as well stop by. The reception room was empty of both nurse and patients, but the chairs looked so comfortable I sank down gratefully to rest. Maybe grasshoppers like me didn't deserve help. But at least I was trying to do what I could for my child. Each morning I'd sit, nauseated, at my typewriter, trying to write, but it was small use; everything sounded as sick at its stomach as I was.

"What are you doing here, young lady? I told the nurse I was through for the day . . . Why, you're crying! Tell me about it."

The doctor was tall, concerned, and his suit must have cost enough for Rick's layette, but when I had finished telling him about the baby that apparently nobody wanted, the chief of staff of the great hospital leaned down to pat my shoulder. "Don't worry, child. I'll take care of you and your baby for whatever you can afford to pay. Or for nothing."

So Rick would have his Cadillac doctor, after all; maybe Rolls-Royce. I was so excited that the next morning I wrote a heartfelt magazine article about how to select a good doctor in a strange city; I called it "Balancing the Baby Budget." It explained the plight of so many young married people with little cash that *Reader's Digest* condensed it for their readers; after that, orders for other articles flooded in, more than enough to pay for the hospital and layette. Jock and the doctor had agreed upon one month of Jock's salary as a reasonable medical fee.

As Mother used to say to Ike and me when things went well, "And the band played and the monkey danced!"

To me a marriage isn't truly adult until it includes a child. Couples who start out with the spoken or implied proviso, "If this doesn't work out, we'll get a divorce," are just living together, happily perhaps, but as adolescents, since one comes of age only when he realizes that lasting happiness includes not only sex but compassion. Certainly babies are smelly, helpless creatures who keep you nearly bankrupt and from going to the movies, whose teeth always need fixing just when you yearn for a fur coat. But they can also bring wonder back into daily routine, as you see again through a child's eyes how interesting is even a bug in the garden, how enchanting a butterfly. Having a child can be as creative as painting a picture or writing the Great American Novel. Motherhood taught me a great deal. If both generations have eyes to see and unstopped ears, a family can be a mutual adventure in living.

Practically everything that could went wrong when Rick was born; he was an eight-months baby and I had more complications than a centipede has feet, it seemed. We surely needed that Cadillac doctor who, with the help of Jock's sister, Hilda, a nurse who came swiftly from England, brought us both safely through. While I was in labor, Jock, who was suffering more than I, was whisked off by Charles, who was to be Rick's godfather, to a neighborhood party, for it was New Year's Day. Jock phoned my room in the hospital every ten minutes, but when Rick finally did put in his appearance, I was so limp that I begged, "Don't come! I want to sleep and sleep and sleep. I don't want to see even the baby till tomorrow!"

But when Hilda brought Rick in proudly the next morning, the great rush of mother love I'd expected didn't flood over me. Could this scrawny little pencil of a creature, lying on a pillow because he was so weak, be my strong son? Rick even had a pimple on his cheek. Charles was there with his camera, urging Jock to hold Rick still till he snapped the picture of his day-old godson. "Put your hand, Jock, under the baby's head. It wobbles."

"Rick's so skinny Jock's fist looks like the Hand of God," I said crossly.

"He's a preemy," Hilda protested hotly. "Give him a month and he'll fatten up to the prettiest little chap in town! He's nice and tall, as a man should be."

Rick reacted to Hilda's care exactly as she had predicted, became fat, rosy, loudly demanding, but I was too weak even to feed him for three months. It wasn't until he was my very own to care for, howling, spitting milk down the back of my neck, that I fell in love with my son. "Do you suppose love is tactile? A matter of feeling him, helpless, close in my arms?" I demanded of Jock.

"Affection is nine-tenths being needed," Jock agreed. "What's wrong with that? The boy's strong! Just look how he's grabbing at that goatskin lampshade we got in Spain! We'll send him to Christ's Hospital, my old school in England."

"Over my dead body!" I rescued the lampshade. "I don't believe in caning a child because he can't conjugate 'Amo, amas.'"

One thing about Rick both his father and I agreed upon —he was perpetual motion from the day he could walk on his fat little legs. I lost ten pounds running after him, so Jock put an eight-foot-high wire fence in our backyard to keep Rick safe while I made a bed or two. I had barely got to the bedspread when the phone rang and a neighbor announced, excited: "Did you know your baby is down on the state highway, directing traffic?"

I dropped the phone and ran. There he stood at the busy crossroads, wearing his ridiculously small corduroy overalls and striped cotton shirt, holding up first one hand and then the other to regulate the cars! The drivers were so amused they let him get away with it.

"I'm a cop, Mom!" Rick called, pleased.

The "cop" roared with anger when I snatched him up, for this was his first real quarrel with The Establishment. We finally devised an overhang for the top of the fence which his head hit when he climbed up, so he couldn't get out. Roar and wiggle as he would, he was safe while I got my first half-hour to write the articles we sorely needed for cash.

These first lovely, strenuous years taught Jock and me as much as they did Rick. My parsonage upbringing had been avidly Methodist, while Jock's had been British and Anglican. After Rick joined the family, Jock got a job in Boston and we moved to Sudbury, Massachusetts, where he suggested, "I've gone to the Methodist Church with you for fourteen years, Susie. How about you and Rick going with me for the next fourteen? I'd like my son to grow up in my home church." This seemed a reasonable exchange. Since there was no Episcopal Church in Sudbury, St. Elizabeth's was organized in our living room and merely enlarged our family, for Jock later became warden, I was on the Altar Guild, and Rick served at the altar. So now we had Episcopal sherry for communion instead of the Methodist grape juice. How to teach our son the middle course of temperance in eating, drinking, and sex?

Rick was only six when Jock fell and fractured his skull. A blood clot big as a dollar formed on his brain. I left Rick with Mother while I went to Boston to stay with friends till we knew whether Jock would live or die from the resulting operation. The first evening the three of us were reunited back in our own living room, Jock and I sat there, deeply content, drinking our sherry before dinner. When Jock was working and got home from the office tense and weary, we used this quiet time to relax, to share our days with each other.

" 'Wine is a mockery!' " our six-year-old roared from the doorway. " 'Strong drink is raging!' "

"Mother's been getting in her licks," Jock murmured. He smiled at his son over the top of his glass, inviting, "Why don't you go to the icebox, get some ginger ale and join us, son? But, mind you, we all have only one drink. We're *Methodist* Episcopalians, not whiskey-palians!"

These quiet hours together at the end of the day were the reason we three stayed so close-knit a family. Dad, Mother, Ike, and I singing together had achieved the same purpose, for unfortunately Jock's resonant voice was always half a note off-key, so guitars were out.

Parents who swear they won't make the same mistakes with *their* children as their own parents did with them invariably proceed to make different, worse ones, in spite of themselves. Just as kids do. How much misunderstanding could be avoided if children understood that parents are human, too, and vice versa! Our first big lesson that Rick was an individual in his own right came when Tarzie, his pet raccoon, joined our family.

Tarzan came from "Tinnessee" in spite of the fact that we had plenty of native raccoons to rattle our garbage pails—they lived in the wooded swamp back of our Sudbury house. Bartholomew, Third, a schoolmate of Rick's at St. Mark's School, had found the time too short to go home to Tennessee, so he had spent the three-day Thanksgiving holiday with us. "I'm sendin' you-all a hostess gif', Miz Fletcher," Third had promised when he left. From the pleased look that shot from him to Rick, I knew something I wouldn't like was up.

Two weeks later our phone rang and a man's voice said,

"This is the express company. We got a wild animal down here that belongs to you."

"There must be some mistake," I interrupted. "I didn't order . . ."

"You Mrs. Vivian Fletcher? Well, it's yours, all right. Come git it, quick, before it tears up the joint!"

Third's hostess gif' was a raccoon from the mountain his family owned near Nashville. It was half-dead with fright and thirst, for it had refused both food and drink, but when I phoned Rick at school, he announced gleefully that he and Third had a cage ready, wired on all four sides so Tarzan couldn't burrow out.

"I'll Tarzan you if you don't get home right now," I snapped and hung up.

The cage was six feet square, and I contributed an old-fashioned mahogany victrola for Tarzie's house. Laid flat on its side, with the little doors that opened and shut, the coon could have dark privacy or come out as he chose. Water, lettuce leaves, and patience worked wonders. Tarzie soon got so that when Rick whistled, the coon would open his victrola doors and amble out for food; after a few weeks he was so tame Rick could take him down the road on a leash attached to a little red collar. Half the kids in the neighborhood lived in our yard, and I couldn't keep any lump sugar on hand, they loved so to feed it to Tarzie, watch him wash the sugar in his bowl of water as he did all his food, then stare in dismay when there wasn't any sugar left in his tiny five-fingered hand that looked so ridiculously human. The kids would roll on the grass with laughter.

Rick had made the soccer team at school, but he was having trouble in class because his handwriting was so poor; he said he couldn't help it, his fingers just wouldn't work right, but the school said, "Nonsense." We took Rick to Children's Hospital for tests and they said that the small muscles of the boy's hands had atrophied because of a tumor on his spine which had to be removed. "It's a wonder he can write at all," the doctor said. "He must come in for an immediate operation."

When Rick went out to say "Good-by" to Tarzie, he wasn't there! He'd cut the wire on the bottom of his cage with his teeth and had gotten free to visit other neighborhood coons. Rick flatly refused to go to the hospital until the pet was found; neither my protests nor Jock's commands moved him an inch. He called and whistled, "Tarzie! Here, boy!" No scramble in the bushes. The Boy Scouts did their good deed by helping him search everywhere, down the road, all over the neighborhood. They even got hold of a part-bloodhound, let him smell Tarzie's cage, and followed him, sniffing, down the street. Still no Tarzie. Rick was due at the hospital for his "prep" for the operation at four that afternoon. At five-thirty Jock took him aside.

"Son, do you trust me?"

"Sure, I guess so."

"I promise you Tarzie will be found this night if it's humanly possible. If you'll go on to the hospital."

Father and son stared at each other for long moments. Rick went. When we got back from the hospital that afternoon, the Boy Scouts had located Tarzie up in one of our own pine trees in the backyard! One intrepid boy had climbed up to wrap his coat around Tarzie's terrible claws that could rip out a dog's intestines, and had brought the coon safely back and put him down in our cellar in the cage he'd traveled in from "Tinnessee." I was so relieved I treated twenty kids with Cokes.

Next morning, however, when I got to the hospital, I couldn't tell Rick about finding Tarzie because the lad was already in the operating room. I waited four endless hours for him to come back to his room, watching the green baize swinging doors his stretcher must return through, listening to the nurses busy at the station nearby.

"There's an emergency in the operating room," I heard the head nurse say into her phone. "The Fletcher boy." I began to run toward the green baize doors. What was wrong with Rick? I had to know . . . "How can I find the doctor?" I gasped to the nurse.

"He's coming now."

The doctor, still in his rumpled operating overall, took one look at my white face and steered me into his office. He explained quickly, mercifully, "I cut the motor nerve to your son's right leg. It was involved in the tumor so I didn't see it. I sutured it immediately. Maybe that will work out and the boy's leg will be O.K. Or he may never walk again."

How did you tell a boy, proud of being the speedy back on his soccer team, that he might never walk again? I said, "Thank you for telling me the truth," and sleepwalked to the telephone to call Jock. He caught his breath, then said practically, "There's nothing we can do now. Meet me at the lobster pound. We'll have a good supper, then come back to see how Rick's getting along."

An Englishman can hide his jitters from everyone but himself. When we'd finished our lobsters, Jock and I found that neither of us had a penny; we'd both been so upset we'd forgotten our pocketbooks! When we explained how this had happened, the sympathetic restaurant owner took Jock's check; he must have had boys of his own.

Back at the hospital, Rick looked barely alive, more like a mummy wrapped in bandages from his chest to his knees, his face colorless and very still against the too smooth pillow. One intravenous needle was dripping liquid food into his right arm and another needle, blood from another bottle into his left arm. I bent close, assuring him silently, fiercely, "You'll walk again. You must!" His hand moved just a little; he was coming to. As he opened his eyes, I bent closer. "Darling, I'm here. It's Mom!"

"How's—Tarzie?" Rick murmured.

Not even, "Hi, Mom." I might as well not be there at all. I didn't matter. Only his Tarzie.

"He's fine. He's home in the cage, waiting for you to come home."

Would I never learn that Rick belonged to himself? That mine was merely the womb that had sheltered him? For a little while only. I'd better learn for both our sakes.

Rick walked again. As soon as he could hobble, he insisted upon going back to the soccer team, although moving his leg, running and blocking, was so painful his face looked white and grim. His studies suffered, but the exercise was good for him; he even got so he could kick the ball so accurately that coaches of competing soccer teams would warn, "Look out for that Fletcher! He's dangerous!" He was proud of his team and of his place on it, but I'd already learned that he was essentially a loner, as I was, who liked people but was still sufficient unto himself. But once Rick loved, he was fiercely loyal—as he was to Star, his first Morgan horse.

He had yearned for a horse of his own ever since he was a small boy. Most of our neighbor children rode; he used to tag along behind them, wistfully, on his bicycle and clean up the stalls in the stable just "to sniff horse."

"Kids need to belong to their gang," Jock worried. "We might manage a horse for him, but we certainly couldn't afford to build a stable."

When a friend offered Rick his registered Morgan mare, which was too old to hunt but was still fit for a boy to ride, Rick was in seventh heaven. I'll never forget the light on his face the day Star backed out of her trailer and the two met each other, the mare brown and aristocratic, the boy's face so radiant my own throat hurt, just watching the two of them. (I must be getting old, fearing too much joy.) Rick pulled a carrot out of his dungaree pocket and offered it to the mare. Star ate it cautiously, whinnied, then wiped her nose on his shirt.

"She knows me already, Mom!" Rick exulted. "Hi yah, baby!"

From then on they were practically one person, and our house smelled happily of manure and horse liniment. Our neighbor across the street had offered Rick a stall in her big barn, but Jock warned Rick, "If you forget just one time to feed and water Star before school, to clean out her stall, back the mare goes!"

Rick never forgot once. He who had to be urged ten times to cut our lawn set his own alarm clock for 5:30 A.M. to trudge up the hill across from us even when the temperature was near zero, when he had to break the ice on his mare's water bucket. For Star and he belonged to each other, surpassing the love of Damon and Pythias. The two of them went on "horse picnics" with the other kids, riding up our mountain mornings and often not returning till after dusk while I listened for the clop, clop of horses' feet to know they were safely home. Rick even taught Star to jump.

"But, son, she's an old lady," I protested. "She's twenty-five!"

"Morgans can do anything!" Rick boasted proudly.

How could you puncture such perfect faith?

Not long after that the blow fell. It was bitter cold that fall and Star's ankles had begun to swell, so I sent for the vet. He came down after looking her over and sat uneasily in my kitchen chair, twirling his stained old hat in his hand, not wanting to tell me what he had to. Finally he burst out, "It's dangerous, Rick's riding the old mare! She's got a bowed tendon and arthritis in both her hind legs. She's in dreadful pain. She's apt to fall any day and kill both of them." He hesitated, then made himself go on. "But I'm not going to be the one to tell Rick she has to be shot!"

*Shoot Star?* Coldness crept up my own legs into my whole body. It would kill Rick, too—the part of him that mattered. But if his life were truly in danger . . . I asked, "How . . . I mean, who would . . . er . . . do it?"

"The S.P.C.A. would shoot her for you." The vet, relieved, got up to go. "I'll phone them to come tomorrow morning. You don't even need to be there, at the barn. They'll do the job, then take the carcass off in their truck. I wouldn't tell Rick till it's all over, poor kid."

I felt like Judas the next morning when Rick went whistling gaily up to the barn for the last time. Jock and I had debated all that sleepless night whether to tell Rick or not, and we just couldn't face it. If only we could bear this for him! After he'd fed and watered his Star, Rick got on the school bus as usual, swinging his books on their strap. I tried to make comforting cookies for his afternoon snack when he got home from school, but after I'd burned three batches I gave up and just jittered. Every truck that rattled by shook me, too. Was that the S.P.C.A.? Would I hear the shot, know when it happened? Surely the—the murder must be over by now. About two that afternoon I decided nervously that I'd better go up to the barn. If Rick got off the school bus, went up there and found the stall empty before I had a chance to explain why Star had to be put to sleep . . .

I fairly ran up the hill, my heart thumping, but everything looked peaceful. The barn door was wide open with Star's blanket neatly folded on the floor with her bridle on top of it. What was that rustling in the stall? Merciful heaven, was it possible Star was still alive?

I tiptoed over to the stall to look inside. Rick was there, sprawled out on the hay he'd tossed down that morning for his beloved, his face hidden on his arms, sobbing his heart out. He must have heard us talking last night or maybe just sensed that something was wrong. He had not gone to school at all! Oh, my dear—I wanted to rush to him, to kneel beside him, but I knew his tears belonged to him alone. I tiptoed back down the hill and waited, as

women have for years and years, for my son to come to me
of his own will. A thousand years went by before I heard
the latch click on the back door and turned to face him.

"Star's gone, Mom," Rick said slowly, clearly. "You
know something? She lived a good life. She always came
to me on willing feet. But she won't be cold any more and
her legs won't hurt."

It was Star he was thinking of, not himself! As his bedroom door banged, I rejoiced that my son who had gone
up that hill a boy had come down a man.*

The three of us were so happy, so self-sufficient, that it
never occurred to me I might lose both Jock and Rick in
different ways. When he went away to Charlottesville to
"The University," as Virginians, with unconscious smug-
ness, call Thomas Jefferson's lovely campus, Rick came
home for holidays frequently. Even when Jock became
noticeably ill, I didn't worry too much for we had an
excellent doctor friend to whom we went for a checkup.
While Jock was dressing again, the doctor called me,
alone, into his office and his sober face was a sharp arrow
to my heart. I said slowly, "Jock isn't going to live very
long."

"I share your concern," the doctor agreed.

"How long ... I mean, could we go back to Spain where
we had our last honeymoon?" Where we grasshoppers
had been so deliriously happy.

"Go if you like," the doctor decided. "The end will be
the same. But when Jock begins to fail, bring him home,
fast."

Jock and I didn't discuss the doctor's prognosis, but I
wrote Rick and he drove all night in his rickety Model A
Ford to get home the next weekend.

"Go to Spain, by all means," he urged. "Does Dad know
how sick he is?"

* *Woman's Day,* October 1952.

"I don't know what the doctor told him and I'll never ask." He wouldn't want to worry me; he'd rather face what he had to, in silence, I explained to Rick, and he agreed, "Yes, I suppose so. Write me often from Spain, will you? Don't wait too long to come home."

Our second look at Puerto Sóller was disillusioning: huge hotels had been built where only fishermen's small homes had stood before; even the seashore, where we used to sit with no one in sight except the old woman mending her nets and humming, had been subdivided by barbed wire clear down to the water so that only the guests at that particular hotel could bathe there. No laughing Irish Quakers to be fellow pilgrims . . .

"Let's get out of here!" Jock urged. We took a coal-burning steamer to Ibiza, a smaller island as yet not over-crowded with tourists and noisy Hondas. Our faces were black with soot, but the countryside and the Ibizans were just as independent and friendly as Majorcans used to be. We took a taxi to the end of the road where "Las Arenas" (The Sands), a tiny pension, sat close to the lovely mile-long crescent of white beach. Pepe, our host, had to ride three miles to Santa Eulália on his bicycle every day for provisions, as there was no other way except to walk; but the shaved-cork mattresses at Las Arenas were comfortable and the thick, stone-walled bedrooms cool. We lived in bathing suits. Jock, who was a much stronger swimmer than I, used to swim out a mile or so in the gloriously warm, blue Mediterranean till his bobbing head was out of sight and I'd wonder if he'd ever make it back to shore. What did it matter if he was happy? Drowning, they said, was an easy death; easy for him, not for me. When he strode back up the beach with great red lumps on his body from the poisonous jellyfish but triumphant at his conquest of sea and space, I'd draw a deep breath of relief.

Pepe gave us good meals, though it was hard to wait until 11 P.M. for dinner, and the way he opened cans made me wince watching him. He'd take a huge butcher knife and hurl the blade down upon the tiny can with abandon. What if the knife missed? "The next time we go to town, I'm going to get the poor man a can opener," I told Jock.

Taking a cab to Ibiza town meant walking three miles to Santa Eulália, and then paying about three dollars' fare to the city, but we discovered a bus which had no regular schedule but left whenever it was full and cost only six cents. Since time meant nothing to us these days, we ambled thus to Ibiza's main street, where Jock went to the bank to cash a check; this process frequently took all morning, especially if the bank teller went out to take a snack during the proceedings. I went to the hardware store to buy Pepe his can opener, only to find that I didn't know the Spanish word for this instrument vital to American housekeeping. I tried hard to imitate a can opener but couldn't get the idea across, although the salesmen gathered around and offered me knives, strainers, and eggbeaters. In desperation I went outside to see if I could find anyone who looked as if he might talk English.

The elegant Spanish officer coming down the sidewalk had enough gold braid and shiny leather to indicate he might be well educated, so I smiled and stopped him. "Pardon, señor! Would you please tell me the Spanish word for 'can opener'?"

There's no one more gallant than a Spanish aristocrat. The officer bowed, smiled, and offered, "I would be most pleased to accompany you to buy one, señora."

As we went inside the hardware store, the clerk gasped, bowed to the ground, and produced like magic a can opener with so many gadgets all it could not do was cry "Mama!"

I thanked the officer profusely.

"Delighted to have been of service," he murmured, bowed, and left.

The clerk marveled. "You are most fortunate in your

friends. The military commandant of our island!"

"Well, he sure picks a swell can opener!" was Jock's comment during our leisurely ride home. Pepe, of course, refused to use the can opener. He still disemboweled the cans with his butcher knife; what was good enough for his father and his grandfather (if they had cans then) was good enough for Pepe. He put the can opener on his shelf as an ornament.

Jock and I had a "studio" beyond the beach, high up on a yellow cliff, with a flat rock for my typewriter (I was finishing *No Marriage in Heaven*) and a place for him to set up his easel to "mess around," he said, as he did not pretend to be "an artist." Out of a clear sky one day when he was bored waiting for me to finish typing, he'd decided to paint pictures in oil. "How do I know I can't till I try?" He looked out over the jade and dark-blue sea, the golden rocks. "All this gorgeous color!" Jock had an assistant, a tiny salamander who came out from under his rock each day to get his breakfast from Jock's palate. We named him "John"; we could tell him by the ocher paint upon his little snout. John never ate from any other tube.

"Because it comes from the rock he lives under," Jock explained.

But one morning when Jock tried to get out of bed, he fell back limply. He said, "If you don't mind, I think I'll skip the studio today. It's such a long walk, isn't it?"

It was time to go home, as the doctor had warned me. I called Pan American in Barcelona, explained my urgent need, and they promised us two seats to Boston soon, even though it was their busiest season. We left Ibiza on the first tiny plane to fly from the island. As we bumped over the brown cow pasture, rushing close to the edge of the tall cliff with the hungry sea below, I thought how nice it would be to die together as we had lived so long. No such luck. Rick met us at Logan Airport in Boston. I could see he was shocked at how worn and flushed Jock looked; he was very gentle with his father and played endless games of cards to keep him amused. But in only a few weeks Rick and I heard a thump upstairs in the bathroom where Jock had fallen. He had had a massive stroke. It was all over in two weeks.

"Why didn't you let us know?" demanded one of his GI pals from the 55th Coast Artillery Corps, after the funeral services at St. Elizabeth's. "We could have made it a military funeral. With Taps."

Taps made me cry on Memorial Day even when I didn't know anyone; it would have finished me then. I said gratefully, "The big flag Washington sent was enough." Even that I couldn't bear to look at for long. I sent it to a new school in New Hampshire where the children needed the Stars and Stripes to salute.

Fortunately Rick and Sylvia fell in love and wanted to be married almost at once. With him still in college and her working, I was needed again, helping her to pick out her trousseau evenings, addressing envelopes, all the silly little things that keep you from thinking how lost you are, how useless. So you can drop into bed too tired to weep.

The red and white Christmas wedding in our little chapel across the street from our house, where Rick had been an altar boy, was perfect; Sylvia in white, with her arms full of red roses, was radiant; Rick was so proud of her he glowed like the altar candles, and when she drew his face down to hers and kissed him full on the lips, I remembered the first time Jock had kissed me up in Maine, with the sea whispering at our feet and ecstacy running down my spine. I had that to remember, to hold onto. As the children came down the aisle, holding hands, the words of the ceremony tolled again in my mind, "Cleaving only unto her so long as you both shall live . . ." Sylvia came first now with Rick; it was right; I *wanted* it that way. The lonely ache in my heart came not from envying my lovely, talented new daughter-in-law but because, with Jock gone, I would never come first with anyone any more.

But Rick gave me a wedding present. He said, reading my mind, "Good-by, Mom. And thank you. My father was a *good* man."

And I remembered, comforted, that a part of Jock was still here, in the compassion of my son.

# CHAPTER 4

# Unugly Americans in Japan

Jock might be "going from strength to strength, in a life of perfect service" wherever he was in the next world, but I was no angel. My stomach felt squeamish, to say the least, that sunny morning when Polly and I took off from Los Angeles via Hawaii for Japan. What was I doing, going to a country where I knew no word of the language, not even how to find the ladies' room? But that wasn't what we were looking for on our first day in Kyoto.

"Dozo, which way do we go to visit the great Shinto shrine where the Emperor worships?" Polly asked a pleasant-looking gentleman complete with horn-rimmed glasses, smile, and the camera without which the modern Japanese looks naked. Clickings and snappings took the place of the twittering of country birds as we got out of our taxi whose driver spoke only Japanese. But modern trappings are misleading; for, underneath, the Oriental is essentially the same as he has been for several thousand years. Unlike the strange mélange of cultures which somehow emerges as what we label "an American," the Japanese remains, polite, unchangeable.

"Reft and then light one mile," the pleasant gentleman, bowing low, told Polly and me.

After we'd wandered about shrine-hunting for a few hours, we finally took a taxi and discovered that the directions should have been exactly reversed. Polly, who had lived here before, shrugged. "He had to tell us whether he knew the way or not. Otherwise he would have lost face."

On this first trip around the world as a merry widow, I not only learned plenty about "face," but also how *not* to influence people.

It is not always the Ugly Americans who act like barbarians in the Orient, brashly trying to impose their adolescent ways upon older civilized cultures; the misunderstandings lie chiefly in the difference in the sense of values between East and West. In Hong Kong a dying woman lay in the street for hours with passers-by stepping over her inert body simply because helping anyone meant you became involved, that the victim became your responsibility. The Oriental is a practical man who finds immature, friendly-puppy advances suspect.

Miss Helen Quack, the Korean assistant conductor of the New York Philharmonic, in explanation of the energetic way she uses her whole body to draw out from the players the musical effect she desires, said frankly on the Today show recently, "In the Far East, if you really want something, whether you are talking to a merchant or to an orchestra, you ask it in a demanding fashion."

The first month I spent in India I went all "buddy-buddy," trying to show that I did not consider myself superior; the result was that at customs in Delhi I remained at the end of the line while an icily aloof English woman sailed by me out of the dreadful heat. When at last the customs officers came to me, they cried, as if I were secreting a machine gun, "Aha! A typewriter!"

"I wasn't planning to sell it," I pointed out. "I need the thing." They made me sign a two-foot-high pile of papers before I was released, while they obviously enjoyed watching me, an American, sweat. The next time I entered India, I decided to go English. I thumped down my typewriter on the counter and demanded, very courteous but firm, "I want a receipt, please, at once. I'm in a hurry." I got the receipt and a smile. What the Oriental wants is equality, not servility, *on either side.*

In Japan I could understand the psychology of the well-dressed Osaka businessmen who nearly knocked Polly and me down in their rush to mount the plane ramp before we females did. For thousands of years Japanese women had been walking behind the men, carrying the bundles. Why should two American women be an exception? But when a bunch of strange men took over our stateroom on the Kansai steamship (for which we had paid plenty to sail down the lovely Inland Sea), I finally lost my temper. The usurping men were calmly having tea in our room, talking and laughing, ignoring my attempts to show them our tickets to prove the room belonged to us; we might have been a couple of flies, buzzing. First we had been stepped on at the airport, now ignored here. Maybe Japanese women liked being carpets, but not I!

I rushed out into the big ship's saloon, full of luggage and white-jacketed stewards demanding tips, and broadcasted loudly, "I wish to see the captain of this ship! *Right now!*"

If I didn't stamp my foot actually, I did so metaphorically. The result was miraculous; every single white-clad steward melted away into the woodwork so that Polly and I were alone. But not for long. A fat little Japanese, heavy with gold braid, with two gold teeth showing in his anxious smile, came rushing up. "Iss everysing allite, radies?"

"No! It's all wrong, Captain!" When I showed my tickets and explained about the invading tea drinkers, the captain soothed, "I get you better loom. Come, plizz!"

The new stateroom had everything, four bunks to rest

upon, a table and seats next to the plate-glass side of the ship where you could look out to see the passing little rocky islands as clearly cut as Japanese prints; there was even a place to put our calling card so our nonexistent friends could drop by, and, at the clap of the captain's hands, delicious tea arrived in small thin cups.

"*Arigato gozaimasu!*" Polly thanked him and he beamed. If you know only two Japanese words, those are useful. "Thank you very much!"

Every hour on the way to Beppu, the captain would push the doorbell of our suite and demand anxiously, "Iss everysing allite, radies?" We'd thank him, he'd bow and we'd bow, and that was that.

As soon as we were alone, Polly began to laugh. "You looked like a kitten having a fit," she told me.

"I'm sorry if I . . ."

"Don't be sorry. They are disappointed if we Americans buckle under when we're right. If we aren't a little crazy, where is their sense of superiority? It's all in the ear, anyway." When I looked mystified, she explained, "Like the missionary from Japan who came to speak to our Women's Guild at home and was asked by the lady in charge of devotions to lead the Lord's Prayer in Japanese. But in Japan she'd taught it only in English! I bowed my head with the rest but lifted it suddenly for I couldn't believe my ears! In order not to disappoint the dear ladies, she was reciting rapidly the names of all the railroad stations between her mission and Tokyo!"

The nice little Japanese, courier for a couple of wealthy Americans, whom we met on board telephoned from the ship to the Hotel Seifu in Beppu for reservations for Polly and me. It turned out to be a marvelously comfortable international hostel. The manager shook hands with us, beaming, "All the same Miami!" He had been there and I had not. But here you could go East or West according to your taste; in the elevator we met a whole family going down to the communal pool to bathe naked together, but our bathroom had a modern Western seat so you didn't have to squat, and our tiny balcony looked out, over beautifully clipped little trees in pots, to the sea. Our *futons* on the floor had innersprings and satin coverlets topped with embroidered sheets. Polly's masseuse was silent and deft. What if we had to stand up in the four-foot-square bathtub to bathe? We could adapt, too.

Polly was smart enough to go shopping next morning instead of climbing a hundred steps or more to see the monkey god. She said firmly, "Have fun. Meet you at the naked lady by the railroad station at train time," and took off. I took a taxi to the monkey temple, looked, dubious, at the many steps, but started up, as the monkey horde descended upon me. They chattered loudly, yanked at my skirt, pulled my hair, and nearly knocked me off the stone steps, demanding the cookies I didn't know I was supposed to bring them as a bribe to behave. The guards standing around just laughed. When a vicious yank of my hair brought tears to my eyes, I decided this was no place for a Methodist minister's daughter. I didn't want to see the darn monkey god, anyway. When I arrived at the station, Polly was waiting below the naked-lady statue who was clutching her marble head.

"What's the matter with *her*?" I puzzled.

"She's saying, 'Mon Dieu, I forgot my clothes!' "

When we arrived at Nara, Polly all but wept over how many of the huge trees, which had been magnificent when last she saw the forest, had been knocked flat by a hurricane. But the deer were still there. A sign warned that this was the rutting season and visitors should please look out for the males. Polly bought some cookies from an old lady in a nearby hut, to feed the deer. One old buck kept pushing his lady friends aside to grab the food out of Polly's hand; she glared at him, turned around, and butted the buck right back with her own rear end, snapping,

"Keep in line, you!" Like the ship's captain, the Japanese buck obeyed meekly in sheer surprise.

People or animals en masse, regardless of nationality, often exhibit atavistic tendencies of which, as individuals, they would be ashamed. Polly and I avoided "conducted bus tours" like the plague; but one rainy day we weakened and joined a band of tourists and rode by bus to visit the well-known monkeys who see, hear, and speak no evil, as they lurk over the lintel of the "sacred stables" at Nikko. The battle scene in the parking place at the Toshogu Temple was unbelievable; each of the many conductors of groups of tourists held his little flag aloft over the struggling multitude, yelling, "Forrow me!" and dived into the melee of blue-uniformed schoolchildren seeking credits for "visiting historic places." We emerged battered but unbowed. Polly was reluctant to step in her stocking feet on the wet floor of the temple. She took from her shopping bag a pair of bright red sandals and put them on, while the doorman shrieked, "No shoes!" "These aren't cowhide, they're just Buddhist rubber soles," Polly explained. "Do you want me to get pneumonia?" Being Polly, and he a man, she got away with it, but I had to patter mournfully in my wet stocking feet to look at dripping "royal chrysanthemum doors." They were magnificent, but I refused to duck-paddle to the stables. "I've bought those blind-and-deaf monkeys at Woolworth's," I snapped. "I'm freezing. I'm going back to the bus."

"I'm going shopping," announced Polly happily. "I'll join you when the bus gets back from the Falls. I suppose you're hellbent to see Lake Chuzenzi? The pamphlet says, 'The Kegon Falls is greatly noted for committing suicide.' " She looked around her at the wet, milling tourists, determined not to miss a monkey paw, sniffed, and was gone.

The trip to the lake in the rain was a nightmare. The bus smelled of steaming bodies and cigar smoke, and the road corkscrewed up a mountain so sharply that the rear end of our bus frequently hung out over nothing; mist shrouded the invisible falls when we arrived. "Hear it? Wonderful!" cried our leader optimistically. Again, Polly had chosen the better way. Wet, cold, and despondent, I went inside the inn and was comforted with hot sake in a lovely little jar. Sake proved as smooth as mother's milk but a little more heady in its results.

When our bus got back to Nikko, our leader stood up front, counting and recounting heads; he'd scowl, scratch his head, then begin again. He looked as if he were about to burst out crying as he muttered, "Ole rady rost! Ole rady rost!" Finally what he was saying got through my sake-happy mind. "Old lady lost!"

"No, she isn't," I told him. Polly would kill him for calling her that; maybe I'd better just leave her in whatever store she fancied. But it was a long way to Tokyo. "Drive down Main Street," I urged the bus driver. "We'll pick her up." Polly was easy to find, standing there under a huge paper umbrella gay with chrysanthemums. "Just what I always wanted." She beamed as she swung lithely aboard. "Gorgeous? It cost only sixty cents!"

I sighed inwardly. One more thing to push under the seat of the next jet, along with my typewriter. Polly rushed on, full of energy. "How about going to that tempura place tonight, when we get back to Tokyo? The one the hotel recommended?" I decided not to tell her just yet that she was an old lady because that would make me one, too.

Polly and I both loved the Old Imperial Hotel, not because of its beauty (useless bits of mirrors stuck here and there in the lava-like gray stone gave it the raffish look of an ex-brothel), nor because it had survived the earthquakes, but because, unlike the new building which was infested with Americans, the Old Imperial was dear to the heart of the Japanese, and the service was wonderful.

Little maids in bright kimonos snatched up your laundry almost before it hit the floor; even if the tiles that lined the bathtubs left checkerboards on your bare rear end, there wasn't anything you could ask for that the help couldn't produce. Once in the usual tourist rush, I'd ripped off an orange-colored blouse so carelessly that a button came off. I tossed the blouse onto the bed, reached for another, and hurried off. When I came home that night, the blouse had been laundered and all new buttons had been sewed on because the tailor couldn't match the one I'd lost. No charge or tip, just good public relations. Ah me, part of the Old Imperial is now a museum in a park, moved stone by gray stone; the New Imperial bedrooms have plastic walls that pretend to be wood, and you turn on the overhead lights yourself without getting out of bed, by pushing a button on your radio. No friendly little maid to run in to do it for you. Progress?

Polly and I got back to the hotel, ravenously hungry, and had dinner there that night. "The High Priest of Tempura" we called the fat little Japanese Buddha who sat cross-legged presiding over the twin kettles of oil. "You're a joy to me. You don't mind barging off into the dark in a strange city where you don't even know how to say 'Hi!' " Polly said as our taxi tore madly through dark, winding, rain-wet streets. "We might be halfway to Kyoto or en route to a bordello, for all we know."

"There's a bright light! That must be something important."

In front of the tempura restaurant were rows and rows of shoes on the three steps leading to the front door. We climbed in our stocking feet to meet the Buddha of Abundant Eating. Imperturbable and round-bellied, as if he regularly sampled his kettle of fat, he sat in the exact center of a tiny garden of potted plants amid the incense of his pots. He waited, beaming, for us to select what we wanted from the feast spread out in front of him ... bits of raw fish, bean sprouts, carrots and a rainbow of vegetables, ginger root, seaweed, other unidentifiable tidbits, and prawns looking as fresh as if they'd just been drawn from the sea by a line out the window. We'd point to whatever we wanted to eat, Buddha would pick it up with his chopsticks, dip it into the batter and fat, and drop it smoking hot and delectable onto our plates. We ate till I was sure I'd never make it up from the pillow upon which I sat, replete, upon the floor.

"How do you cry Uncle?" Polly gasped.

"Just stop eating, I guess."

When we indicated we simply couldn't chew any more, Buddha bowed, pushed a button, and he and his paraphernalia turned slowly around on a turntable to leave us gaping at another garden of tortured potted trees, while he fed the people in the adjoining room. A small maid trotted in with such delicious iced pears we couldn't resist; at worst, it would be a pleasant way to die.

"This sure beats the automat," Polly decided. "Let's find a Japanese inn when we go to Hiroshima tomorrow. I didn't come six thousand miles to see Americans. I'm fed up with being asked, 'Are you from New York? Do you know Whosit?' "

In spite of the greenish liquid they call "ceremonial tea," the charm of Japan had gotten under our skins.

Polly went inside the Japanese Tourist Bureau at Hiroshima to finagle the name of a native inn from a clerk harassed by assorted tourists, while I waited outside in the taxi to keep an eye on our luggage. The inn looked charming as we drove up. Beyond a walled garden the host and hostess were waiting with assembled waitresses and bellhops; they bowed to greet us. They spoke no English, but Polly dug out her bits and pieces of Japanese, enough (we thought) to secure us a private bath; certainly the price of our room was high enough to warrant something extra. We shuffled along behind our host, in plastic slippers so big I lost one in the brook when we hopped from one stone to another to reach the wing we were to be in. As we entered the large room furnished only with pillows and a tiny vanity so low you had to kneel to see in the mirror, a couple of giggling Japanese maids began to take off even our underclothes, to substitute two blue-and-white, crisply starched kimonos.

"I could almost fly, I'm so airy!" I flapped my long sleeves. "What's the name of this place?"

"I haven't an inkling. The Tourist Bureau just gave me the address." Polly grinned. "Some people can lose a drum in a telephone booth. But it takes real genius to lose the place you're in!"

"Bass?" murmured one of the doll-like little maids.

We followed her happily until we saw twelve tooth-brushes lined up around the basin in our "private" bass. Polly decided it took too much effort to gripe in Japanese, so, unprotesting, we went on beyond the screens to the tub. It was about four feet square, filled with lovely hot water for our travel-weary limbs. Polly shot the bolt on the door, bathed decorously in the Japanese manner by wash-ing herself with soap and water before getting into the tub, then sank with a sigh of content into the hot, hot water. "Your turn," she told me finally and pulled the plug to the tub. At the sound of the outrunning water such an uproar arose outside the locked door I could hardly hear her say, "For what we're paying here we can at least have private hot water. Let 'em pound."

But when we emerged, the little maid grabbed me by the kimono sleeve, making strange motions of listening to her cupped hand. "Someone wants you on the phone. The only one I saw was in the robby-lobby," Polly interpreted.

"How could anyone know where we are?" I wondered.

"Probably called the police; they know all, see all."

Naked as a plucked chicken under my starched kimono, I followed the little maid to the robby where, sure enough, the receiver was lying on the counter of the reception desk. But as I picked it up, the innkeeper's wife gave a yell, rushed at me, yanked open my kimono. "Hey, quit that!" I tried in vain to cover my nakedness, but she insisted upon the kimono being refolded in the opposite way from which I had tied it, all the time shrieking in Japanese. Meantime the phone was asking, "Mrs. Fletcher? Are you there?" I gave a sort of gulp into the mouthpiece and the English lady I was supposed to interview the following day asked, "You sound peculiar. Are you all right?"

"Sort of. I guess I wrapped my kimono the wrong way."

"Maybe you folded it like a prostitute or a dead person?" She waited for my answering laugh and then went on, "I just called to ask if you needed anything to be comfortable."

"Pillows," I decided. "The *futons* are fine here, but my pillow is a bean-bag."

"I'll send a boy over with some. Until tomorrow, then."

Shaken, not daring to look anyone in the face, I hopped back across the brook to our room. Polly, already lying luxuriously upon her *futon* on the floor, murmured, relaxed, "I've sent for a couple of masseuses to rub us to sleep. All this and heaven, too . . ." A knock on the door interrupted her. It was flung open to reveal an attractive, very young Japanese man rolling up his sleeves. I told him, doubtful, "We sent for a missis, not a mister!"

The young man looked us both over carefully; what he saw seemed to please him.

"*I* don't mind," he told us. But he sent us two girl substitutes.

There's nothing like a Japanese massage to relax tense bodies. But afterward I began to laugh. "What's so funny?" Polly asked drowsily, shifting her bean-bag under her head, for the pillows had not yet arrived.

"I just wish I knew if I looked like a prostitute or a dead body!"

The next day we waded into horror at the Atomic Museum, where we looked at pictures of what was left of people and houses after the Big Bomb; all that remained of one man was a mere shadow burned into the rock of a stone doorway that miraculously still stood. There were whole schoolrooms of children whose hair had turned white and who would later sicken with leukemia. The effect was a crescendo of horror. Polly looked pale. She refused to go with me to the Red Cross Hospital, where many leukemia victims were still being cared for after twenty years. "There's nothing I can do about it," she explained and took off, shopping.

The head of the hospital, Dr. Shigeta, who had not gone home for a month after the bombing while he tried his best to succor victims until he fell asleep at his job, was suavely, professionally welcoming in his white coat. He led me through wards full of more victims than I could stomach—bodies half eaten away, one woman with the pattern of her dress burned into her skin, patients with hair burned white, dying slowly of leukemia years after the bomb had exploded. All our modern medicine was unable to help any more than the paper cranes hanging over the patients' beds that their friends had brought them instead of flowers to ward off evil. A little late. I shivered as the horror went on and on . . . I demanded, swallowing nausea, "How can you possibly forgive us for all this?"

Dr. Shigeta shrugged. *"Shiktagami.* That is our national saying. 'It can't be helped.' "

"But it was an *American* bomb that did this!"

"We Japanese brought the first bomb on ourselves by starting the war," the nurse in rustling white, who was following the doctor, interrupted suddenly. "But why the second one so soon?" Tears streamed down her face as she told me, "I lost my whole family at Nagasaki."

"Please take care yourself," Dr. Shigeta urged as I left. "Don't tired too much."

Tears ran down my cheeks as my taxi rattled away. "The lives of a million American soldiers might have been saved by those two bombs," we'd been told. But Japanese civilians, adults and children, were people too. "Someone else would have dropped the first atomic bomb if we hadn't." Only we had; the onus was ours eternally. After what I'd just seen, for the first time in my life I was ashamed of being an American. I cried all the way back to the inn.

Polly took one look at my wet face and dropped a tiny black Buddha about one inch tall into my hand. "I knew you'd have a hard day. I brought you a present," she said. "He's three hundred years old. Isn't he cute?"

*"Shiktagami . . ."* If I had had this awful decision about the bomb to make, knowing that it meant my Rick would die, what would I have done? I did not know. *"Shiktagami"*—it can't be helped now. My hands closed gently about the little comforting Buddha. Would East and West ever understand each other? Would we Americans ever understand *ourselves?*

"A modern Japanese speaking of the Emperor as 'divine' does not mean the same thing we Westerners do," my English friend explained the next day when I returned her pillows. We'd been so afraid they would be stolen that Polly and I had carried them along with us wherever we went to eat. "They do not mean that he is God with a capital *G;* simply, that there is a spark of divinity in every man; this spark is fanned to a flame in the Imperial Family since they are the symbols of the entire nation. It was not hard to get the Emperor to say in his New Year's radio broadcast that he did not consider himself divine; he never thought so in the first place.

After all, he is a modern marine scientist."

"The more I see and know the Orient, the less I understand it," I mourned to Polly. "I must be stupid."

She looked at my new bright-blue Thai silk suit that even I knew was becoming, put on because we were going back to Tokyo for a few days before we took off for Hong Kong and the grand shopping spree. She comforted, "You look bright-eyed and bushy-tailed to me! If you can't think like a Japanese, neither can they think English. Remember the conductor on the train to Kyoto?"

The train ride from Tokyo to Kyoto had been as smooth as silk; even a cup of coffee set upon the window sill by our car seat had not rippled. (If we Americans were so smart technologically, why couldn't we build a train like this to run from Boston to New York?) The conductor had proved as proud of his English as of his crack train. When I had asked where the ladies' room was, he'd explained, "In the next car. But look out. It is coeducational."

The nice young doctor whom some friends in Boston had alerted to squire Polly and me around Tokyo, because he'd studied at Harvard, phoned us soon after we had returned to the Imperial Hotel. He said cordially, "I would like for you to meet my wife and family. Come to tea? But, first, is there any other place in town you'd like to see?"

"Yes," I answered. "I'd like to go to a geisha house."

The ensuing silence was dark and prolonged. Finally the doctor said coldly, "I know very little about such things. But I have a friend who does. I'll call you."

"That does it. I've offended him." I dropped the receiver ruefully. "Of course he knows plenty. We can't possibly go without an escort. They'd tell two lone females politely that everyone had smallpox, so solly."

"I'd like to talk to a geisha, girl to girl," Polly agreed. "See what makes her tick, men or money."

But the good doctor did call back. When I picked up the phone the next evening he said abruptly, "I'm coming for you in a car in an hour. I've arranged for a private room at the Tall Pines on the Ginza. It's considered one of the better geisha houses," and he rang off abruptly.

"We're still not very popular, but we're going," I told Polly.

She picked up her knitting bag and we went to the robby to wait. The huge black limousine the doctor had provided was impressive; he did not sit with us, however, but up in front with the chauffeur. Naturally a Japanese gentleman wouldn't take his wife to a geisha house, but he certainly couldn't think that Polly and I were infectious . . . or could he? Polly winked at me and I knew she was thinking the same thing and enjoying it hugely.

This turned out to be the most fascinating evening we spent in Japan. Our car stopped at a brightly lighted entrance where the delicate leaves of tall pines right in the heart of the city threw flickering shadows upon the surrounding skyscraper walls. On the polished front steps were hundreds of men's empty shoes but no women's. I dropped mine as I entered, wondering if I'd ever find them again among so many. A little maid in a kimono, with black hair standing out from her head, led us in our stocking feet down immaculate, empty corridors behind whose closed doors we could hear the roar of men's laughter and the thin tinkle of a samisen.

The private room the doctor had reserved for us was about twelve feet square, the floor covered with thick tatami upon which were a low table and pillows to sit upon. At one end of the room was the *takonoma*, "showing the beauty of good harmony," with its delicate scroll, below which stood a priceless jade vase with three cherry blossoms. "It is the place of honor," the doctor said. "Please to sit down in front of it, ladies."

"I can't see the lovely scroll this way," Polly protested. "Why do you seat your guests with their backs to 'harmonious beauty'?"

"It is the honored custom." That settled that. Thousands of years of iron rules did cramp your style; I was glad I was a careless, hybrid American. But the little waitresses pattering about in their flowered kimonos were darling; their tiny steps were far more graceful than those of the modern city girls on the Ginza striding about in dungarees or short skirts which showed their bowed legs. The first course of the dinner was cherry blossom tea, which tasted like nothing but had a lovely painted bloom in the bottom of the black lacquer bowl. The hors d'oeuvres were raw white fish in a sauce (very good) and caviar on thin slices of cold cooked rice; the soup was rich with mushrooms, served with a slice of lemon on a jade-colored dish.

"If we serve a thin soup, the bottom of the bowl is decorated so you can see as well as taste beauty," the doctor explained. "With thick soup we decorate the cover of the bowl."

The next course was also mushrooms arranged in a pattern on a silver platter with a chrysanthemum in the center.

"Thank heaven, we don't have to eat the chrysanthemum," Polly muttered to me. "If I'd known we were going to have so many courses, I'd have gone easier on the first three."

Course followed course, thin slices of pork to be dipped in soy sauce and horseradish, a salad in a gray pottery bowl to show off the orange of carrot slices, the clear white of radishes—or were they turnips?—a delicate bouquet of queer watercress whose leaves were red underneath. Each dish was intended not only to eat, but to feast the eyes. You'd open a plain lacquer bowl to discover a mother-of-pearl flower inside the cover, or perhaps a delicate spray of bamboo was visible when you finished with your chopsticks, like a small boy eating his cereal and finding Mickey Mouse in the bottom. We had tempura, thin broiled fish, pink and luscious cuttlefish and other tidbits better anonymous, ginger dipped in batter and smoking hot. But each dish, in some way or other, included mushrooms.

I thought, No wonder hungry girls learn to be geishas! But probably they ate only after the men had finished. I told our host, "I can't even swallow any more. Would it be impolite if I passed up this tenth course?"

"Just move the food around with your chopsticks," the doctor advised. "To please the cook."

Gauguin could have painted the final course of luscious fruit, a black-and-white-striped bowl in which were heaped persimmons, mandarin oranges, and grapes as big as small pears. Polly drank only tea; she disliked alcohol as much as foreign missions. We listened to the loud laughter of men in nearby rooms.

"But where are the geishas?" my lifted eyebrows asked Polly.

The door opened quietly to admit a little maid who put down a red satin pillow for a beautiful girl with a sad face and gentle hands, who sat down to tune her samisen, which emitted low moans. Dramatic against the frame of a panel of cherry blossoms, the head geisha appeared. Her hair was a shining black tower scattered with tiny ornaments that tinkled, her gown a lingering sheath of dark blue decorated with wavering lines of foamy white, while her long train was lined with a red satin which showed when she kicked it aside.

"It is the 'Dance of the Waves of the Blue Sea,' " the doctor murmured, pleased. "Prince Genji danced this for the Emperor's pleasure a thousand years ago."

Lady Murasaki, a novelist writing in the year 1008 A.D., had described Prince Genji's performance thus:

> Never had the onlookers seen feet tread so delicately, nor heads so exquisitely poised. . . . So moving and beautiful

was this dance that at the end of it, the Emperor's eyes were wet, and all the princes and great gentlemen wept aloud.

How the Japanese still clung to ancient ways under their modern acumen in business! As if a computer had grown out of a tree, with roots deep in history. If we wanted a pragmatic foreign policy, all of our Washington State Department striped-panted diplomats should be shipped to Tokyo to study geishas dancing a thousand-year-old dance.

"The Dance of the Waves" was indeed languid, beautiful, finished, enchanting. The smooth movements of the head geisha's limbs were like water flowing along a sunny shore, like a bird singing at early morning, or the hushing sound of the delicate foam as the wave breaks along the seashore, draws back, then gives itself as a lover to the sand. We hardly dared breathe for fear of shattering the magic. When the geisha had finished, there was an instant of quiet tribute before we could come down to earth to applaud her art. Then she and a younger girl danced together a sad love story, but it was obvious the younger girl was an apprentice, less controlled in her motions. After they had finished, the doctor invited them to sit down at our table to talk to us, with him as interpreter.

"The head geisha says she is forty and has four children," he explained, adding proudly, "One of our most popular geishas in Tokyo is seventy-five!"

"And the girl?"

The doctor shrugged. "She says she comes from up country."

The two geishas were chattering like magpies in Japanese, waving their tiny hands with fans, very earnest. "What do they say?" Polly demanded. "Or is it another sitting dance?"

"They want you to take them with you to America!" The doctor smiled, for he was familiar with New York. "They think you pick up gold nuggets in Times Square!"

I sighed, thinking of the wet newspapers blowing around my wet ankles, the dirty subway train where people were crowded like cattle; I had once seen the starter push the last passenger inside with his foot in order to close the car doors. I said, "Someone as gifted as the head geisha might find gold of a sort. Ask her how she ever builds that contraption on her head every day."

"She doesn't. She sleeps on a wooden pillow that fits her neck. The hairdresser comes to her house every third day, and it costs her plenty. She has to have help even to get into her elaborate costume."

With a husband and four children she could hardly be a prostitute, but the younger girl looked healthy and willing. I was deciding this was one question too delicate to ask the doctor to translate when the door to our room burst open and the little waitress came rushing in so fast in her tight kimono that she almost tottered and fell. She whispered in the doctor's ear; his face, too, grew grave. What could be the matter? He snapped an order in Japanese and the little maid hurried out. Polly and I tried to pretend nothing had happened, but the doctor was obviously distrait. Was one of his patients perhaps seriously ill, needing him? We'd better go. I was sure of this when the maid came back looking even more upset.

"I hate to tell you this, but there seems to be no alternative," admitted the doctor. "It is disgraceful this could happen in Japan." Was he about to commit hara-kiri? He told Polly, *"Someone has stolen your shoes from the front step!"*

"Oh, no, they haven't!" Polly reached cheerfully under the table and drew out her shoes. "I put them in my knitting bag."

The little maid began to laugh hysterically, then the

geishas, while the doctor joined in. They laughed and laughed! As soon as one would stop to draw breath, another would start and the wave of merriment would rise again. They were still laughing as we wended our way to the street where the big car was waiting. "Sayonara!" Still convulsed, the geishas bowed us away politely, but we could hear loud giggles even after we turned the corner of the street. Those crazy Americans!

"It was a most delightful evening and we do thank you," Polly told the doctor as we drew up to the door of the Imperial; it was long after midnight, but the time had passed so swiftly we hadn't realized. It must have been pretty expensive for our host, to give such a sumptuous dinner to two, well, ladies who were young only in spirit. The Tall Pines certainly couldn't be cheap, transplanted right into the Ginza. Since I had suggested the trip to the geisha house, did I dare offer to share the expense? After all, the good doctor was merely a friend of a friend. I did not dare. I told him, "We will be forever in your debt. Do come back to the States so we may return your hospitality. Sayonara!"

He bowed gravely and drove away. We never saw him again. But it was not until the next morning when our jet had cleared the Tokyo airport en route to Hong Kong that I said, "You know, Polly, he never asked us again to meet his wife!"

## CHAPTER 5

# Hong Kong Fireworks

*Bang! Boom! Whoosh!*

"I know the Chinese love fireworks even at funerals . . . This wouldn't be the Hong Kong Fourth of July, by any chance?" I asked Polly as our dining room shook the first night when we were having dinner at our Kowloon hotel. When I am traveling, days run all together in a pleasant blur, in which anything can happen and usually does.

The burst of light coming in our dining-room window that overlooked the harbor was almost blinding. "Let's go up on the roof," Polly suggested. "This must be something special."

We rode up as far as the elevator went, then climbed some dimly lighted stairs into the vast night which, instead of being dark, was full of earthbound stars and flashes. Against the black sentinel hills brooding over the harbor, the sky blazed with fire-painting from horizon to horizon, magnificent and eerie; rockets that spilled stars, others that merely roared, "Boom, look at me!"; dozens of set pieces of the Emperor's horses and of the fire-breathing dragons the Chinese love (as I do, incidentally). As we watched, fascinated, a spinney of fairy bamboo trees grew bright leaves against the peak across the harbor at Victoria. Down below, the harbor, which boasts seventeen miles of shoreline, was tipped with fire-crested wavelets, reflecting the long string of festive electric lights hung from stem to stern on Navy destroyers from England, France, and the United States. Half a dozen floodlighted cruise ships were tied to the Kowloon docks, while the busy little ferries twinkled back and forth like fireflies looking for a mate.

"Nice of them to give us such a 'welcome to our city,' " Polly said approvingly.

A horrified, unmistakably British voice came from the darkness behind us. "The Crown Colony is celebrating the arrival from London this morning of Her Royal Highness, the Princess Alexandra!"

"Indeed," I murmured.

"Bress her little heart," added the irrepressible Polly.

The Britisher choked and moved hastily away from two irreverent Americans who could jest about royalty. Actually, when we saw Alexandra close to, we liked her immensely, though we did not envy her her job—a fresh-looking, pleasant English girl trying to put a Band-Aid over the deep wound that was already tearing apart the British Empire. Red China had only to cut off the supply of water she now sold to the Crown Colony, or perhaps to move her regiments across the bridge to take back the bit of land that had long belonged to her own Chinese Empire, and she could disrupt Hong Kong's life in hours. All of the four million refugees who had fled Red rule would be slaughtered before the United Nations could even pass a resolution. Both the Chinese and the English knew this, but they counted for safety upon the fact that China needed the dollars, pounds, and francs she earned in Hong Kong to shore up her shaky economy.

Meanwhile the dogged British went valiantly forward, doing their best to feed, clothe, and teach hygiene to the desperate millions of refugees who had chosen freedom. The silent battle of Hong Kong was rather like the Battle of Britain under the buzz bombs, the man on the street refusing to accept defeat. Today they had sent into the front line even the slim young Princess Alexandra.

"We could do with a princess or two in Washington," I suggested as the final Union Jack flamed bravely above us in the sky. "A hostess to meet VIPs at the airport, to pin on medals, and kiss babies. Then the President could get on with the nation's real business."

"But he wouldn't have any fun," Polly pointed out.

Our first close view of the princess was at the military tattoo given in her honor. We drove to the great open-air amphitheater amid paper decorations and flags fluttering from even the Red Chinese banks and stores, and got to our seats very near the Governor's box just as Alexandra arrived, poised and erect; in her white dress with the great sash of royal blue across her chest, with her crown of shining brown hair, her pleasant, fixed smile, she managed to look both amused and regal.

"No balloons?" I murmured, looking about. "You know, when I watch our Presidential candidates at the nominating circuses, dummies which the hard-faced political bosses manipulate openly for their own ends, I cringe . . . All I can do about it is to turn off the TV. Democracy, my eye!"

"Those bagpipers put on a good show," Polly yelled over the rumpus the Scottish band was making for Alexandra, home, and country. She hadn't heard a word I'd said. Oh, well . . . everyone to his own racket.

The big show for the princess didn't miss a trick; each regiment or whatever went on and on through the night, performing deeds of derring-do. There were hair-raising pyramids of soldiers on motorcycles, bridge-building races led by little Gurkhas from Nepal, pride-of-the-city traffic squads as they whirled about like ballet dancers on their raised platforms. As fighters they are tough as steel, quicker than the blink of an eye. But when the Army rescued a fallen climber from the top of the mountain across from the amphitheater, the sled roared down so fast that I decided that if I ever got in such a tough spot I'd rather be dead than rescued. Through all this wind of excitement, not a hair of Alexandra's brown head got out of place; it wouldn't dare.

"She looked lonesome, always having to do what is expected of her, never what she feels like," I commiserated on our way home. "I do hope she finds someone nice to marry." (Alexandra did later, thank heaven.)

Polly's and my greatest hazard in Hong Kong was the Battle of the Air Conditioner, which is so new to the Orient that they turn it on full blast on the theory that Western visitors are all Eskimos. After driving home through the pleasantly mild night, we found our room so near freezing that I rushed to turn off the icy blasts while Polly flung up the windows so that the roar of the city blew in on the damp night air. Hong Kong never sleeps, or if it does doze, it snores; the racket is unbelievable but preferable to being frozen as you sleep. But even when we disappeared for a few moments into the bathroom, our room boy would rush in, slam down the windows, and turn on the air conditioner. The laws of the ancient Medes and Persians had nothing on Chinese rules which, once issued, are carried out to the letter, or else. A friend of mine once took an old coat and materials for a new one to her tailor, with an order to copy the old one exactly; the tailor obeyed, even to cutting a slit where the lining had been torn and mended, and sewing it up again neatly.

"What happened to our room boy? I haven't seen him today," I asked Polly. "He hasn't cleaned off that black ring around the tub I spoke to him about yesterday.

He seems to have disappeared entirely."

"Of course. He lost face. You'll learn," Polly comforted. The room boy didn't return for two days, during which we had to make our own beds.

Try getting one poached egg for breakfast when the menu order quotes two! Day after day, hugging my sweater about me in the frigid dining room, I would beg for "Just one egg, please." "Yes, yes, madame." The waiter would beam and return placidly with two. Changing a Chinese mind is as hard as digging a hole with your finger in a pond; it simply closes right up again. But we did win out in the Battle of the Coffee Cups, mostly, I think, because the waiters found Polly and me ready to laugh with them, even at ourselves. I am simply not human until I get my first sip of coffee, but Polly likes hers at the end of her breakfast. Morning after morning I would stagger to our table with one eye open, begging, "Coffee *now,* please." The little Chinese waiter would rush for the silver-plated coffeepot, then try to fill Polly's cup also, but she'd cover it with her hand, explaining, "No, no, coffee later."

Each morning as Polly and I came in we would see the white-clad little waiters clustered about the door, waiting for customers, giggle and poke each other in the ribs. Finally I had to know what it was all about.

"What's so funny about us?" I asked our waiter.

He blushed; the rose-pink shade under his yellow skin made him almost orange-colored. "Nothing, madame!" But I pressed him, "Nonsense, tell me!"

"They give you two ladies Chinese names," he explained uneasily. "Call you 'Coffee Now' and 'Coffee Later.'" When we laughed, he joined in uproariously, much relieved.

We liked our Chinese names so well that we still sign our letters to each other in the Hong Kong manner.

Hong Kong is, of course, a shopper's paradise, where you can buy a twelve-transistor Japanese radio cheaper than in Tokyo, and Thai silk dresses for less than in Bangkok. Since there are two shifts of tailors working day and night, I picked out some woolen material from England one morning, had it fitted that afternoon, and wore it the next night, which was chilly. Tailors' shops are social centers where they press upon you drinks, soft or hard, and coffee flavored with the story of their lives while you wait for a fitting. Norman, my tailor, happened to be a clever Indian, but he had a Chinese head fitter. When Norman heard I was going on later to Nepal, he offered me a letter of introduction to the two queen mothers, one the mother of the present king and the other his aunt, both of whom had been married to King Mahendra's Hindu father. Every year Norman went to Kathmandu to spruce up the family wardrobes. He lived, he said, in a little house on the palace grounds in order to facilitate fittings, though how one could fit a sari, which is merely a piece of cloth you wrap around you, was more than I could figure. I accepted the introductory letter with proper gratitude but never used it; it seemed a bit odd to be introduced to royalty by one's tailor.

Shopping with Polly was such sweet folly; never had I been separated from my cash so painlessly. Polly always wore white cotton gloves which she washed every night, for she had a horror of contracting an Oriental skin disease. I who hated gloves went with carelessly bare hands, sunburned in India. We would sally forth from our hotel in the cool of the morning to bargain happily for articles which we wanted and many we didn't but which were just too enticing. Guess who got the skin disease? Polly, of course. Horrified, she rushed into a chemist's shop and was met by the Chinese proprietor who had three solitary hairs dangling from his chin. He soothed, "Aha, I fix." The remedy he handed her was labeled "atomic ointment" and may have been ground-up frog's legs, but it worked.

Bargaining in the Orient is at once a game and an art

in which Polly was so proficient that both she and the vendor enjoyed themselves thoroughly, while I was merely the cheering section. We would enter a shop, lured by the window display of gorgeously embroidered nightgowns or blouses in the window. Polly would beam at the proprietor and say flatteringly, "You have beautiful embroidery on your nightgowns. But I am looking for a sweater. A jumper, perhaps you call it?"

"Alas, we do not sell sweaters," the proprietor would regret. Already Polly had him on the defensive. He would rush around and offer us a Coke or some of that awful orange fizz the English bottle up; Polly would take a sip while I looked frantically for a potted palm into which to empty my fizz. She would say graciously, "Well, perhaps since we are here we will look around."

Great piles of the most exquisite underwear from which we could make our selection would appear on the counter. Polly would praise the workmanship, absently ask the price, then raise her eyebrows. She'd look the shop proprietor straight in the eye. "You're sure these lovely things were not embroidered in Red China? You know we are not allowed to take anything from there into the States."

The proprietor would wring his hands. "No, no. On the word of my wife's cousin once removed, these were all made right here in Hong Kong!"

"You can give a certificate of origin?"

"Well, no, Illustrious Lady," the proprietor would admit. "Not for these." Whereupon he would bring out from under the counter even more beautiful embroidered silken undergarments. "Does China make nylon? Obviously these are from the West."

But not necessarily embroidered there, as we all three knew.

"These are more expensive, but to you only I will sacrifice them at the same price as the cotton ones. Think of that!"

"A certificate of origin costs ninety cents," Polly would observe, so he would agree to give us one and to knock off the ninety cents. Finally we would emerge from the shop carrying our exquisitely handmade purchases at the exact price which Polly and the proprietor had decided upon the moment we came in the door; but neither of them would have missed the game of wits they had played.

We were not the kind of Americans who cheat their own government; besides, the nightgowns would have been confiscated by the customs if we had tried.

But sometimes in their zeal to carry out the letter of the law "which kills rather than the spirit which gives life," our American officials could be just plain stupid. So it was the American Consulate for me, and I explored its labyrinthian corridors on the Monday morning after Polly and I (as two proper Episcopalians) had attended early communion at the Anglican Cathedral. The great gray stone church is comfortably Victorian in feeling and hospitable to visitors; we went down the long aisle to the communion railing in a procession of Chinese, British, and Americans, coolies, shopkeepers, and the titled wife of the Governor of the Colony. I should have been looking down at my clasped hands and thinking holy thoughts, but I noticed at the left of the altar a tiny chapel where hung a faded wooden plaque with red flowers in a vase on a little shelf below. The faded, red-painted, carved letters ended in "Richard something," which, of course, intrigued me. After the service I went closer to read the words.

"This was carved by a British prisoner of war here in 1941 during the late unpleasantness with the Japanese," explained Mr. Kwan, the Chinese verger. "It hung in the prison chapel until after the war, when it was presented to the Cathedral by the Reverend Charles Strong, who later became our dean." The little verse spoke to me strongly, as it must have to the war-weary Englishman in a prison camp:

Thanks be to Thee, my Lord Jesus Christ,
For all the benefits Thou hast given me.
O Merciful Redeemer, Friend and Brother,
May I know Thee more clearly,
Love Thee more dearly,
Follow Thee more nearly
Day by day.

ST. RICHARD OF CHICHESTER, 1197–1255

"This is exactly what I've been looking for as a memorial for Jock!" I told Polly excitedly. "It's so like him, don't you think? British, with its roots deep in history. His philosophical acceptance of life was like these two other Englishmen, St. Richard and the British war prisoner, generations apart. I wonder . . . Could I have this copied to send to the States? If the vestry of St. Elizabeth's in Sudbury approves, it could be added to the war memorials already left in the personal chapel of Ralph Adams Cram. But we hold worship there now."

"We could ask the dean for permission."

The dean not only agreed but offered to have his own Chinese artist, who did all the carving for the Cathedral, copy the little shrine for me, and the verger would see to shipping it. I gave the latter a check for $200, together with my home address so that if more cash were needed he could let me know. Just to be sure there could be no possible hitch in sending the memorial later to Massachusetts, I dropped by the American Consulate. Was it possible that one had to have a certificate of origin for a prayer seven hundred years old, sent by one church to another?

The official to whom I was directed had a very plush office with wall-to-wall carpeting and violent air conditioning. He wore striped pants and a morning coat but must have been up late the night before, for he kept yawning all through our conversation. Finally he reached for a thick book on his desk and flipped through the pages to announce, "No wood carving may enter the United States from Hong Kong. Undoubtedly it was made in Red China."

"But this isn't even carved yet!" I gasped. "The dean of the Cathedral is hardly a Red. The work is to be done by his very own artist. What possible connection could *they* have with Mao Tse-tung?"

"The book says, 'No wooden carved article allowed.' The law is the law."

If he hadn't yawned again, I probably wouldn't have been so angry. I wanted to sputter, "You striped-panted idiot!" With difficulty I held back the words. I merely told him, "It's people like you, tied up in red tape, who are making us Americans the laughingstock of the entire East! I shall report you to Washington!"

He stared at me as if I were at last visible. I rushed on, "I am a member of the Press Club. I could make you a lot of trouble if I choose. And I do choose!"

"Now, now," he placated. Who could suspect such a harmless middle-aged lady could go off like a rocket? "Do not worry, madame, I will personally see that the gracious memorial to your husband is sent without delay when it is finished."

Oh yeah? I thought vulgarly. Stupidity affects me that way.

But he kept his promise. The memorial plaque arrived in Sudbury shortly after I returned there. But alas, it was very different from the quiet, faded words painted by the British prisoner of war. Gilt and bright red are so closely associated in the Chinese mind with temples and churches that the Cathedral carver had generously improved upon the original. The new horror boasted bright gold letters with gilt scrawls here and there, the whole as highly varnished as an advertisement for a chop suey joint. Jock would have risen from his grave at the very sight of it. Appalled, I hid the thing for a time in my attic and finally gave it to a friend to destroy for me since I couldn't bear to watch a dream burn.

Visitors explore a strange city in different ways. To Polly, Hong Kong was a vast storehouse of lovely things, jade to be found in the dark shop of an ancient Chinese, a copy of the T'ang horse I'd always wanted but couldn't afford, pale pearls that illumined the neck of the wearer, all of them to be carefully, appreciatively handled. Other tourists, their noses buried in guidebooks, scurry from page to page to be sure they haven't missed anything the neighbors will ask about back home in Iowa. Once I watched an American woman rush through a magnificent collection of jade, soft green, dark brown, lustrous white, worth a king's ransom, and remark, "There, that's checked off! Gosh, my feet hurt!"

To me, the most exciting discoveries were the people who lived in this strange, fascinating city, finding out how they lived, thought, and acted. I wondered, "Are the millions of refugees to freedom actually better off here than in Red China? What can an individual American who hasn't very much money do to help them?" I had the theory that while great grants of food and technical assistance from one government to another were necessary, real understanding between the Chinese and American people could come only person to person. I spent most of my days with S. Y. Lee, Chinese secretary of the Hong Kong Christian Welfare and Relief Council, exploring both the city's dives and beauties. Together we drove in a jeep to visit huge gray concrete apartment houses where 2500 Chinese were crowded together and where, even though each apartment consisted of only one ten-by-ten room, if the family did not boast six adults, they had to take in a "boarder." Yet these people were clean and merry, for the Chinese prefer companionship to privacy. S. Y. and I drifted in a sampan down the South China Sea to visit the islands around Hong Kong where the refugees were replanting gardens and trees on the denuded hills. We spent an hour talking to a withered crone who was younger than I was, who had been born on her family's sampan moored to the shore. Afloat she had had her babies and would eventually die there, still in her tiny world. She *was* China, ancient, yet crackling with vitality, with her own special wisdom of endurance, the living China which few tourists, scrabbling for beaded sweaters, come to know.

S. Y. Lee took me to lunch in a tiny village inn on the main highway in the New Territories. (His baptismal name was "Albert," but everyone called him "S. Y." What these initials stood for in Chinese I never did find out.) We climbed up a flight of steep, dirty stairs, flanked on one side by a tank where the diner could choose his special fish to be cooked to order; in other cages were partridges, also doomed to the table . . . if one had the time to wait, which residents of Hong Kong who can afford to eat such delicacies usually have. The day was blazingly hot and the room into which we pushed was loud with a babble of many languages, for the newspaper reporters who were following Princess Alexandra on her trip to the New Territories (leased from China for ninety-nine years, two-thirds of whose days of grace had already elapsed) were lunching here, too, waiting for the royal cavalcade to arrive. The waiter brought us chopsticks, a great bowl of steaming hot water in which to dip them, and our rice bowls. Amid shouts of derisive laughter, an American reporter was trying to absorb a great bowl of Chinese noodles, wrapping them around his chopsticks and shoving them into his mouth by the yard. S. Y. ordered for us tiny packages of prawn and pork wrapped in cabbage leaves, a huge dish of rice scattered with bits of squid, sausage crisped in brown batter, and an ocean of hot, strong tea for which I was grateful as I was suspicious of the drinking water. After the meal we were given damp towels to wipe off the remains, a courtesy which I, for one, sorely needed.

"All this for two costs less than five dollars, Hong Kong," Mr. Lee boasted. "About fifty cents apiece." I had paid three dollars for lunch yesterday at my hotel. Small wonder they welcomed tourists.

Back in the car, we were headed for St. Christopher's Orphanage, where, besides older homeless children, they took babies found in ashcans by the police, kept them in the hospital until they had been tested for physical and mental health, then flew them by jet to be adopted in both Europe and the United States. But S. Y. found his parked jeep could not be moved! It had been shoved by the police to the side of the road till Princess Alexandra and her escort had passed by. All we could do was sit and sweat. The sidewalks were massed with white-clad Chinese children holding tiny British flags in their hands; they must have been waiting in the sun for a long time for they were restless, noisy, and milling about. Add to this the excited voices of hundreds of adults, rolling over us in a hot wave of sound, till we felt like screaming, too, "Hurry up! Get on with the show!" One small Chinese expressed his irritation dramatically. He had put his head on the edge of our jeep door and had been regarding me with flat black eyes that demanded, silently, a coin; but I knew if I gave it to him, I'd be overwhelmed by a horde of youngsters yelling, "Me too, Auntie!" When he had satisfied himself I wasn't going to come across, the small boy turned his back and relieved himself disgustedly into the gutter.

When the princess finally arrived, I was too hot to even turn my head but was merely conscious of her green hat and fixed brave smile. Being the Band-Aid for an empire was a weary, frustrating business.

At the end of our separate days Polly and I would meet to have tea together in the vast lobby of the Peninsula Hotel, where "If you sit there long enough, everyone you know will pass by." The tea there was delicious, with such delicacies as asparagus tips wrapped in soft bread and little cakes frosted and abundant which the waiter counted as you chewed to know how many to charge you for. Meanwhile the orchestra played nostalgic melodies, "Smoke Gets in Your Eyes" and "I Want To Be Happy, but I Can't Be Happy, Unless You Are Happy Too."

"Good afternoon, ladies!" The young man from Ohio whom we'd picked up on our jet flying to Hong Kong sauntered up to our tea table. He grinned mischievously. "Don't you two know that sitting on the left-hand side of the orchestra here is merely hanging out a sign that you are . . . well, ladies of the evening? Just waiting to be picked up?"

"Left which way?" Polly demanded practically. "As you come in the front door? Or counting from the lobby desk?"

He refused to tell us and just went away laughing.

"Well"—Polly shrugged—"one can always hope."

We had heard of the Shanghai Market, held once a week, where the government cordoned off from traffic eight blocks of city streets so the merchants could display their very cheap merchandise upon the pavements for the immigrants from Red China who could afford only a few Hong Kong coins. It seemed to be about as near visiting Communist China as we were likely to get, so we wanted to go. But when we asked at the hotel desk just where to direct our taxi driver, the desk clerk was horrified.

"That is no place for two ladies, alone!"

Of course that made us more determined than ever. When we finally got it across to him that we were going, willy-nilly, he urged, "Well, if you must go, please to put all your valuables, passports, traveler's checks, jewelry, here in our safe and carry only a few coins tied in your handkerchiefs! The market is thick with thieves."

We put our stuff in the safe but could hardly tie coins

in our handkerchiefs since we used Kleenex. Everyone seemed to agree, however, that we were being foolhardy. Even our taxi man, when we told him where we were headed, protested, "No, no. Dirty place. Dirty people!"

*"Young man!"* Polly said, very *grande dame.* He went.

For some reason, instead of electric streetlights, the Shanghai street market was lighted by flaming oil flambeaux tied to the posts, which gave an eerie glitter to the scene. When we got out of our taxi, which rushed, hooting loudly, away, the myriad Chinese eyes turning to stare blankly at us intruders were unnerving. Hundreds and hundreds of strange ivory faces, and ours the only two white ones in sight. Far from being the wooden-visaged Orientals depicted in Dr. Fu Manchu, the Chinese are a gay, volatile people, rather like the Italians, whose emotions are easily stirred to laughter or rage. I wondered uneasily, "Maybe the people who live here know better than we. If these refugees decide to mob us, who would know? We would disappear like a grease stain in soapy water."

"Hello, America!"

A ten-year-old Chinese boy was pushing his way toward us through the crowd, his face alight with welcome. Proud of his schoolboy English and of recognizing that we were not British, he offered, "Come, I will go with you. To translate. What did you wish to buy?"

We went with him gladly. Lying on blankets or old coats spread out upon the street were cheap plastic sandals, nearly worn-out secondhand clothes, battered pots and pans priced for the thin pocketbook, pens that did not write but that looked official in the coat pocket—all the flotsam and jetsam available to the very poor. Even if we did not buy anything, the merchants were polite and smiling. Our small guide led us from blanket to blanket, introducing us in Chinese, while everyone bowed deeply. In short, it was the jolliest, most friendly evening Polly and

I had had in Hong Kong, for here you could feel the heart of a great people beating.

The only one who bothered us at all was an Englishman, three sheets to the wind, who happened to stagger by. Seeing us, he rushed for a policeman, demanding, "Officer, take care of these poor ladies! They are lost!"

"Lost, indeed! We are here by invitation!" I told the officer indignantly. The little Gurkha smiled and went away, but the drunk continued to follow us till finally we got rid of him by going into a doorway marked LADIES. Encouraged by the success of our independence, we took a bus instead of a taxi back to our hotel. Polly, holding out a handful of coins for the conductor to pick out whatever he wanted, said, "We probably never were safer in our mothers' arms!"

Certainly all the Chinese we met in Hong Kong treated us Americans as equals. Perhaps this was because, as British-protected refugees, they were for the moment free of fear of reprisal from their Communist masters. Certainly the Chinese had small reason to love the West politically. We had forced opium upon them, a practice which had boomeranged by degrading our own slums as much as theirs. We Americans had made the Chinese lose face by denigrating them as immigrants to our supposedly "free" country, because the farmers of California hated to work as hard as the industrious Chinese. We had chosen to back Chiang Kai-shek even after we found out that his regime was as riddled with bribery and crime as that of the Communists. When Chiang was banished to Taiwan, we had turned that island into as bristling a fort as Hawaii after Pearl Harbor, furnishing, besides guns and ammunition, limousines for his generals to throw dust in the faces of the farmers working in their fields. As the apex of our stubborn refusal to admit our foreign policy could possibly be wrong, we had failed to recognize Red China's government even after its twenty years in office and currently were doing our best to wreck its economy.

"How can we pretend six hundred million people are invisible?" I demanded of Polly hotly. "I hold no brief for Communism, certainly. Mao Tse-tung is a decaying horror. But our children and grandchildren will have to deal with China whether they want to or not. Couldn't we at least speak to each other? One of the craziest evenings I ever spent was watching the Chinese and American ambassadors sit side by side at an official dinner in Nepal, and neither one could speak to the other or let on that the other ambassador was there!" I sputtered to Polly, "If they go on hating us, heaven help our kids when the Red Dragon wags his tail with the bomb in it."

"Speaking of dragons, I got you one." Polly changed the subject deftly by reaching into her knitting bag and drawing out a small package wrapped in bright-red brocade. "I bought this today for your birthday. When is it, anyway?"

"I don't have 'em any more. Oh!"

The little gold dragon had jade eyes, rubies and opals in his tail, and fitted exactly the curve of my delighted arm. Thank heaven for friends who can prick your pomposity so delicately.

As our big bird took off from the airport the next morning for Calcutta, I dug down into my bag for my notebook and began to scribble.

"What's so important you can't say good-by to our nice harbor?" Polly demanded. "Can't you even wait till we're aloft?"

"I'm just jotting down the names of people we can do without . . . Mao Tse-tung, Charles de Gaulle, the stuffed shirt at our consulate." I glanced, irritated, at the jet's overhead TV screen barking busily. "And Lassie. Isn't it queer? Not even God seems to want them!"

# CHAPTER 6

# *Island-Happy*

I have a thing about islands, sea-lulled islands. I prefer them to the mainland any time because, whether one wanders through the sun-dappled cathedral pines of Maine or lies on a tropical shore where waves and palms whisper together, he has time and peace to be himself. Some are born islanders, others are adopted only after a proper period of probation, but all have salt water in their veins. For love of the sea is not so much a matter of geography as of the spirit, an enduring passion for the awesome beauty of nature.

Cap'n E. Gray, postmaster at Newagen when I was a child, used to make us all, islanders and summer people, wait for our mail on an evening when there was an especially beautiful sunset he wanted to see. What did a few stamps matter, measured against being enfolded in glory? Dangling his great legs in their sea boots over the end of his fishing pier, he would sit staring out at the explosion of red, yellow, rose, and gold enflaming both sea and sky and murmur, as I settled down beside him to dangle too, "Handsum, ain't it?"*

*Reader's Digest, August 1948.

The true reason that my brother, Ike, and I yearned to get back to Newagen, which is the sea end of the island of Southport, Maine, was that the rough, unpainted cabin, perched there on a gray-yellow cliff within the sound of great waves and the screaming of hungry gulls, was our only real home. For a parsonage, such as we lived in ten months of the year, is only a sort of holy hotel, a place where parishioners come to park their troubles. Dad, Mother, Ike, and I hardly ever had a meal alone because of assorted hungry parishioners frequently bearing complaints about the sins of Ike and me, for which they held Dad's training (or lack of it) responsible; such as Ike's getting mad at the hard-hearted neighbor across from the parsonage who, when the baseball the kids were tossing about in our street happened to fall on his front lawn, deliberately built a bonfire in his driveway and, while the small fry watched in agony, dropped the baseball into the flames. Ike retaliated by throwing an egg at his front door. Dad made Ike go over with a bowl and water to wipe the door off.

"What kind of a minister of the gospel will people think I am," Dad demanded, "with a son who throws eggs at the neighbors?"

We Preacher's Kids knew that we were loved deeply by our parents, but we also understood early in life that when we wanted something and the parish needed something, the church always came first. This was a fact of life like the sun rising. Once when Mother was curling her front bangs to get beautiful to speak on missions in India at the Ladies' Aid, I accidentally laid my arm upon the hot iron. Mother smoothed butter on the red streak of pain, protesting, "You shouldn't be so careless, Susie! You know I have to leave for the church." And she went. I was only three, but I still wear the pale scar on my arm and in my memory.

But once safely at Newagen, Ike and I had our parents

back again; we came first with them as other kids did with theirs. I exulted, "We don't have any doorbell! We don't have to open our front door again ever if we don't want to!" Small wonder we children lived from summer to summer in anticipation of the great hegira. For even getting to our island was fun. The "Big Boat" from the Eastern Steamship Company left Boston for Bath at 5:30 P.M. We knew that Mother had packed us a delicious basket supper because we couldn't afford the dollar apiece it cost for the whole family to eat on the boat; but we could sniff delicious odors of steak and lobsters from the dining room, as remote as heaven. We knew full well we would have to change at 4 A.M. at Bath to the small, sturdy steamer which wound downriver among the wooded islands, but when we were sent to bed early, Ike and I could never resist peeking through the tiny holes in the top of our stateroom bunks, watching for hours, listening to the orchestra sawing away in the red velvet saloon. Consequently our eyes would be glued shut with lost sleep when we were hauled out of our warm bunks and onto the cold deck the next morning. And Mother once packed suitcases so frantically that when she needed a rag to wash Ike's face awake, she tore off by mistake the tail of Dad's only Sunday white shirt. Since the shirt had cost $2.98, he couldn't afford to buy another but had to keep his coat on, Sundays, for the rest of the long hot summer.

It was bitterly cold, however, on the deck of the island boat where we hunched uncomfortably on wobbly canvas-seated stools, watching the battle of Hell Gate where the river narrowed and the tide ran so fast it was nip and tuck whether our boat would win through; we didn't much care if we made it or not until the miracle occurred. The sun came up in red splendor behind the pointed pines, reminding us that we were nearly home! We were back in Maine and free as the gulls squawking over our heads! Warmed by this knowledge and by paper cups of hot cocoa, we felt as proud as if we had sparked the new day ourselves.

"I wonder if John will be there waiting?" Ike shivered happily. John was his pet gull who all last summer had come at the sound of the tin bucket from which Ike dumped the garbage over the cliff into the sea.

A spanking pair of big black horses pulling a buckboard met us at Southport landing, then clopped briskly down the orange dirt road through the crisp air to Newagen, where there were no parishioners, only gulls, squirrels, and close-mouthed invisible fish. We began to run along the shore, screaming our delight that we had once again safely shed our parsonage skins, and were born again as lovers of the sea, of our deep silent woods, of our own beloved island.

In times of danger, pictures from one's past life are supposed to flash through the mind. Do you know what I thought of recently when I was a prisoner in an Asian relief bus on Route 4, the main road down on the Mekong Delta in Vietnam? It was impossible to move because of the South Vietnamese and American Army vehicles rushing down the narrow paved road to fight the Vietcong in the rice field beyond our bus. All we could do was to park on the dirt shoulder of the road, hoping that the mines which the VC put there every night and which our side tried to clear out every morning had been removed. Pray heaven that the whirlybirds roaring over our heads would not drop a napalm bomb our way by mistake! I wondered (my mouth dry with fear) if I'd ever eat another real Maine island breakfast with mugs of hot black coffee, with pancakes with real maple syrup and—gifts from the neighbors' pots—sweet, cold, little "short" lobsters. Greedy me. But it worked. I forgot to be afraid.

So when Polly and I decided to visit assorted islands of the Pacific on our way home from Asia, I was ecstatic.

Would the old island magic hold true in the strange, lush tropics as in cool, pine-scented Maine?

Our first glimpse of Penang in the Straits of Malacca was clouded by indignation because the Malayan Airlines, alone in the Orient, had refused to honor the forty-four pounds of luggage allowed by our Pan American round-the-world tickets, and we had to pay excess baggage. "It isn't the money; it's the trickiness!" Polly exploded to the young, handsome captain of our jet, with whom we were walking out to the plane. He wore his four stripes jauntily and had an eye for the ladies. "Do you need new uniforms?"

He grinned. "Well, we're not rich Americans." He glanced admiringly at Polly (all men from seven to seventy did) and suggested, "Why don't you two ladies ride up in the cabin with me?"

So Polly and I watched with wonder while the lovely island of Penang rose like Venus from the silken light-blue sea. I wondered idly whether the cane my father used to carry on occasion had been named for the Straits or the Straits for his cane. Nonsense comes easily in such light-hearted company as that of this young air captain. As we swooped down to the airport, he urged proudly, "Don't miss the Temple of a Thousand Buddhas. And go up the cog railway to the top of Penang Hill. Queen Elizabeth of England has a big house up there, the view is so marvelous. You can see almost to heaven."

"Were you born here?" I hazarded, one island lover to another.

"Penang belongs to every Malayan," he said evasively as our plane touched its wheels down lightly.

Penang residents, like Newagen's Cap'n E. Gray, cling to their own ideas and are equally allergic to change. The E and O Hotel hadn't discarded a red velvet cushion or a heavy window drapery since Queen Victoria's day.

Advised casually by the desk clerk to find our own room—"The porter will be up later with your bags"—we couldn't make the big iron key open our door.

"The clerk did say room twenty-three," I said, bewildered.

Polly sniffed at the delicate perfume which filled the air. "Smell the frangipani," Polly murmured. "Try the key upside down."

It turned, of course. Every Oriental gadget works backward, as I had discovered one night in Tokyo when I was trying to find the light in our hotel bathroom without waking Polly.

"You happy?" a voice behind us demanded. Instead of our bags, the porter carried a tray of steaming hot tea and biscuits which he put down on the table on our balcony veranda, which looked out over the sea to Mt. Kedah, an enormous biscuit someone had taken a bite out of. Our room was at least thirty-five by twenty feet, with lazy fans moving the soft air overhead. "Grand Central Station with a veranda," said Polly.

"Like being at sea without being seasick," I agreed. I hate big ships. Even the smell of linoleum and bilge from a pier makes me ill. But a small boat with the wind blowing free and the sea spray fresh on my face is a joy. The quiet of our Penang veranda was heavenly after the milling bazaar, violent and vocal, at Singapore. There was no sound at all except for the whisper of tiny waves along the shore below us and the clear voice of a girl singing down under the frangipani tree. We watched a freighter glide silently along the horizon. Not even the fishing boats had engines, only quiet sails or oars that rose and fell, boats in an artist's preliminary sketch where the finished painting is about to be but never quite is. The cool sea breeze flowed past our cheeks like water. I drew a deep, satisfied breath.

"I'm going to phone and cancel my interviewing dates

at Kuala Lumpur," I announced. "All capital cities are alike, tall buildings, slums, and politicians. I can learn more about real Malayans here than sitting in an office, yakking."

"You happy?" The porter was back with our bags, beaming, and chanting the only two English words he knew. They were enough. He never woke us up for early morning tea but waited till we rang. Every day when we tossed aside our nightgowns, he would collect them, wash them, and put each one, neatly folded, on the foot of the proper bed. There were always flowers on our dressing table and plenty of soft, thick towels in the bathroom. What more could a tired traveler desire, or a weary home-comer? I said dreamily, "Queer, isn't it, how mainland people think islanders are a little touched in the head because they know that their sons will always come home? When Cap'n Gray's son, Scott, went off to war, his mother, Sooney, used to look for him every night with a lantern. Often I went down to the post office late to mail a letter. I'd see her light coming toward me down the fog-misted path. 'Have you seen my Scott?' she'd ask anxiously. It was kind of eerie, but she wasn't mad. She simply knew that everyone born in Newagen eventually had to come home. It might be tonight—who knew?"

Wherever he may roam the seven seas, by sail or steam, in the end, dead or alive, the islander is welcomed back where he belongs. I know a country graveyard where the arm of one Maine sea captain lies buried with full ceremonies because it is all the sharks left of him. The inscription on his gray slate tombstone reads:

> Home is the sailor,
> Home from the sea . . .

Whether they be Mainiacs, Malayans, Ibizans, Ceylonese, Fijians, or Tahitians, island lovers are independent, strangely happy people, glorious and stubborn in their pride. Cut off from the mainland for generations, they are not—like city dwellers—carbon copies of each other. At least the old-time New Englanders whom I know best are not. What will happen to the next generation, suckled on radio and TV satellite programs, I shudder to think. Without salt in their veins, they'd do better to move their tasteless carcasses back to the mainland.

Penang proved to have the same compelling enchantment as Newagen when we drove around the island the next day, only instead of sharp pine fragrance, here the tropical air smelled of spices, cloves, nutmeg, and cinnamon. Our driver stopped the car to climb a steep bank to pick us a sprig of cloves growing on the tree; it looked, with its bright, shiny leaves, rather like a sprig of New England lilac before the buds burst into blossom. He showed us how to cut away the thick green covering of the nutmegs to discover the delicate red veining which, of course, had disappeared when we bought them dried or powdered at home. He didn't seem to care if we tipped him or not, so long as we, too, appreciated Malayan spices. When he showed you how they milked the rubber trees, you'd think the plantation stretching for miles beyond the road belonged to him. It did, in proud spirit.

Even the mosquitoes in Penang are polite.The mosquitoes at Bangkok are military marauders. They attack as single scouts, as squads and whole battalions. In Penang they don't boast, as the Bangkok ones do, "I'm going to bite, I'm going to bite, *I'm going to bite!*" The Penang mosquitoes simply do their stuff and fly away, and live to bite another day.

As the Malayan airship captain had suggested, Polly and I went up the slow cog railway, which clicked through the jungle to the top of Penang Hill, where we could see the kingdoms of this world spread out before us: Mt. Kedah, the wide, pale-blue satin Straits of Malacca, the mist-veiled mainland beyond, and all the small coral islands and lagoons we had flown over. As always at a very high place, I had a sudden sharp temptation to jump off the cliff into the lush green so far below.

I asked Polly, "Do you suppose His angels would bear me up with wings, lest I dash my foot against a stone?"

Polly drew me hastily toward the hotel, reminding me that lunch was ready and we'd miss the tram down if we were late.

The returning car was mobbed with native holiday makers as well as with tourists, for the people of Georgetown are as enamored of their mountaintop view as Cap'n E. Gray had been of his sunset. A Chinese family of three sat opposite us, the man dressed in a black tailcoat and striped trousers, his plump little wife in a Burmese dress, and their small son of three, who piped to us, "Hi!" and then hid his face in embarrassment in his mother's brown silk lap. They were the Lu family from Singapore, where the father taught in the university, and they were on their way home from the World Council Assembly at New Delhi.

"I was there, too!" So we were at once close friends.

Polly grumbled under her breath, "Susie, you could go into a strange jungle and come out with a bishop on each arm!"

The professor said that they were going on to see the Temple of a Thousand Buddhas and if we ladies cared to join them, he'd translate the Chinese inscriptions for us. I accepted instantly, but Polly pled a previous engagement. It was her afternoon nap; besides, she said that sightseeing in churches made both her conscience and her feet hurt. But she cheered up when Dr. Lu remarked that the Buddhists had formal worship services only at the time of the new or full moon.

"That sounds like a good idea," Polly said. "Maybe I'll join." After her nap, naturally.

The stone steps leading up to the temple doorway were

lined with dark little shops selling everything for both gods and men, paper prayers with tiny brocade bags to put them in—they make marvelous coin purses—food for both humans and fish, and small silver bells to ring to wake up the Buddhas. The enchanting Lu baby and I were torn between buying a carp or a turtle from the temple pool; by buying a fish we could save life and so gain future merit, but if we turned loose a turtle we could insure ourselves of long life on this earth. We eventually bought both carp and turtle. I wondered if this magic worked for Episcopalians.

The temple itself was huge, peopled with darkly peaceful gods, pious Malayans, and tourists. Dr. Lu interpreted the Chinese inscription under one Buddha as the inevitable *om mane padmi hum,* "Oh, the jewel in the heart of the lotus!" and another as "The lotus flower of forgetfulness." Would Fiji, where we were flying tomorrow, be Buddhist, too? It would certainly include animists of a sort, for trees, rocks, and sea are neighbors to an islander. I finally thanked the Lu family and left because Polly had been right; my feet did hurt. But when I got back to our room it was empty except for a note on my bureau: "Have gone shopping for jade for Toby's West Point ring." Which was more precious to collect, jade or bishops? Well, jade would last longer . . . unless you counted on eternal life.

The coral reef curving out from the long white beach at Korolevu in Fiji was even more exciting than the pools left behind by the tide which Ike and I had explored in Maine, for the reef was an apartment house for all sorts of sea creatures which had been building their homes for hundreds, perhaps thousands, of years. Fiji air, unlike that of languid Penang, had a vigor more like Maine's and the wind was strong with salt. Our *bure* at Korolevu Beach, with tiny waves whispering almost at our doorstep, looked like a native hut; but beneath its thatch were comfortable beds, a tiled bathroom, screens, and a telephone by which to summon a waiter who carried his tea tray on the handles of his bicycle, miraculously without spilling a drop. We could talk with Suva or with New York. Not that we wanted to; the murmur of the sea along the white beach spoke the international language of peace.

"Let's explore the reef," Polly urged. "Right away, while the tide is out."

We clambered over the uneven, sharp coral excitedly, poking with sneakered feet at orange sea cucumbers which turned black when out of water, collecting bright bits of rose, red, and pink coral which later bleached to gray-white in the sun, admiring blue starfish and blood-spotted crabs and strange crown-of-thorns starfish. We needed our canvas shoes to wade through the pools because even a slight scratch from the coral might not heal easily; but even if I'd had to hobble for weeks, it would have been worth it to explore this strange world of tropical sea creatures.

"I wonder what I was a billion years ago?" I said dreamily. "A sea urchin who grew legs?"

"Perhaps 'a shell more rare,' as our neighbor in Concord said." Thrusting some bright shells into her dress pocket, Polly began:

> My life is like a stroll upon the beach,
>     As near the ocean's edge as I can go;
> My tardy steps its waves sometimes o'erreach,
>     Sometimes I stay to let them overflow.

She was always dredging up pertinent bits of verse while I marveled that she could remember all the words. "Oh, it's because I never went to college. I had to educate myself," she explained. But all poets do not write verse; many only feel sea magic. Since Thoreau had lived practically in my back yard—or, more properly, I in his—I did recall the rest of what he had said:

My sole employment 'tis, and scrupulous care,
   To place my gains beyond the reach of tides;
Each smoother pebble, and each shell more rare,
   Which ocean kindly to my hand confides.
I have but few companions on the shore,
   They scorn the strand who sail upon the sea;
Yet oft I think the ocean they've sailed o'er
   Is deeper known upon the strand to me.
The middle sea contains no crimson dulse,
   Its deeper waves cast up no pearls to view;
Along the shore my hand is on its pulse,
   And I converse with many a shipwrecked crew.

We ourselves looked rather shipwrecked that evening as we were too hungry from the sea air to change for dinner. Polly stared at our waiter who wore a lava-lava wrapped around his bare middle; his huge brown feet were bare also, but he sported, surprisingly, immaculate, white gloves! "Because they are likely to put their thumbs in the soup," the headwaiter explained.

Nearby on a tiny rock in the Pacific we met the ex-doctor of medicine from Suva, the islander with a college degree who'd come back home to act as the barefoot chief of his tiny native village, to which we traveled by bus, canoe, and finally by piggyback over the shallow water. As I slid down from my carrier's brown muscular shoulders, I asked the chief, whose fat, naked stomach rolled comfortably over the edge of his lava-lava, "You got tired of doling out pills to petulant patients?" He said seriously, "I got tired of rush." And I remembered the bill Cap'n Gray had given Dad when we'd asked him to haul his lobster pot for some unexpected visitors at lunch; after the cost of the lobsters he'd written, "Ten cents for hurry."

"Could be, tourists are more profitable than patients?" Polly murmured pragmatically as we followed the chief up to his *bure,* which was the largest in the village. The single room was carpeted with smoothly woven bamboo that waved up and down as you walked but was most comfortable to sit upon. The chief boomed hospitably, "Now I must introduce you to kava, the nectar of the Pacific! We celebrate tomorrow—New Year!" I watched, dubious, while he produced a handful of droopy bushes, their roots still dripping dirt, mashed them in a great wooden bowl, and poured on water to produce a milky drink which he passed around in a tin cup. With mounting concern I saw the Australian, some Germans, and several Americans take a sip from the tin mug, trying politely not to grimace. Would I vomit when it came my turn?

"Do we have to drink that, dirt and all?" I murmured, horrified, to Polly. "Will it hurt his feelings if we don't?"

"Of course not. I wouldn't think of drinking the stuff." Polly had lived long enough in the Orient to know how to handle delicate international crises gracefully. She dropped a couple of shillings into the chief's tin cup and handed it back to him. "Would you mind if we took a walk around your beautiful island?" The chief didn't mind at all.

I said defensively, as we climbed the steep cliff, "Lobsters go terribly high-priced in Maine, too, during the summer. The men have to make enough in two months to feed themselves all year."

"It's an old island custom," Polly agreed.

That night Polly and I were the only visitors to the village who were able to appear at dinner; the rest were depositing kava into basins.

The loudspeaker from the hotel desk announced with the dessert, "Fijian war dance begins out on beach! Will all guests please sit on lawn chairs?" The management wouldn't like a guest to be injured by a stray spear.

"Station WBZ-TV," I sniffed as we sat down. "I'll bet that tall guy with the biggest mop of hair is president of the local Chamber of Commerce."

The warriors were all dressed up for New Year's Eve in

their best tapa cloth lava-lavas and had yellow powder in their hair, which stood up stiff as a potato brush, but the spears were sharp all right. We could all but see the warriors' tonsils when they rushed, yelling, right at us. Ladies squealed happily, but before the spears pierced us through, they turned aside, of course.

"Phony, like all New Year's celebrations," I grumbled. "What's so groovy about making resolutions you know you're not going to keep? Getting so high you enjoy kissing a perfect stranger in Times Square?"

Yet the sitting-down dance of the Fijian women in their bright holiday finery, with flowers in their hair, as they crooned and swayed in the pavilion by the sea to the beat of the guitars and violins, was enchanting—the calm after battle. The moon overhead, the endless murmur of the waves, the wavering light of the big bonfire on the beach wove island magic again. A few of the guests got up to dance, too, but they waltzed slowly; even by flickering firelight, they all looked over forty, and were.

"I wish my son and his wife were here," I murmured to the Australian who'd settled down beside me. I was tapping my foot in time to the beat of the music. "One should see Fiji when he is twenty."

"Oh, I don't agree. Your young people walk about plenty," he insisted. "High-school exchange students, college kids hitchhiking all over Europe. They're even snapping up jobs in Sydney at the moment. Australia's the last frontier, like the Westerns they see in the films. Did your son join the Peace Corps?"

"No. There wasn't any when he was sixteen. But he and a bunch of teen-age boys and girls bicycled through eight European countries. Crazy kids, they rode motor scooters through that awful traffic in Rome and had a marvelous time singing in Irish pubs. You should have seen Rick when he landed in New York! I almost didn't own him. The soles of his shoes were tied on with string, and the customs official simply couldn't believe that all the luggage Rick had was wrapped in his raincoat. The officer said, 'After four months in Europe? Nuts!' "

"His luggage wasn't in suitcases." The Australian chuckled. "I'll wager he fell in love on shipboard."

"She came from California." I grinned. "When we drove her over to Grand Central to get her train home, the kids said good-by in the middle of Forty-second Street. They kissed so long that the traffic cop started to blow his whistle but, being Irish, he winked at me instead and waited till they had unclenched. I don't think they ever saw each other again."

"Naturally. It takes a while to find out that love that lasts is salted with compassion. Will you dance?"

Intoxicated with the mingled fragrance of sea, frangipani, and hibiscus, we glided slowly over the floor to the sound of violins and drums. Our kids could take care of themselves; I wouldn't go back to the agonies of adolescence for all the jade in China. Being a merry widow was more fun. A silly verse echoed in my mind as we whirled in a waltz.

> I don't owe nobody nothin',
> The world is my oyster, Baby.
> If I can pry it open
> We eat . . .

Polly slept late on New Year's Day, so I decided to go alone to church, whatever its creed, Christian, Moslem, or even pagan voodoo. I had no idea what or whom the Fijians had chosen to worship. "Services will begin about 10 A.M. in the nearby village," the hotel bulletin board reported vaguely. Couldn't they make up their minds?

My guide, when he finally turned up half an hour late, had a black eye. Last night's celebrations had been loud with firecrackers and fistfights under our windows, but surely the pugilists were not pillars of the church? I followed his brown feet, their soles white with calluses an inch thick, down a narrow path through tall thickets that widened finally into a deserted village green surrounded by a circle of quiet huts. Not even a chicken was in sight so early in the new year.

The little church with its tin roof, its windows innocent of glass, proved equally empty when I ventured inside; but immediately I heard the drums begin to talk, first a whisper, then a clamor, beating faster and faster. "Church drums!" I realized. "Instead of bells!"

One after another the shy brown Fijians began to drift into the pews, one mother holding a nursing baby at his Sunday breakfast, older women in their yards of flowered cotton, grandmothers more sedately covered. The astonishing thing about the gathering congregation was the large number of men. One huge Fijian seized me by the arm and propelled me down the aisle to a dais where there was also a lectern; he beamed as he sat down below me with a group of twenty-five men, half-naked and still with the yellow powder from last night's war dance in their hair—they were the choir, and how they could sing! My giant sponsor lined out the song and the rest joined in *a cappella*, harmonizing and improvising, much as our rich-voiced American Negroes do, until the chant became a swelling, soaring shout of joy. The theme sounded vaguely familiar, but whether it was a Christian hymn with variations or a Buddhist mantra I'd heard in a Bangkok temple, I couldn't decide, for the words were strange to me.

Suddenly a shy little brown man in a white lava-lava, over which he wore a shapeless brown tweed jacket, arrived through the back door and took his place at the lectern. When I saw the hole in his sleeve I knew who this little man, smiling at me, was! Once when my dad couldn't afford to have his shoes resoled, he'd put a couple of postcards over the hole, assuring Mother no one would see the bottom of his feet. He forgot that he knelt at communion.

No one could deceive a Preacher's Kid—this Fijian was a Methodist minister!

I didn't understand a word of the service, songs, or sermon, but the smell of innocent piety was as strong as that of my childhood. After the benediction, the little minister in his torn jacket took me down with him to the railing where we both shook the hands of the congregation as they filed by. One plump naked baby leaned out of his mother's arms to give me the pink hibiscus flower he'd been chewing on, then howled so loudly at its loss that I gave it back to him. Looking at this small brown baby, I remembered the words of the hymn I'd been searching for in my memory:

> For the beauty of the earth,
> For the beauty of the skies . . .

And suddenly I was at home in a strange island.

Tahiti was a disappointment after Fiji, for it seemed more like a colored advertisement of girls, wreathed in flowers, continuously shaking their rear ends, than an island where real people lived and loved. Worse, the Hollywood movie people had just left Papeete after filming *Mutiny on the Bounty* and teaching the Tahitians that nothing less than a dollar was an adequate tip. Perhaps things would be different if we went upcountry. So Polly and I hired a small car to drive around the island.

I put on my bathing suit under my dress just in case I found a good place for a swim. Polly dislikes swimming in strange seas, which are all too likely to harbor sharks and other varmints, but when I got hot enough, I'd say, "Phooey," and dive in. I must be an unappetizing morsel, for I haven't been eaten yet. The road was dusty and the sun scorching, so when we drove over a bridge where Tahitians were bathing down below in the cool-looking river, I asked Polly to please stop while I stripped to my bathing suit. The water rushed over a sort of wooden watershed divided into sections, in each of which was a gay Tahitian wearing his or her single wet garment, letting the crystal-clear water roll deliciously over him. Naked youngsters screamed and splashed alongshore.

I joined a tall brown man in a wet hibiscus-flowered skirt, who stared at me, then closed his eyes again in content. The cool water was blissful, but after a while it seemed ungracious, when you were bathing in the same tub with someone, so to speak, just to ignore him. So laboriously I concocted a sentence in French which we'd spoken in the shops in Papeete.

*"Très belle ici, n'est-ce pas?"* I ventured. (Jock, who was bilingual, since he learned to say, *"L'eau—water!"* in the first grade on the island of Jersey, used to remark that I spoke French with a Jewish accent.) *"J'aime votre île enchantée."*

The Tahitian opened his eyes, nodded, and went back to sleep. Maybe his mother had warned him not to speak to strange women, especially merry widows. So I gave myself up to enjoying the coolness slipping over my shoulders and body, the voices of the children chirping like birds, the kiss of the hot tropic sun. Suddenly my bath mate spoke.

"Swell, ain't it? I used to live in Brooklyn. But I was born here."

As we laughed together uproariously, I decided I liked Tahitians, after all.

All islanders are a breed apart who love the sea in spite of its being a moody mistress, giving generously today, tomorrow lashing out at her lover, perhaps even killing him as a queen bee does a drone after the mating. The islands that bejewel the sea's swelling bosom are heavy with history. Picnicking on the Maine shore, Ike and I had often dug up hidden mounds of clamshells, debris from an Indian meal which predated the United States of America.

More important than the past, the sea was still spitting up new islands, the process of creation was continually going on, proof that ours is not merely a decadent, unchangeable world run by an Establishment whose members are dead at thirty but don't know it, as the young people seem to think. On our way back home to our own island state of Hawaii, the captain of our Air France jet pointed out a volcanic island that had recently erupted from the sea, first as a smoking rock and now with birds bringing seeds to green its naked slopes. Henry Beston has put my feeling of wonder into singing words:

> . . . one's first appreciation [of islands] is a sense . . . that the creative forces are as great and as active today as they have ever been, and that tomorrow's morning will be as heroic as any of the world. *Creation is here and now.* So near is man to the creative pageant, so much a part is he of the endless and incredible experiment, that any glimpse he may have will be but the revelation of a moment, a solitary note heard in a symphony thundering through debatable existences of time. Poetry is as necessary to comprehension as science. It is impossible to live without reverence as it is without joy.*

Islanders also live with fear, but they have learned to harness the dangerous steeds of the sea. Shortly after Polly and I arrived in Honolulu, a terrific storm broke over the island. The following sunny morning so many cars rushed by us, as we stood on the sidewalk, that we asked a bystander, "Where are they all going?"

"Down to the beach to watch the surfers. It's a sight!"

So we hopped a car and went too. The thunder of the great waves shook not only the shore but our little rented Falcon while we were still blocks from the beach. So many cars were parked on each side of the road that we had to walk perhaps a quarter of a mile, while the roar of the surf grew louder and louder till we stood there, watching,

---

*From *The Outermost House* by Henry Beston. Rinehart, New York, 1949. Reprinted by permission of Holt, Rinehart & Winston, Inc.

awed. The waves were thirty feet high, mountains of dark-green water toppling into cascades of angry white foam as they crashed their tonnage onto the sand. The wind blew salt against our faces, beat back our clothes from our bodies.

"Dear grief, look!" Polly screamed in my ear.

A slender brown Hawaiian boy was riding his surfboard down the frightening slope of a giant wave. He slid cross-ways on the toppling water on his little bit of wood, balancing himself with exquisite timing. Imagine doing this for fun! When the wave broke, he'd be crushed to death! I closed my eyes, there was a trumpeting crash as if the world had come to an end, but when I dared look again the boy was still there. He had steered his fragile craft back into deep water and safety; a true islander, he had pitted his cool timing and lack of awe against the everlasting sea and had won.

I licked my salted lips and the knot in my own stomach relaxed as I remembered another long-ago day when fearlessness meant power. Dad, Mother, Ike, and I were sailing home over a stormy sea after a picnic on one of the outer islands beyond Newagen. Our motorboat was little more than a bucket propelled by a two-cylinder engine, which just left room for the four of us to squeeze into; Dad had bought the boat because it was cheap, so we could wander about among the islands that summer. It was good going when the sea was smooth, but the joker was that it didn't always stay that way. We had started home earlier than planned that afternoon because "it was breezin' up," but the wind had increased so rapidly that our puny little craft could hardly make any headway against the great swells rolling in from Spain. It was frightening to be tossed up and down like a chip, willy-nilly; then the engine would sputter and we'd inch ahead in the trough of the waves. Would we make the harbor? Only if the little engine kept going.

"Let's sing," Mother said.

So we sang—silly songs, grand songs. "Mary had a William goat," "White wings, they never grow weary," "Unfold, unfold, unfold, ye portals everlasting!" "He shall lead His flock like a shepherd" . . . Finally the welcoming, rocky hands of the little landlocked harbor reached out for us and we chugged, drenched and bone-weary, into quiet water. As we putt-putted up to land, I saw that the fishing pier was crowded with Newagenites, year-round lobstermen, sailors, and their wives, and I wondered what so many were doing down on the wharf at suppertime.

"Kinda choppy outside," Cap'n Gray observed as we climbed up the slippery ladder to the deck of the pier. "Thought we'd dodge down to see was you safe home."

They'd been worried about us in our cockleshell boat. Did that mean we were no longer "summer people," that we'd been accepted, really belonged to Newagen? Now that the terror of the sea was gone and we were safe, I began to shake all over. The salt on my lashes was so white I could barely see the path we were going up, but I could smell the sweet fern and the crushed bayberry. When I stumbled, Dad put his arm around me and I leaned back for a moment against his strong, wet body.

"Susie," he said, "don't you know there's nothing to be afraid of in this world or the next?"

CHAPTER 7

# Cleopatra's Wig

Not everyone has the great good fortune to be adopted by a friendly Arab family from Cairo or to walk through the dark, clamorous bazaar hand in hand with the nephew of the mayor of Giza, home of the Pyramids, as I did when I went alone on my first visit to Egypt.

This second trip around the world had as its aim spending several months in Kathmandu, where I was to write a book about the Fabulous Flemings,* who had introduced modern medicine into Nepal, an equally fabulous country which I was to come to love and to yearn for all my days. However, ever since, as a lonely adolescent, I had seen a picture of Cleopatra floating down the Nile on her barge, I had yearned to sail, too, on her romantic river. So I had arranged to stop off in Egypt en route to Kathmandu and, after exploring Cairo, to sail three days upriver to visit the great temple of Rameses II at Abu Simbel. Certainly, if there was ever a river sacred to merry widows, the Nile was it! For being merry and independent had little to do

*The Fabulous Flemings of Kathmandu. E. P. Dutton & Co., Inc., New York, 1964.

with whether one was maid or matron. Perhaps I should meet a descendent of Cleopatra's who could give me pointers, who knew?

My mother had tried hard to teach me how to manage a man without seeming to do so. All her life, from the day when she was seventeen and voted "the prettiest girl in Ft. Worth, Texas," to when she was seventy, she had only to flirt her long, curling eyelashes, to look feminine and helpless, and every male within sight rushed to her aid. She called this process "feebling up." This allure was not put on or coldly calculated but was as much a part of her as breathing, and as innocent. She and Cleopatra had a lot in common. But would it work for an ugly duckling who had inherited her dad's big nose and who wore glasses? Time alone would tell.

Traveling alone in the Orient without Polly was, at first, as tasteless as a cup of Irish coffee without the "stick" in it. But unless one is a deaf-mute, she can hardly bump elbows with the man in the next seat of a crowded jet for twelve hours without speaking. Especially when he was reading one of my books with my picture on the back cover which, strange to say, he recognized. We parted at Cairo with exchanged addresses and a promise to get in touch later in New York; so I was feeling pretty cocky when I got off the plane at Cairo.

The screaming mob of urchins who descended upon me at the airport, yelling Arabic and more incomprehensible English, terrified me. What on earth did they want? Would they tear me limb from limb? The sound of a man's authoritative voice shouting something in Arabic caused my attackers to melt away like snow before an April sun.

"They want only to carry your bags. You're Mrs. Fletcher?"

My rescuer was a tall, handsome Egyptian in long, flowing maroon robes which swept the floor regally; his turban made him look seven feet tall. (How on earth did his wife ever get the bottom of his skirts clean?) "I'm Ismail, Bill's friend. Any friend of Bill's is a friend of mine."

The card he handed me was almost as impressive as he:

Ismail Mahdi Khattab
Shepheard's official dragoman No. 3
Contractor of Upper and Lower Egypt
Camping out in the desert and sailing Dabieh on the Nile

Sailing Dabieh on the Nile! Hallelujah, here I come!

"Am I glad to see you!" I held out my hand. "Bill said he'd write." My friend Bill was interested in archeology and had been in Egypt so often it was his second home. "But I'm not staying at Shepheard's . . ."

"I know. The Semiramis." Ismail didn't like being interrupted. "Where Bill stays. He says the plumbing is ancient Egyptian, but you can see the Nile, which is more interesting than bathrooms." Ismail clapped his hands and my bags appeared like magic; he clapped again and a big black car with driver drove up. If Aladdin's genie had been the chauffeur, I wouldn't have been surprised. "I have sent roses to your room to welcome you to Egypt!" he announced. When we got to the room of the welcoming roses and found that it did not have a balcony overlooking the Nile, Ismail's wrath was so magnificent that bellhops and porters flew about until in a matter of minutes I was ensconced in a new room, complete with a river view and a midnight supper of soup and fruit on the table. "I decided you'd be too tired to go down to the dining room," Ismail announced. "I will be here tomorrow morning at nine. We will go to the Pyramids. I have a hundred and thirty Japanese who wish to ride camels there, also."

"But I don't want to ride a camel!"

To go to Giza without riding a camel is like going to Mecca without circling the Kaaba, Ismail's glance implied reprovingly. He said firmly, "Until tomorrow, then?"

Well! If Ismail said I would ride a camel, obviously I

would. I wondered, sipping my delicious hot soup, if I should buy a yashmak and go purdah all the way. But remembering the howling urchins, I decided that I rather liked "feebling up," for once. After all, this was Ismail's country and I was only a lone female to be taken care of as he had promised Bill. Not having to make decisions was rather restful at that.

The Pyramids and the half-man, half-lion Riddle looked exactly as they had in my history book. Riding the camel over the sand wouldn't have been so bad if only the creature had gotten up all in one piece, but his behind rising tipped me almost over his head, and his front, unlimbering, all but shot me over his tail; I hoped he wouldn't decide to turn his head and spit, for I'd read that was most unpleasant. Any animal Ismail had picked was well-behaved, however, and 130 Japanese on camels were quite a sight. The Pyramids filled me with awe at what midget man could do. As Ismail and I went back to the hotel to lunch together, he told me that his family had been mayors of Giza for four hundred years; but after his grandfather died, his father decided that guiding tourists was much more rewarding, so now his uncle was mayor. Ismail pointed out to me their family compound with a high wall enclosing the many houses for the different generations, but he didn't invite me to stop. I wished he had, for I found people much more interesting than the Sphinx. Who cared what it was thinking? But how did modern Arabs live? Did the papas decide whom the girls had to marry or else? Or had the ladies gone unhappily modern like the girls in Tokyo who had discarded their lovely kimonos to show their bowed legs? After all, independent females were nothing new in Egypt. What about Queen Hatshepsut, a merry widow who'd put on men's clothes and the king's ceremonial beard and who'd ruled as Pharaoh for twenty-seven years? She antedated our bloomer girls in the States by some three thousand years. I decided that wearing a yashmak would not only be un-American but un-Egyptian.

Ismail took such good care of me that I began to feel fragile and jade-precious. He not only decided which sights I had to see, but he ordered all the meals we had together so that I tasted the specialties of Egypt, and they were many and delicious. When we went to the bazaar to find a truly old native knife for Rick, who was making a collection of ancient weapons, and a lamp like the foolish virgins carried—empty—for Sylvia, Ismail held my hand tightly, guiding me down the dark alley between narrow open shops whose salesmen shouted at us in vain, till he led me to a friend's who agreed to make me "a necklace like Cleopatra's." Its intricate golden pattern scattered with turquoises was gorgeous but so bizarre that I never got up my courage to wear it. Perhaps Rick could put it in my tomb like the golden furniture in Tutankhamen's, to wear in the spirit world. Ismail couldn't have been more careful of my spending if the money had been his own. He once made a grumbling merchant cut into a large hunk of lapis lazuli, six inches in diameter, so I could have a bit of the inner, bluest stone for a ring. He had arranged for a friend of his named Amen—pronounced like after a prayer—to guide me in Luxor, and before he'd allow me to get alone onto the plane for Aswan, he bought me some amber "worry beads" to finger if I got upset.

He needn't have bothered because my seat on the plane was next to Atia Abulnaga, a Moslem woman I was to come to love.

How can I describe Atia? To say she was slender and gentle with eyes like a startled brown deer is to mention only the outer shell; when you are fond of someone, you see the inner self. She is the wise woman of the East who mothers not only her family but everyone else she meets. Atia introduced me to her husband, whom even his children affectionately called Jimmy, and to Sherif, her son who was in his last year in medical school. Her daughter, Mona, said how glad she was to meet me because she was majoring in English Literature at Cairo University.

"I am studying Shakespeare and *Pilgrim's Progress*," she told me, flirting her long, curling lashes, and when I said well, that was a varied program anyway, she laughed ... such a clear, merry sound that half the jet riders turned to look at us. She reminded me of someone ...

"Jimmy, Mrs. Fletcher is going up the Nile to Abu Simbel, too, on tomorrow's boat. Why can't she come today instead, with us?" Atia suggested. (Dr. Abulnaga's real name is Mohammed Abdel Azin. When I asked how she came to call him "Jimmy," Atia laughed. "Well, I found Mohammed Abdel Azin too much of a mouthful and I thought he looked like James Cagney!")

Jimmy said hospitably that to have me as a companion would be a pleasure; I thought he was merely being polite until we got to the boat that belched steam and soft coal. The captain said yes, he had an extra stateroom, but he wouldn't take my traveler's checks for $130; he wanted only "real money," Egyptian.

"But I don't carry that much currency."

"That's easily fixed." Jimmy took out his wallet, handed over the cash. "You can repay me when we get back to Aswan. Now we'd better go down to select our table in the dining saloon."

*Our!* He was including me! Thus simply did I join the Abulnaga family and sail up the fabulous Nile with the Egyptians to whom it belonged. We were three days gliding over the dark waters that had already engulfed the drowned temple of Philae. The golden sands of the desert stretched beyond the Nile, its banks dotted with the deserted mud-brick huts of the Nubian villagers who were being evacuated before the waters from the Big Dam at Aswan rose to cover them. For the Abulnagas this was a voyage of mingled pride and apprehension, for the great

temple of Rameses II at Abu Simbel was being cut out of
the sandstone cliff to be precariously raised two hundred
feet to higher ground. Whether this tremendous feat of
engineering would be successful or not, no one was entirely sure, so pilgrims from all over the world were rushing to take what might be a last look at this miracle temple
of ancient Egypt. There were German, French, and English groups mingling with the Egyptians on our ship, but
I was the only American. As the long, sunny, quiet hours
passed on deck and as we lingered around the Abulnaga
family table, Atia, Jimmy, and I got better acquainted
than we might have done in months ashore. I watched
how a Moslem family chaperoned their young lovely
daughter without seeming to do so. Mona was a charmer;
she had that "come hither" look in her dark, melting eyes,
and in the curve of her small, rounded hips, that drew men
as inevitably as the Nile drew thirsty travelers. She was
springtime, innocent yet instinctively alluring. Every
male on the ship watched her hungrily. But she was never
alone; somehow Atia, Jimmy, or Sherif always turned up
at her elbow.

"How do you Moslems manage marrying off your
daughters?" I asked Jimmy one evening as we sat watching the moon paint the Nile with silver. "Would you make
Mona marry someone you picked out, even if she didn't
want to?"

"Of course not," Jimmy said. He smiled at me in the
moonlight. " 'Accentuate the positive.' I just see to it that
she meets the right people whom I *do* approve of. Meanwhile ..." Our eyes went to where she was "having a date"
with a fellow passenger, leaning over the rail and smiling
up into his fascinated face ... with Atia on one side of the
couple and Sherif on the other. "Meanwhile, we take care
of her."

Thus we sailed together, my Moslem family and I, as
merry as grigs—whatever they are—and arrived at Abu

Simbel, where the tall cliffs were made magic by the moonlight. The great temple, cut into the living rock, towering above us, was magnificent, an architect's dream; here had been cunningly welded together both nature and art so that they were one. On either side of the entrance, blazing with electric lights, were two huge statues, sixty-seven feet high, of that P. T. Barnum of Egypt, Rameses II. As we docked—if you can use the word for teetering over a wiggly plank into the sand—we could see that beside the Pharaoh was his Queen, Nefertiti, who did not quite come up as high as his knee, while the two children (he was reputed to be the father of 187) merely topped their father's ankle. Easy to guess who wore the pants (excuse me—ceremonial beard) in the Pharaoh's family!

Rameses II could have given the modern public relations man pointers. As we entered the bright mouth of the temple, we were brought up short by another statue of the ubiquitous gentleman and then by a third statue which depicted him as a god. He had made the headlines ever since he, at twenty-five, had made sure of the throne by murdering his elder brother and marrying his half-sister, the princess royal. Rameses had then proceeded to pull down the statues of the other Pharaohs and to put up his own; if history didn't do him credit, he twisted it by the tail.

"Look over there on that wall!" Jimmy pointed to the pictured story of the battle of Kadesh where, in colors still gorgeous after three thousand years, Rameses was shown magnificently charging the Hittites, single-handed, until he had shamed his troops into backing him up and winning the battle.

"Actually, the Hittites won or, at best, it was a draw," Sherif put in. "But the old smoothie settled their differences by marrying a fifteen-year-old Hittite princess, adding her to his harem. Those old Pharaohs had it made.

That big I Am reigned for sixty-seven years!"

"Well, he did dig Queen Nefertiti. He built her that chapel beyond his own temple." Mona defended him, giggling. "Of course, it's much smaller than his." They could jest about Rameses because he belonged to the family and they were so proud of him. I felt very small and insignificant trailing these magnificent Egyptians whose civilization went back thousands of years to when my ancestors in Europe were still painting themselves a pagan blue. It was a mere blink of an eye from the Pharaoh to Sherif, standing there, today's young Egypt, dark, strong, sure of himself also. Mona might well have modeled for whom? Why, of course! That's why she had seemed so familiar. If I shut my eyes, would I wake up dreaming back in Sudbury, Massachusetts? Could this possibly be me going down the Nile with a modern Cleopatra on her barge?

Back in the Cataract Hotel, colorful and shabby, in Aswan with the Abulnagas, I began to realize how well-known in Cairo my doctor friend and my adopted family were. Jimmy knew everyone. If we wanted to visit the Big Dam, he knew an Egyptian engineer who would lend us his car. We had dinner with a factory owner who employed ten thousand Sudanese and who had been host to the governor and the Begum the night before. The Begum, of course, was the widow of the famous Aga Khan, who got fatter and fatter because his subjects had to pay him tribute in gold according to his weight. She wintered in a great white house near her famous husband's tomb, across the river from our hotel. Her companion was the Aga Khan's Parisian girl friend who'd been with him in the terrible automobile accident from which he died. "Bettina isn't very pretty but she wears lovely clothes," Atia remarked. It was all very civilized, modern . . . and Moslem. And why not? But it was rather a shock to me when our host at dinner walked through the lobby later, where Atia and I were chaperoning Mona and her date, a fair-haired German engineer, who were sitting together and chatting across the lobby. (At least we couldn't hear what the young people said to each other!) I smiled at our host and said, "Nice evening, isn't it?" but Atia's face was wooden as a cigar-store Indian's as she stared straight in front of her.

"A Moslem lady never speaks to another man unless her husband is present," she explained.

Goodness, I had a lot to learn! I watched the arrogant Russian in his rumpled civilian suit, decorated with so many strings of medals one could hardly see the fabric, parade across the lobby, followed by his humble flock of lesser engineers. Would we Americans have done better not to have given up building the dam? Would the Egyptians have liked us any better? Atia was chuckling. She said, "I know a chief of police who wears plastic medals!" You couldn't really fool these ancient people; they'd seen too much and lived too long.

Next morning I was awakened at sunrise by a terrific bang. Had Israel attacked? I leaped out of bed, reached for my blue nylon negligee. I wasn't going to be shot in my nightgown! But Mona stuck her head in my door, yawning reassuringly. "It's only the cannon for the beginning of Ramadan, the month of fasting. The orthodox can't eat anything, or even drink a sip of water, till the cannon goes off again at sundown."

Would the Abulnagas keep Ramadan too? Was it only the man in the street who fasted? Jimmy announced that we were invited for tea with the manager of the big fertilizer factory which employed some twenty thousand Nubian refugees. Our host—who called Dr. Abulnaga "Uncle Jimmy"—had an impressively huge home with an army of servants to do everything for you except breathe. The hostess, in a clinging tea gown that shrieked "Paris," sat at the table, spread with an enormous epicurean tea.

Suddenly it dawned on me that nobody was eating or drinking except me! I was left, embarrassed, with my teacup in hand, chewing alone. So Ramadan *was* for rich *and* poor. In courtesy to me, the host spoke English, complaining because he'd fixed up modern apartments for thirty thousand families, had put in electric stoves, air conditioning, everything, but the Nubians had preferred their charcoal burners for cooking. They set them on top of the electric burners, which were ruined. Did we have such problems in America?

"Certainly," I assured him. "I know a small town in rural New Hampshire where, when they built their first modern school, the children had to be taught how to flush a toilet."

Everyone beamed and relaxed into a rush of Arabic. I was glad of the chance to put down my solitary teacup. Aswan was dirty, overcrowded with refugees, full of flies —except here in this elegant home. These hosts of mine were educated, wealthy, cream of the crop; they could joke about Paris and New York, where they had visited, and could welcome me warmly, a Christian. Yet my hosts kept Ramadan without apology. I remembered how often when I had been shopping in the Aswan bazaar our bargaining had been interrupted. Five times a day at the call of the muezzin from the tall tower of the mosque, the merchants spread their prayer rugs and bowed toward Mecca.

> Allah, el Akbar,
> La Illah, Illah, Allah,
> Siadnah Machmud Rasoul, Allah-h-h-h!

How often did I stop shopping on Boylston Street, Boston, to pray?

"I do hate to leave you here alone. It seems as if one of the family should stay with you," Atia mourned next morning when I went to the airport with them to say good-by. "You will come to visit us in Cairo?"

I promised and kissed her.

When I got back to Cairo, the faithful Ismail was waiting at the airport to take me to the Museum, which I'd missed before, to show me the marvelous golden furniture taken from Tutankhamen's tomb, designed for his use in the spirit world. There was even a golden royal barge with tiny oars. Did he still haunt his beloved Nile, on a dark night?

Even more eerie was the Mummy Room at the Museum, where soldiers with muskets marched round and round, guarding Pharaohs who had been dead for three or four thousand years. We peered at each other, they from their ancient tattered wrappings. "One mummy's got red hair!" I exclaimed. He got lice, Ismail explained, and the chemicals used to exterminate them had changed the color of his hair. But you can't keep a good man down. Although he'd been embalmed since 1234 B.C., Rameses II had recently made the front pages of the Cairo newspapers!

"One morning the guard saw him raise his forearm!" Ismail related the tale with relish. "The guard was so scared he dropped his gun and rushed outside, shrieking bloody murder. The scientists who investigated discovered that the sun had been coming through that high window over there, hitting Rameses' left arm in the same place for so many years that the joint had contracted chemically and had raised the forearm!" Ismail's face was solemn except that his eyes were twinkling.

"Believe which you like, but the poor guard is still in the lunatic asylum!"

The Abulnagas and I wrote back and forth, of course, but it was two years before I dropped by their apartment on the Nile to visit, under such circumstances that I wouldn't have blamed them if they had slammed the door in my face. I had given them the airline and flight number of my arrival from Athens. I told them I couldn't bear to miss seeing the Parthenon and Mars Hill where Paul had preached and the place where Socrates had calmly drunk the fatal hemlock; it would have been like by-passing the family homestead. I also wanted to see the island of Rhodes. But unfortunately I was taken so ill en route in the jetliner that I was met at the Rhodes airport by an ambulance and driven in it to my hotel, where a doctor was waiting. I spent three reluctant days in bed chewing antibiotics. On the very day I was to fly back to Athens to change to my plane for Cairo, the plane from Athens crashed in a terrible storm. Naturally everything was grounded. I went to the hotel desk to cable the Abulnagas of my dilemma.

"Send a night cable," advised the desk clerk. "Day cables are very expensive."

"But my friends are meeting me this afternoon in Cairo airport at six P.M.! No, I'll send it straight, please."

The cable cost me twenty dollars, but it was worth it to put not only my friends' minds but my own at rest. Two more days went by before a plane finally set off for Athens, but we arrived too late at night to make connections for Cairo. So I sent another wire to my hosts on the Nile saying I had a seat on the plane arriving the following evening at 11 P.M. and went happily to bed. When our plane landed, I went unconcernedly through all the hocus-pocus of entering a strange country as an alien, and it wasn't till I saw Mona and Sherif rushing madly toward me that I realized something was wrong.

"Where have you been, Auntie Grace?" Mona gasped. "We thought something awful must have happened to you. We've met every plane from Athens for the past three days!"

It was my turn to gasp. "But didn't you get my two wires?"

No wires. Had that miserable hotel clerk pocketed the twenty dollars or had the cable company lost the address?

When we got to the car, I looked around for Atia and Jimmy. Mona explained, "They stayed home. They're exhausted."

Great day in the morning, what must they think of me? Relations had worsened considerably between our two nations during the two years since we had met. Would they realize this was no more my fault than the crashed plane? After all, they'd known me only a few days. Would they think me an arrogantly casual Ugly American?

Jimmy was at the phone in the entrance hall of the apartment when Sherif let us in with his key. "Your wire just arrived," Jimmy explained, holding out his hand cordially. As I babbled explanations, he said, no, they hadn't received the earlier cable from Rhodes; this was from Athens. Atia rushed up with a welcome and yet . . . Did I only imagine a chilly undercurrent? Not that I'd blame them. We chatted about Sherif's new fiancée and he said he'd bring her over to meet me; Atia offered me something to eat and I said that I'd eaten on the plane, thank you. It was like a stage scene, smoothly polite but surface talk. We were making conversation like utter strangers! Finally Atia inquired, rather desperately, "We wondered if you'd like to go out to the Pyramids tomorrow night? There's lights and the lecture is in English."

"No Pyramids, please," I begged. "I live near Concord where the American Revolution began. I've shown the battlefield where they 'fired the shot heard round the world' so often that my feet hurt whenever I think of it. I came to see *you,* to meet your friends."

"Thank God," Atia said. "No sightseeing." Suddenly the warmth between us was as real and deep as it used to be, and I was at home with my Arab family again.

"Mona has given you her room because it's not on the Nile so it's quieter," Atia explained. The apartment was block-long; one really needed roller skates to get to my bedroom from the two living rooms and the balcony overlooking the busy street, beyond which flowed the busier Nile. "Don't forget to lock your bedroom door and your suitcase whenever we leave the house." Atia herself locked the pantry in the kitchen after putting away the coffee and sugar we had been enjoying. "The cook will be in early tomorrow morning. You can hardly blame them for pilfering when they're hungry and have so little."

Atia herself brought us early coffee and every meal was a banquet. Sherif's fiancée was also named Mona but was shyer than my Mona. Sherif explained that they'd tried to hurry up their marriage rites so I could be there to see a real Moslem wedding, but the contract wasn't yet signed and after that so many days had to elapse. It was not possible. "My best wishes. I will be here in spirit, anyway," I told Sherif. The nice kids . . .

The Abulnagas took me literally. I went with them to their clubs, met their friends, had coffee with their banker cousin. Mona drove Atia and me daytimes through the raging traffic of Cairo; she was working now on a newspaper, but she still had her "come hither" magnetism. A young handsome Egyptian was always rushing up to ask her for a date, but Mona always shook her head. "Later, perhaps. My Auntie Grace is visiting me from America." Strangely, it was an editor of the most popular woman's magazine in Egypt, with whom an author should have had much in common, who gave me an uncertain welcome.

"Is it because I'm American?" I asked her bluntly.

She didn't pretend she didn't understand me. "Admit it, now! You hate blacks like me!"

"Hate you?" I gasped. "Why . . . why . . . some of my best friends are Negroes. I never even see the color of anyone's skin! I have two Chinese daughters of my own in Hong Kong and a Chinese granddaughter, for that matter! I couldn't love them more if I'd borne them myself!"

"Well, that's not what we read in your newspapers . . .

terrible riots, student sit-ins, black lynchings."

"You, of all people, shouldn't believe all you read!" I was really indignant. "I'm not just white, *I'm me!*"

She reached a soothing hand across the table; I grasped it and we both began to laugh. But the mountain of misunderstanding piled up by news media and movies that show all Americans either stinking rich or abysmally poor, still fighting Indians or clubbing down Negroes and students, almost makes me wish we had no TV satellites. At home, we Americans adjust automatically to events, interpreting them in the light of our knowledge of their background, but overseas they see only crooked bits of the jigsaw puzzle that is the United States. The editor asked, "Do you think you'll ever elect a woman President?"

"If we do, I hope she's an honest woman like you."

The entire Abulnaga family came down to the airport to see me off for Bangkok, to which I was flying via Indian Airways. Jimmy even paid my exit tax, since I'd forgotten to save enough Egyptian coins. "Don't wait," I urged. "We may be late taking off and it's such a bore." But they did wait. The last thing I saw was their hands waving, waving, till they became mere specks of motion.

"Did you get something in your eye, madam?" The air stewardess in her lovely rose silk sari bent over me solicitously.

"Yes, I guess I must have." I could hardly admit I was crying because I'd left those I loved behind, for a time . . . Why am I such a fool that I can't stand Taps playing, or an airplane leaving? Or the sea sighing alongshore? Was it tears for some former life which I had lost forever? Yesterday is like a harp upon which we chose to play a tune, but after the song is ended, do the strings still vibrate in the subconscious? Mona wrote me a year later, a vibrant, happy paean:

My Dearest Auntie Grace, I'm going to be married! To Maquid who is a scientist but who knows more about English Lit than I do! The most handsome, the nicest man in the world! Can't you come over, please, for the wedding?

I was in the hospital when her invitation came, so I sent my sincere regrets and a small check for a wedding present. Mona wrote back, with the unexpectedness of the "now" generation, that she'd spent the money for what she'd always wanted—a wig! It seemed an odd wedding present. But after all . . . if the regally independent Queen Hatshepsut had worn a false beard, why not a wig for Cleopatra?

# CHAPTER 8

# *Wild Hospitals
I Have Known*

If, as biologists tell us, everyone begins to die a little in his twenties, it is only to be expected that even a merry widow's machinery may begin to squeak and need greasing. Imagine if you tried to run your car for fifty years without a grease and oil job! Modern medicine offers the oil of healing but the body can't give top performance unless the patient has, as Solomon advises, "a merry heart [that] doeth good like a medicine—but a broken spirit drieth the bones."

Since my ambition for what I want to accomplish frequently outruns the performance of what one doctor called "your rather delicate internal machinery," on my various trips around the world I have found myself suddenly catapulted into hospitals or sickrooms in seven countries, Nepal, India, England, Kenya, Greece, Hong Kong, and Singapore, and have been frequently under the care of a doctor whose language I do not speak. Always my stay in bed was interesting and sometimes hilarious.

I shall not easily forget the first time I was offered a bedpan with greetings in Shanta Bhawan, the Palace of

Peace hospital in Kathmandu, Nepal. I had arrived in this lovely valley, watched over by the high Himalayas, to write the story of the Fabulous Flemings who had pioneered modern medicine in this developing country less than ten years earlier. But I sprang a mysteriously high fever and was hustled into the square cracker box on four poles carried by four sturdy Nepalese which serves as a stretcher, and hoisted, squatting precariously and holding onto the wooden sides, up the forty-six steps to my hospital room next to the men's ward. Through a haze of fever I looked about at the bare, uncompromising concrete walls, at the cold marble floor, at the four gray concrete steps leading down to the bathroom, which consisted of a hole in the floor and a cold-water faucet which dripped maddeningly. The only furniture was the high hospital bed upon which I lay and a table to hold the cowbell that I was supposed to ring if I wanted the nurse. I needed a bedpan urgently, so I tolled my bell. The brown little Nepalese man who answered wore a turban and a ragged army jacket over his nurse's uniform since it was March and bitter cold, but he understood my gesture if not my American. He disappeared and returned with an immaculate bedpan which he put carefully upon the floor while he bowed to me with folded hands.

"*Namaste!*" He beamed. "Greetings!"

By this time my need was so urgent that I snatched at the bedpan, only to wonder minutes later what I did now that I'd finished with the thing. I folded my hands upon the blanket and murmured back, "*Namaste* yourself!" My nurse took the pan with a ceremonial bow. But would he empty it? Not he. He yelled so loudly I all but fell out of my high bed, till a small ragged boy appeared—untouchable caste, I surmised—who took the pan, emptied it gravely down the bathroom hole, washed it out at the cold-water tap, and returned it, bowing, to the nurse. We went through this rigamarole several times a day and each time I laughed aloud; it did me more good than a shot of penicillin.

"*Memsahib* want sati?" my nurse demanded.

"What for?"

He shrugged. "Sit under bed. Call *me*, nurse. Run errand."

"No! Nobody's going to sit under my bed," I said firmly, closing my dizzy eyes. "What I do want is a shot of painkiller, I ache so."

"Doctor order," he agreed. He returned almost instantly with a hypodermic and tossed the blankets off my rear end. I reflected that this Nepali man to whom I had not even been introduced did a much more painless job than many nurses I had known in the States, bless him. Smiling, I drifted away into happy slumber.

It wasn't until several days later while I was being transferred, squatting again in the box stretcher, to a better, private room downstairs that I glimpsed the men's ward. Under each of its twenty beds was a small boy or a female relative, ready to alert the nurse or to bring the patient food that he—the sati—personally had cooked for him. Many Hindus would be defiled by eating rice prepared by lower castes or by the Christians who ran the Shanta Bhawan kitchen.

"In the early days when I made my night rounds, I often stumbled over vegetables or firewood hidden under the patients' beds," recalled Dr. Bethel Fleming. "So we built those little cubicles out in the back yard, each with a charcoal stove, where any man's family may cook what he pleases. Only about half the patients are fed from our kitchen." In spite of this bowing to local custom, one Hindu woman, from a family so wealthy that two of her boys were at school in England, flatly refused to eat at all in the presence of patients of a lower caste; she simply put her kerchief up over her head, turned her face to the wall and died.*

My new room downstairs had a bay window with a marvelous view of the garden, planted by the former wealthy Rana owner, filled with budding trees, statues, and greening grass, while beyond lay a wide golden field and beyond that rose the eight-thousand-foot-high Mountains of the Moon, green and brown against the sky. I could watch the villagers going along the winding paths, and once a helicopter from the American expedition on its way to climb Mt. Everest came buzzing down, transporting a woman badly burned because she had tried to rescue her cow from her fire-gutted home. The expedition, passing by, had come to her rescue. Because of a storm, the Americans couldn't raise Kathmandu, but they radioed New Zealand which contacted Calcutta which finally alerted Shanta Bhawan hospital, so they were ready for the poor woman and saved her life.

But usually the only drama of my hospital day for six weeks was when Maia, the little maid with the long pigtail and wide smile, came in to stir up the dust in my room with her twig broom and then to wash the floor with some horrible-smelling disinfectant. She was barefoot, although outside my window sleet often lay silver upon the grass and the room was icy cold since kerosene was imported from India and her troops fighting the Chinese on the borders of Tibet needed the heat themselves. When I got well enough to sit up, clothed in two pairs of pajamas, my thick wool bathrobe, and a couple of blankets, Maia would lift up my feet carefully to wash underneath with the disinfectant as if I too were a germ. We had but two words in common.

*"Namaste!"* I would beg, holding out my hot-water bottle, cold from the night before.

*The Fabulous Flemings of Kathmandu*. E. P. Dutton & Co., Inc., New York, N. Y., 1964.

"*Pani* [Water]!"

She would beam and disappear, to return with the bottle, hot and toasty. I never dared inquire whether she begged, stole, or borrowed the hot water.

At first I had been heartbroken because I had to stay in bed instead of rushing around town to interview people for my book, but when friendly visitors poured in to comfort the poor sick American, it finally dawned on me that when you're writing about medicine, inside a hospital is the best place to be. For one thing, my visitors didn't realize they were being interviewed, so they talked freely. These nice people came from all walks of life, from the Rana lady in her silken sari with a diamond flashing in her left nostril to the street cleaner from the front of the hospital who smelled loudly of the mustard oil with which he rubbed his skin to ward off the cold. The Indian technician who took my x-rays used to drop by to chat, as well as fellow Americans from the USAID, Peace Corps boys and girls who were staying in the hospital till they were cured of "Delhi belly," and a gay and marvelously gifted Roman Catholic priest who came on a motorcycle to regale me with stories about the villagers who lived near the school for boys where he taught. All of this was rich grain to be ground in my mill of words.

The only joker was that I—like the lately deceased Hindu lady, but for different reasons—was unable to eat the hospital food; it came up about as fast as it went down. This was partly because the cereal and bread were made from wheat that was mildewed, the canny Nepalese farmer having kept it in his damp house to wait for the high winter prices, and partly because my insides rejected water buffalo. Since this was a missionary hospital with little cash and a hunk of water buffalo was the cheapest meat available, we had water buffalo steak on Sunday, water buffalo ground up on Monday, stewed on Wednesday, and so on. Weak from hunger, I dug out the letter of introduction my congressman at home had given me and enclosed it in a note to the American ambassador to Nepal, asking him if, rather than starve, I couldn't please buy a few cans of soup at the PX.

A mere half an hour later a messenger with a huge box on his head banged on my screen door and entered to thrust into my hand a receipt to be signed for thirty cans of soup! The ambassador's tactful note read:

> It is impossible by law for a civilian to shop at the PX but my wife and I are delighted to give you the soup. But don't feel under any obligation. Our home is in Milton, not far from Sudbury, and some day we will drop by to have a cup of soup with you.*

Believe it or not, the soup was labeled S. S. Pierce, the very Boston food store where I had a charge account of my own! The gift fed and warmed me in both body and spirit.

Actually, I "never had it so good" in any hospital as at Shanta Bhawan. Besides the attentions of the seven American doctors on the staff, each day had its surprise. One morning when I responded to a scratching on my screen door, I saw a dirty, rosy Nepali urchin clutching beneath his rags two brass devil dogs, so old they had turned black and so ugly they were enchanting. Next to dragons, I cherish devil dogs who keep away evil spirits, if any.

"How much?" I asked.

The urchin shrugged, so I gave him three rupees, about thirty cents, and he oozed away like quicksilver before he got caught by the nurse. From then on I ran a sub rosa department store. The cautious scratching would come on the screen door, and a Nepali would slide furtively into my room with a treasure which I either bought or did not. The gem of my hospital collection was a *tonka* brought to

* *Ibid.*

me by a desperate Tibetan refugee with a jade earring in his left ear. This primitive picture of Buddha surrounded by a circle of smaller Bodhisattvas (saints who are eligible for Nirvana but who choose to stay on this earth to teach others The Way) was topped by a sort of cloud at whose misty center was a vague figure circled by what looked like angels with halos. The faded painting on canvas was obviously very old, probably from the Tibetan's family altar, where it had been worshipped for generations, and had been brought with him to Nepal as his most cherished treasure when he had fled from the invading Chinese.

"You sure you want to sell this?" I was worried.

He nodded. I knew no Tibetan, but it was obvious from his skinny body that he needed bread.

I gave him twenty-five dollars, which I hoped would feed him and his family for the rest of the year (the annual income of the average Nepali is about $30), and hung up my treasure at the foot of my bed on the bare hospital wall with bits of surgical tape, where I could see it when I first woke up. But when the good nurse, of a fundamentalist creed in the States, brought in my luncheon and saw my pet *tonka,* she gasped.

"Idols! You can't keep that here. This is a Christian hospital!"

"That's exactly why I *can* keep it," I said gently. "To me it is a lovely picture, impregnated with the incense of many prayers. See the beautiful faded rose, greens, and blues around the Buddha? Who am I to disdain what another man worships?"

I knew Dr. Bethel would understand, for she herself, when a Hindu patient was dying, would frequently order the Christian ambulance station wagon to take him to the temple at Pashupatinath so that the pious Hindu could die with his feet in the holy Bagmati River which empties into the holier Ganges, and so might attain his longed-for peace and paradise.

I took the *tonka* home with me as my most cherished possession and, curious to find out more about the painting, I carried it to the Boston Art Museum. "This isn't so very old; only about four hundred years, I should say," murmured the authority on Oriental art. "But it *is* from Tibet." He began to read me the names of the gods written on what I had thought to be an Oriental frieze around the edge of the *tonka.* "Tsong-kha-pa and one of his favorite disciples, Jigs-byed, tutelary deity of Tibet . . . That god up in the cloud is too holy to have a name that may be spoken."

Awed, I asked if to preserve the *tonka* I should have it framed under glass.

"If you don't, it will probably not last longer than another hundred years."

"Neither will I," I pointed out, "so I guess I'll just enjoy it as it is. Thank you for introducing me to the gods who will share my home."

When I look every day at my *tonka* hanging in simple grandeur on my living-room wall, framed in faded rose and gold brocade, which Polly's mother had bought in Japan half a hundred years ago, I remember my friends in the hospital at Shanta Bhawan, the Doctors Bob and Bethel Fleming, the gay little nurses in their white and red saris who sing at dawn, the good priest, and especially the strange Tibetan whose family shrine I cherish, but whose name I'll never know. He wore his hair in a braid around his head, tied with a small pink ribbon. Higher in my memory rise the great snows, each mountain peak over twenty thousand feet high, peering over the Mountains of the Moon, which are mere hills in contrast. Up on one high, snowy peak, the great god Siva is said to look down upon the sweet rich valley of Kathmandu. When the sun rises, the snows turn glorious pink and gold; at sunset, rose, yellow, and lavender, a rainbow of colors so beautiful to behold that a lump rises in your throat. "Good morning!" I say to the god so holy you may not speak his name. He never answers, but I am sick with longing to go back to that pleasant valley so friendly that even the hospital bedpan comes to you with a greeting.

The assorted patients from all races, creeds, and tribes at Shanta Bhawan reminded me of an earlier hospital episode in the mountains of North Carolina. Jock and I had taken Rick's books, clothes, banners, and other adolescent junk to the freshman dorm of the University of Virginia and then treated ourselves to a well-earned vacation in a charming mountaintop chalet. I had been taken very ill in the night with a sharp pain which the doctor in the tiny hospital at the foot of the mountain diagnosed as a clot on one lung and then prescribed bed rest "for at least two months" in his one-room, all-purpose ward. I stared around at the mountaineer with his brass spittoon by his bed, at the very young baby howling its head off beside his mother, at fifteen other patients, several moaning and groaning. When the mountaineer spat and missed the spittoon, that did it.

"I'm not staying here any two months," I said flatly. "I'd rather die."

Naturally the doctor was furious; he made me sign a statement that I was leaving against his consent, and we drove off with his dire prediction that I wouldn't live to get home. Since Jock didn't have a driver's license, I had to drive every one of the thousand miles to Sudbury, keeping at it till the road grew so hazy to my fevered gaze that we'd have to stop for the night. It took us five days, but by the time the ghastly trip was over, I was nearly well. I understand that the modern cure for a clot on the lung is not to stay bedfast, but to move around; I did the right thing, after all. So I merely kept my fingers crossed at a later date when another doctor told me, "I know what you're going to die of!"

"Well, not right now," I murmured. We merry widows

reserve the right to be mildly skeptical of medical prognoses which change with new discoveries.

Accordingly when I later lay, sick and alone, in my room on the island of Rhodes, where the doctor predicted I'd stay for a couple of weeks, I did not despair of continuing my planned trip. I simply lay back on my pillows and enjoyed looking at the most handsome Greek I had ever seen. The doctor looked like the statue of the discus thrower, only he was about twenty years older; but he had the same perfect classical profile, the sinewy body that stretched the shoulders of his well-cut suit. I knew what was wrong with me, anyway; I had simply enjoyed too much boar's head and other oddities at the *taverna* where my friends had given me a farewell party my last night in Athens. Small wonder that the next morning I had quietly passed out on the plane to Rhodes. But it was comfortable to lie there on my soft hotel bed, lulled by the rhythm of the sea waves crashing on the shore outside my window; if I sat up, I could glimpse the far-off misty hills of fabled Turkey.

"This antibiotic must be administered faithfully every four hours, day and night," the doctor ordered the young and lovely housekeeper of the hotel, who was waiting for his verdict.

"Yes, Doctor," she agreed anxiously.

My protests that I'd rather sleep were brushed aside. Every four hours throughout the night an impressive procession would enter my bedroom door; first the housekeeper in an elegant ruffled white negligee, bossing the job, followed by a maid carrying a tray with a doily upon which lay my pill in solitary glory, while behind them stalked a uniformed waiter bearing on his tray a silver pot of tea to wash down the pill. I felt like the sultan's favorite pampered wife. For four days I enjoyed ill health but finally reluctantly discharged myself and got up to explore medieval monasteries.

The patient with a chronic pain knows pretty well how he feels—after all, the body is his own—but a strange bug attacking with weird results, in a foreign country, can, I found, scare the pants off you. This nightmare happened to me in Nairobi, Kenya, on my last trip around the world. I had been out to dine with half a dozen friends in a Chinese restaurant where we had sampled each other's plates. Immediately after I got back to my hotel, my hands swelled up black and fat as bologna sausages, my body displayed big red bumps, and even my throat got so swollen I could barely swallow. It was after ten at night, but I yelled for a doctor. He came at once and was very British, large, urbane, and comfortingly casual. When I couldn't possibly tell him what I had eaten at our conglomerate dinner, he decided my troubles must be some sort of allergy and gave me a shot of cortisone. If I couldn't swallow at all by morning, he announced, he'd send me to a hospital. To do a tracheotomy? I wondered unhappily; one could hardly be allowed to choke to death. I waited for long, dark hours for this dire threat to eventuate and had just dropped off to sleep when the phone at the head of my bed rang loudly. I sleepily took off the receiver. "Hello?"

"Where are my pants?" demanded a man's voice.

"If you don't know, I certainly don't," I croaked.

"Isn't this the tailor?"

"Wrong number. Dial again," I advised. Obviously he was unfamiliar with the phone dialing system in this brand-new hotel which advised, "Dial 3 for room service, Dial 4 for the tailor," etc. Or maybe he was twiddling in the dark. I had barely dozed off when my phone rang shrilly again. I debated answering for a while; then, as it went on and on, I began to think of all sorts of possible tragedies. Perhaps Rick or Sylvia had cabled that one of them was very ill . . . so I answered, finally.

"Mystic," the phone remarked this time.

The native Kenyans who ran this hotel spoke very good English except that they frequently accented the wrong syllable. I said, "I don't understand."

"Sorry, is mystic."

Mistake! He'd rung me up in the middle of the night by mistake. He evidently had his pants. Suddenly it seemed so funny I began to chuckle, then to laugh heartily till tears of sheer joy ran down my cheeks. Relaxed, I drifted off into such a deep, dreamless sleep that in the morning I was so much better I drove twenty miles into the bush to speak to a group of barefoot Kikuyu ladies. I must admit the cortisone had a lot to do with this miracle recovery; but so did my relaxation from fear. Life frequently offers its own antidotes if you have the will to grasp them with a grin.

Without doubt, this merry widow would be pushing up the daisies without the help of the doctors and nurses in my favorite hospital near my home, where I arrive so often by ambulance that the staff merely say, "Well, hi! You in again?" and dump me into a bed with the metal sides up as if I were violent. Usually I am merely dizzy, like on the evening when I was typing busily when the typewriter table tipped over and the typewriter hit my head so hard I blacked out for four hours. Who ever heard of a typewriter attacking a writer so that she landed, concussed, in the hospital? While recuperating there, I happily wrote several chapters of one book and read proof on another. The nurses found it hard to decide if I were still woozy in the head or merely very busy. Not that it mattered much: thermometers and bedpans went on just the same.

On another occasion when I'd been hurt in an automobile accident, since all the hospital wards were full, I was bedded down in the sun parlor, along with five other emergency patients. We had only one bell with which to call the nurse, so the staff checked us frequently. At midnight a bumbling young nurse's aide knocked down the screen around my bed and then blazed her flashlight into my startled eyes. "Oh, you're awake!" She beamed. How could I be otherwise? "I've been so lonesome. Now I have someone to talk to."

My most eerie hospital experience, however, was when I broke my leg skiing in New Hampshire and was taken by station wagon to a small private hospital run by one doctor. My leg was set adequately and put in a cast, but I was barely out of the anesthetic when I sensed something strange about the place. There were six of "us girls" in the ward, and later when lights went out and we could really talk, I found out what was wrong . . . every other patient except me had had an abortion! I could hardly wait for dawn to phone Jock, demanding, "Get me out of here! It's dangerous!" I heard later that the doctor had gone into the Army, which seemed an odd place to practice his specialty.

Any medical catastrophe which I understand I can meet head on; it is the unknown that terrifies. One morning in the huge Ashoka Hotel in New Delhi I woke up to find I couldn't see. I groped for the phone by my bed, asked for the press room at the Vigyan Bhagan, where I wailed to the correspondent of *The New York Times,* "George, get me a doctor, quick! I've gone blind!"

Give me a newspaperman for fast action, even beyond a fireman or cop. In only a few moments the lady doctor arrived to explain that my eyes were merely swollen shut —my face was a balloon.

"Allergy to New Delhi dust and smoke," she diagnosed.

I was beginning to suspect that allergies were a very happy "out" for doctors in the Orient when no other answer was clear. Yet the lovely rosy haze that filled the horizon every evening when the poor families in this capital city of India lighted up their thousands of cowdung cooking fires might have aggravated whatever was wrong with me. In any case, the lady doctor's antihistamine pills worked sufficiently so that I could recognize the VIPs at the World Council of Churches, where I was interviewing, though my nose for an entire month rivaled that of Cyrano de Bergerac.

A doctor with a sense of humor must get frightfully bored at being treated as the Lord High Executioner to whom all hospital personnel, nurses and patients, must bow. Is that why after the operation his daily visits get briefer and briefer? The doctor stops at your room door, chortles cheerfully, "How are we this bright morning?" "Fine," you lie as he gallops off down the corridor to send you a bill. Medical procedures today, however, change so radically and rapidly that the unwary patient should have an early warning system.

I woke up one afternoon after a major operation to find myself lying naked in bed with a row of black rosettes down my stomach. Thinking I was still woozy from the anesthetic, I murmured to the nurse, "Do you see what I see?"

"Sh . . . lie still. They're only stitches. They'll come out soon," she said comfortingly. But apparently she found my aping "September Morn" as embarrassing as I did, for she began to put small squares of gauze over the rosettes.

"Stop that!" The surgeon, roaring in, snatched off the offending gauze, remarking that it was obvious this girl had never nursed a case for him before. He explained to me, "You'll be much more comfortable during the early postoperative period if you can move at will, get rid of the gas. Bandages merely impede recovery. Now both of you shut up, and you, young lady, go to sleep!"

The doctor was right; as September Morn, I did not have a single postoperative pain, which I privately had been dreading from former experience. But my night nurse blushed every time she looked at me. At least no visitors were allowed in.

Nothing, however, disturbed my day nurse, a jolly little

person with short curly black hair who usually came in whistling at 7 A.M. She brought me, that first postoperative morning, as a comforting gesture, a lovely little watercolor of the sea cove whose waters lapped outside my hospital window. She said proudly, "My boyfriend painted this picture especially for you when I told him a writer was my patient. I took a lesson from him last night."

I was so pleased with the little picture that I had her pin it up on the curtain where I could see it. But when my 3 P.M. nurse came on duty, she demanded, "Who gave you that?" When I told her, she rocked with laughter.

"What's so funny?" I wanted to know, but for a long time she refused to tell me. Finally she said, "The nerve of her giving you that! She took a lesson, all right. She's taken up with an artist feller from New York lately."

I still have the sketch because it passed so many weary hours for me so pleasantly, for, wondering about the lesson, I forgot my unpleasant self.

My chief grievance against hospitals, both here and overseas, is that you can't get any sleep, ever, during the day. Nor a cup of coffee before 8 A.M. I'm not human, mornings, until I get my coffee. But at 7 A.M., an hour before your tray arrives, and after a fearful combination of sleeping pills, antibiotics, pills for nausea, and heaven knows what else, you are awakened by an implacable nurse who carols gaily, "Temperature time!"

"Then can I have a cup of coffee?"

"Here's a nice basin to wash your face."

The water is tepid. As you dab, bleary-eyed, at where your face should be, you know perfectly well the trays will not arrive for another hour, so why fuss? If only you could settle back cozily, catch a catnap . . .

"How about a nice drink of ice water?" The white-coated orderly has burst in, murdering sleep.

The heck with ice water, it's coffee you need! When the coffee actually arrives and you lift it to your lips with fingers shaking with eagerness, it has apparently been waiting as long as you have and is lukewarm.

After breakfast comes the equally chancy bath in bed. In these days of nursing shortage they wash only your back, so you sit up naked in bed, trying not to tip over the basin perched precariously upon your bedside table while you reach your toes with slippery soap. Just as you are deciding there's no use to wash any further, there is a sharp knock on your door and the doctor asks rhetorically, "May I come in?" He does not wait for an answer, so you scurry to pull up the big bath towel to cover as much of your nakedness as possible, but either your top or your feet stick out anyway. All of the important questions you've been saving up for twenty-four hours to ask the doctor, such as, "Why do I have to be waked up in the middle of the night by some idiot shooting a flashlight in my eyes to see if I'm asleep?" go completely out of your mind. All you can do is to cower under your bath towel until the doctor leaves.

Then the blessed comfort of smooth, clean, new sheets and pillowcases! Surely now, as the nurse finishes and bustles out to the patient next door, you can nap in peace. But you reckon without the clerical visitors who do not have to wait for visiting hours. There were six such well-meaning early risers in the last hospital I was in, a Roman Catholic priest with a kindly, rosy Irish face who asked each morning, "You're not a Catholic, are you?" and then stayed on anyway for ten minutes to prove how ecumenical he was, visiting a sleepy Episcopalian; as many as five other ministers, Congregational, Unitarian, a couple of Methodists, and once a Christian Science reader who wandered into my room by mistake, broke my post-bath pleasant lassitude to save my soul. The climax came, however, when my own rector came (at my request) to give me communion and the loudspeaker over my head, which was connected with the nurses' station in the corridor, broke into the invocation to demand, "Mrs. Fletcher, do you still want a laxative?"

In sheer despairing fatigue, I finally begged the nurse when she came in to give me a pain shot, which I hoped would send me off at long last, "Will you please put up a sign on my door, *Do not disturb! Especially clergy?*"

In the afternoon it's the kindly volunteers who jerk open your drooping eyelids, pink ladies and little high school pinkies, selling you toothpaste, books, and Kewpie dolls. The pinkies demand sweetly, "Isn't there *anything* I can do for you?" You can hardly reply, "Yes. Get out of here!"

There are advantages, however, to staying awake if you have good ears. You can listen to the patients in the rooms on either side of you complain. Some of their remarks are pleasantly pungent. Like the sea captain I listened in on once up in Maine, begging his nurse to smuggle him in a pint of whiskey. He told her plaintively, "Gal, I'm so dry I'd have to be primed even to spit!" The nurse murmured some negative I couldn't quite hear, and then the captain broke in wrathfully, "Then git! This room's worse'n the depot at train time. In and out, in and out. It's thicker in here than three rats in a stocking!"

In Kathmandu, my next-door neighboring patient was the six-year-old son of a Rana general. (Ranas, the former ruling family in Nepal before King Mahendra took over his regal rights, used to be *born* as majors, colonels, and generals in the Army. Rank was their birthright.) This child patient had fallen off a high wall and might have injured his spleen; in order to do an exploratory operation, Dr. Bethel had to have the consent of the entire family. Grandma and Mama had already moved into the little boy's room, filled it and the corridor outside with their own beds, Oriental rugs, and luxurious divans, while the general-grandpa with a decoration as big as a dinner plate on his chest kept walking up and down in front of my door, trying to make up his mind what to do. The sooth-sayer finally decided this was not an auspicious day to operate, so the relieved general picked up the patient, parents, furniture, and enough toys to start a kindergarten and left, to the great convenience of the nurses, who'd been trying to edge by to get to the patients in the farther rooms.

How many patients would eventually get well without medical assistance I defy anyone but a soothsayer to predict. It's chiefly a matter of faith. Personally, I always feel very much better whenever my family doctor, who knows my foibles as well as my aches and pains, sticks his head in my door and smiles. Yet we merry widows, without modern medicine, would be either in a wheelchair knitting afghans or under a granite slab, RIP. I, for one, am not ready to try either of these avocations. Yet once in Singapore I was cured by a Chinese beautician. I had picked up a bad bug in Vietnam from the ice in my Coke. I forgot the ice would melt into unboiled water, which I had carefully turned down at the table, and I even preferred to brush my teeth with beer because it came safely out of a bottle. I was acutely uncomfortable on the plane from Tan Son Nhut airport to Singapore, where I taxied to the familiar red plush and gold paint of the famous old Raffles Hotel (beloved also by Rudyard Kipling). There I luxuriously took two baths, one to get clean and the other simply to enjoy having enough hot water. The hairdresser there, I knew of old, gave a marvelous shampoo and manicure. When I found she even had my favorite nail polish— Windsor. After the duchess?—I felt so elegant that I was completely cured.

I suspect that all good doctors are, consciously or unconsciously, soothsayers at heart, watching for signs and portents which the mind may interpret into bodily pain. I watched this miracle of suggestion work in a small but excellent hospital where I got waylaid in my travels and where the country doctor, who was chief of staff, was not only wise in medicine but knew his patients so intimately he called the woman in the room next to mine "Marie." She had had a heart attack while mounting the plane steps to go to Florida to visit her daughter. So here she was, flat and despairing. The heart specialist flown in from Boston had just left after telling her frankly that the ailing pump that was her heart might or might not be able to get rid of the water in her lungs. The whole corridor could hear her sobbing, "I'm gonna die! I'm gonna die!"

"Now, Marie, quit that caterwallin'!" ordered her family doctor, brushing by my door to hers. "You got a good chance of gittin' down to Florida if you keep your chin up and saw wood."

Marie wailed, "But the specialist said there wasn't anything more he could do!"

"Maybe not, but you can," her doctor told her firmly. "Knives 'n pills ain't all of medicine by a long ways. You do as I say. Sit up in bed 'n eat that lunch!"

Three weeks later Marie was on her way to St. Petersburg.

I try to spend some time each year with Polly; it's like coming home; she's steady and changeless as a rock, but one mossed over and softened by laughter, wit, and wisdom. Then there are The Children: Chica, the small golden spaniel, and Amigo, the big black spaniel who nearly knocks you down with his riotous welcome as soon as he makes up his own mind that he's really glad to see you. But this last visit I was able to stay only four days, because I became very ill and had to fly home two thousand miles for emergency treatment by my Concord surgeon. Polly and a friend drove me the sixty miles from Las Cruces to El Paso to put me on the plane for Dallas, where, alone and ill, I found the two-hour wait for the plane to Boston agonizing. At long last, aching all over, completely exhausted and fearful of tomorrow, I fell into bed in my favorite hospital. But next day a comforting letter arrived airmail from Polly. Who but she would know what medicine to offer? She wrote, "My friend said, when you left looking so forlorn and alone, 'If that lady wasn't so delicate-looking, I'd say she had guts!' "

"GUTZ," agreed my irrepressible Polly.

CHAPTER 9

# My Chinese Children

I am a very lucky woman; I have a family upon whom the sun never sets. When the sun goes down on Rick and Sylvia in California, it is already rising the following morning on my Chinese daughters, Suet Fah and Yee-tai in Hong Kong. I even have a Chinese granddaughter whom I have never seen, but Suet Fah, her mother, assures me, "She is a delight." So has her mother been to me ever since we met on a high hilltop in China eight years ago, when Suet Fah was thirteen by our count but fourteen by the Chinese, who reckon a child's age from the moment of conception. This difference might well have been a warning to me, but in the first flush of being a merry widow exploring the world, I thought that creeds and customs need not separate us, that just loving someone was enough. And, in spite of all that has happened, the love between us still holds strong if impotent to change the iron rules of paternal control imbedded in the Chinese character itself for thousands of years. In any case, an interracial, intercreedal family is a fascinating way to stretch a mother's horizons, so that I shall not be so earthbound when I meet Jock in our next life and we go, swinging our hands together along the Milky Way, kicking the stars out of our path.

Snowy Flower, which Suet Fah's name means in English, and I just happened to meet one morning in Siu Lam, the small stone village on the barren, denuded hills outside Hong Kong which are being reclaimed by planting trees and tiny gardens, watered and cared for by former drug addicts. S. Y. Lee, then secretary of the Hong Kong Christian Welfare and Relief Council, drove me out to the Chan family's home in his jeep, explaining, as we rattled along, that "chasing the dragon [taking drugs]" costs less here than buying a package of cigarettes. "Many refugees from Red China are driven to drugs by despair. Take the Chan family, for example. He was a farmer from Swatow who had no other trade when he, his wife, and five children escaped into Hong Kong. But one can hardly plow concrete streets. Although he was strong and willing, Mr. Chan picked up only occasional jobs, unloading a vessel or carrying rocks for road building. When he couldn't find work, the family did not eat. The only place they could discover to live in was the Inner Walled City, where I took you yesterday."

I shuddered. The Walled City had been merely a series of dark alleys with an open sewer down the middle where caves had been scooped out of the thick walls of the adjacent buildings for living quarters. Here, where the sun never shone and very little daylight entered, I had watched a whole family, the husband whirring away at his sewing machine with the baby tied to one chair leg by a dirty rag to keep him out of the sewer, the mother squatting by a tiny coke stove, while a very small boy with tears rolling silently down his cheeks was carefully fashioning a spray of paper wisteria. Working all together, they'd be lucky to make enough to buy today's rice. If the tourist who insisted upon his new suit being finished in twenty-four hours could see this dirt, sweat, and tears, he would never have worn the new clothes. There was no outer wall to this dugout to prevent this little family from looking directly across the alley to the "opium den," where ten or a dozen Chinese men were lying inert, "chasing the dragon."

"It is not easy to watch five children starve," S. Y. was going on calmly, "so Mr. Chan found forgetfulness in drugs. The English government, which does what it can for such first-timers, sent him to jail to be cured. Mrs. Chan, already eight months along with her sixth child, in despair was persuaded to push drugs, so that she, too, was sent to the women's jail where her son was born. This left only Suet Fah, the oldest girl who was twelve, to care for her four younger brothers and sisters. She was a big girl, large for her age, so she went to the owner of the factory that makes paper flowers and swore she was fourteen, as the law requires. The proprietor must have suspected she was under age, but the younger the worker, the less he would have to pay her, so he took Suet Fah on; he paid her fifty cents a day Hong Kong—about ten cents in your money—for ten hours' work."

I stared at him, speechless, but S. Y. went on facing facts as one must in Hong Kong or die. "Thus Suet Fah was able to buy rice for her little family. She cooked it on the sidewalk, washed the children daily at the public spiggot on the block, and, nights, she would tuck them, blanketed with newspapers, in a doorway where the store had closed early so, with luck, they wouldn't be disturbed till morning. Each day before she went to work, Suet Fah would strap the two-year-old onto his six-year-old sister's back so he wouldn't get killed in the brutal traffic of our Hong Kong streets.

"This way she kept them alive for four months. But one day when it was very cold, one of our social workers found the four younger children, wet and crying, sitting on the curb with their feet in the dirty water of the gutter. After inquiry, she took them all, along with Suet Fah, to St. Christopher's Orphanage, where you also have seen how happy are the children."

I nodded. The children had certainly been well fed, yet they had been hungry for someone all their own. I had only come inside the door, when one small girl with a runny nose had tugged at my skirt, wailing, "Mama, Mama! Are you my new mama?" When I had asked where the orphanage got so many children, the matron silently handed me a note that had just come to her along with a newborn baby. It read:

*MEMO*
From duty officer, Hung Hom Police Station,
to St. Christopher's Home.
Date July 20, 1961.
Please receive one female baby of about one week old who is found abandoned in Hung Hom district and whose parents are untranced [untraced]. Thanks.

A human tragedy in twenty-four words.

This was the big-hearted home that had kept the five Chan children until their parents both got out of jail. The father, supposedly cured of his drug habit, was given a garden at Siu Lam to care for and a cement cottage in which to house his reunited family.

A group of these cottages stood high on the crest of the hill above us as S. Y. yanked at the car brakes; we stopped with a jerk as he invited me, "Come, we will climb that path to visit the Chans. That is the papa over there, watering his crop from the barrel on his shoulder."

The "garden" of Mr. Chan, sunburned, stalwart but surly, refusing to notice us, was a mere crack in the hills, but the vegetables he was watering looked flourishing and green. Down below, at the bottom of the verdant crack, was the miracle of the little pool with grasses, orchids, and ducks quacking happily. "Until the harvest comes in, we give the wife thirty dollars to buy food," explained S. Y. "Hello, there, children!"

Down the steep path came running a dozen small Chinese, trailed by at least as many dogs, all shouting and barking a welcome. One boy who wore no pants, only a short red blouse open in front, shrilled above the tumult, "Hello, Auntie! Hello, S. Y. !"

"Is the second Chan son," explained S. Y. He fired a fusillade of Chinese at the boy, who grinned, pointing up at the neat cottage against the sky upon whose veranda was a cluster of people. "His mama, Suet Fah, and the prison baby. They have tea for us."

I hate heights, but of course I climbed anyway and was breathless and dizzy by the time S. Y. and I, escorted by our noisy entourage, arrived at the cottage veranda. The prison baby, wearing only a diaper and showing his two new teeth in a wet grin, was perched on his mother's plump arm as she greeted us, beaming. The tall slender girl in the white cotton pajamas, which had shrunk so it was obvious they were her only garment, must be Suet Fah. She rushed at S. Y., grasped his arm eagerly, demanding something anxiously in Chinese. When he shook his head, the light went out of her face, her small hands dropped, and her whole body slumped into despair.

"I told her I would try for a foster parent for her so she could go to school, become a teacher. But is no use," S. Y. said sadly. "All foreigners want small little buds of children, cute, to show pictures of to their friends. No one wants almost a woman."

Yet this was the girl with the courage to fight in the Hong Kong streets for her brothers and sisters, to slave ten hours a day for their rice. It wasn't fair. I said, surprising even myself, "I will send her to school."

When S. Y. told Suet Fah what I had offered, at first she couldn't believe it; then her shoulders straightened. When she looked directly at me, I saw the delicate pink come back under the ivory of her cheeks and her dark eyes were filled with tears. "Tell her I've always wanted another daughter!" Impulsively, I bent to kiss her soft peach-bloom cheek, but she drew away and I remembered too late that the Chinese do not kiss. Oh dear, I'd got off to a wrong start with my new daughter! My dismay must have shown on my face, for Suet Fah reached up to pat my arm and we smiled at each other. Thus simply we became mother and daughter and the tiny roots of our love began to run down into the good earth of understanding.

Suet Fah did very well at St. Simon's School for Fishermen and Workmen's Children, to which I sent her after I'd met the headmaster and inspected the school as I would for any child of mine. The bunks in the dormitory had only chicken wire for a mattress, but the food was good and the teaching staff excellent. The school was run by Anglicans. I had no idea whether Suet Fah was Buddhist or merely an ancestor worshiper; what, after all, did it matter? That was for her to decide. Soon she began to write me letters in Chinese which her teacher translated for me into English. At first the characters were blotted frequently by tears, but then the lines straightened and grew clearer. She wrote:

> I passed all my subjects at the exams but am not doing so well in English. I wish more to please you. I have a lovely school uniform, blue jacket, white blouse and a gray wool skirt which I made myself. I was first in the potato race and sing in the choir.
>
> Lovingly yours,
> SUET FAH.

The teacher had added a note at the foot of the letter. "Suet Fah is not brilliant in her studies but she is one of the best-liked children in the school. She is learning how to play for the first time in her life."

What more could any mother wish?

But on the plane flying from Hong Kong to Bangkok, I began to wonder ... What would Rick and Sylvia think of my taking on another child to educate, at my age? If anything happened to me, would they see Suet Fah through to becoming a teacher? I decided to send them an airmail letter to ask. I mailed the letter at the Thai airport and forgot about it while exploring this city of gorgeous temples, the jade Buddha, and friendly people. One morning just before Christmas, when I was passing through the lobby, the desk clerk called to me, "Mrs. Fletcher, there's a call for you from New York. Will you take it now?"

At first all I could hear was squawks and yowls, but finally Rick's voice came through thinly. "Mother? I called to wish ... Merry Christmas ..." More cacophony, then the words came clear again. "Sylvie and I want the address of our new little sister to welcome her into the family ..." The rest was lost in transoceanic shrieks which the phone operator interrupted to ask, "You want me to call New York back? Get a better connection?"

I was so proud of all my three children I could hardly speak. I managed, "No, thank you. They've already wished me a Merry Christmas."

It was two years before I saw Suet Fah again. I had written the school to ask if the child could spend the week with me at the hotel in Hong Kong, for I wanted to get to know my Chinese daughter better. She looked so endearingly childish and happy in her neat dark-blue and gray school uniform, standing close to her teacher at the airport. She carried a small brown pasteboard suitcase in one hand and in the other a white plastic handbag, very chic and up to date with its brass fittings and handle. "She made it for you," the teacher explained as Suet Fah held the handbag out to me wordlessly.

"Tell her I love it. I shall keep it always!"

"Oh, she understands English. She's just too shy to speak it," the teacher said. "Maybe when she gets to know you better . . . Well, good-by. Have a nice visit, you two."

Suet Fah's cheeks had grown round and rosy on a balanced, adequate diet, and she bore herself with a dignity unusual in a teen-ager; but when we came into our hotel room with its twin beds and the bathroom of pink tile and a huge pink tub, she looked around, startled. Naturally. I remembered only concrete floor and showers at the school; probably she had never had a tub bath in her life. I showed her the big pink soft towel that was hers and how to work the shiny handles.

"I'm very tired. I've been traveling since five this morning, so I'd like to lie down to rest a bit," I explained. "How about your taking a bath before dinner?"

"Yes," she agreed.

She shut the bathroom door and for quite a time I heard no sound; then the water began to run into the tub and finally, with a mighty splash, Suet Fah slid down the back of the big tub into the water. She was singing gaily in Chinese but the tune was familiar, "Here we go round the mulberry bush, mulberry bush . . ." Bless the child! When she came out again, her uniform was neat and immaculate, but those socks she was putting back on . . .

"They're filthy! For goodness' sake, Suet Fah, are those all the socks you have?"

"Yes."

I ought to increase her clothing allowance. I rang for the room boy, who can always pass miracles in Hong Kong, and in no time at all he came back with six pairs of white socks in her size; so with her dark hair still wet, but clean, clear down to her Mary Jane patent-leather slippers, she rode up in the elevator with me to the restaurant on the top floor of the hotel, for I was too weary to look for a proper Chinese restaurant with chopsticks. Besides, I was curious to see how Suet Fah would handle herself in a new situation.

The restaurant was crowded with maybe a hundred American tourists, but there was not a single Chinese guest; the waiters and the orchestra were the only Asians. I heard one woman ask as we passed toward the window table I had reserved, "Why on earth is she bringing a Chinese schoolgirl in here?" Suet Fah's face didn't show by a flicker that she understood; she held her head high and watched carefully to do exactly as I did. When the waiter drew out my chair for me, she waited for him to pull out hers before she sat down. Had she ever seen knives and forks before? Probably not. She took the enormous menu card and held it gravely upside down, for it was printed in French. I had to help her there.

"I'm going to have fried chicken," I told her. "Would you like some too?"

"Yes."

The chicken proved to be of that unpleasantly rubber variety that bounces off the fork. I waited to see what Suet Fah would do. She picked up her knife and fork as I did and tried desperately to cut off a sliver of chicken. No go. So she beckoned to the waiter, said something to him in Chinese. He reached over, deftly cut the chicken meat into bits, then brought her a pair of chopsticks. She calmly began to eat as usual. I didn't need to worry about Suet Fah; she'd make out whether she was cooking rice on the sidewalk or dining in a snobbish hotel restaurant.

Back in our bedroom, she unpacked her cardboard suitcase, which held only a pair of cheap cotton red-and-white-checked pajamas, a toothbrush, a comb, and her brown English schoolbook. She opened the book and began to read, "I see . . . the tiger. Does Jack see the . . . tiger?" "Tiger" instead of the "ball"; that figured, for the book said, "Printed for Malaya."

"You read nicely, dear," I encouraged. "But it's pretty

late. Why don't you get into bed? I'll tuck you in when you're ready."

She looked good enough to eat in her red-and-white pajamas, with the lamplight shining down on her soft black hair spread out on the pillow, but when I tried to pull up the blanket, she pushed it away. Now what? She took my hand, pulled me down beside her, as she knelt, folding her small hands, and began, "Our Father . . ." She was trying to tell me that she'd become a Christian, as I was! I slid my arm around her; I could feel her heart beating hard as we said together, she in Chinese and I in English, "Our Father, Who art in heaven, hallowed be Thy name . . ."

It was two more years before I got back to Hong Kong again. I had boasted so proudly about my own Chinese daughter that five of my friends had asked me to pick them out a child to sponsor, not just anyone, but someone I chose. The Americans differed widely in their interests: there were a blind man and his wife who had no child of their own; another was dean of women in a fashionable college; one came from Maine and another from Massachusetts. I did my best to pick out the kind of child each would enjoy, but I was especially puzzled about two of my closest friends, a college professor and his wife who surely must have a bright boy who would make them proud of him; a child who, perhaps, might even go on to college himself.

When I told S. Y. of my problem about finding the brilliant Chinese, he said, "I know just the boy for them. Yiu Yee-tak. He lives on the island of Chu Lap Kok. He has read every book in their school four times! We will go there tomorrow to see if you like him for your friend. My wife is unwell so we will have to take along my children, Michael and Sylvia. It is Chinese holiday; the ferry will be crowded. But no matter."*

*"Easter Shopping in Hong Kong," *Christian Herald*, April 1965.

The ferry was mobbed with twenty-five hundred Chinese, with me as the lone American. The noise was terrific as we looked in vain for a seat upon the wooden settees crowded with everyone from Grandma down to the wailing baby in an embroidered carryall on the back of his amah dressed in proper black cotton trousers and a very white, stiffly starched jacket. Each teen-ager aboard seemed to have his transistor radio tuned to a different station, bellowing jazz or Chinese opera. Four older men were playing a gambling game together and shouting gleefully when one man won. Smaller boys and girls were running wildly up and down the ship's aisles, screaming with excitement and putting peanuts down each other's backs. "Every day these people work hard, carrying rocks for road, slaving for other peoples," S. Y. explained. "But today is holiday. They throw away tomorrow."

Dizzy with heat and the din, I was glad when Michael induced one family to push over, and S. Y. and I sat down gingerly on the edge of the settee, while he deposited upon the floor at our feet a paper bag of vegetables, dried fish, and seaweed. "For the *congee.*" He had to mouth the words over the noise which grew to a crescendo as the ferryboat hooted its way down the harbor through the thick traffic of sampans, foreign destroyers, cruise ships, and other ferryboats. My ears hurt. I felt sick at my stomach. Then I remembered what Bishop Fisher had told me about the fever bird in India that had so upset him, shouting outside his study window. He had discovered, "Put yourself in tune with the racket and you won't hear it at all." So I began to sing loudly myself, " 'I want to be happy, but I can't be happy unless you are happy too . . .' " It worked so well that a tiny Chinese girl in a red dress climbed up on my knee and offered me a slightly damp peanut. I belonged to the gang.

After about an hour the ferry docked briefly at a pier, and Michael and Sylvia, shrieking in Chinese, tore down

the gangplank and then down wet stone steps to where a
thin man in torn black cotton pajamas was trying to keep
a small pirogue from banging against the dock.

"They greet the friend who taxis us over to Chu Lap
Kok," explained S. Y.

It was such a small canoe-like boat that I didn't see how
five of us could possibly fit inside; indeed, as we climbed
cautiously aboard while the taxi man stood erect with
crossed oars, the sea was within an inch of lapping over
the gunnels. As the ferry hooted away and we rocked
precariously in its waves, I resigned myself to drowning,
but miraculously we stayed afloat; Black Pajamas began to
row with his crossed oars, and excited Chinese crackled
about my head. What on earth was I doing in a sliver of
a boat rocking in the South China Sea, alone with a bunch
of strangers? I wondered. If the boat sank, who would
ever know what had happened to me? Yet as I stared back
at the mainland hills with the ragged nylon clouds about
their peaks, they seemed to open their arms to me in a
strange peace. When I slid hesitant fingers into the jade-
green water slipping by, it was smooth and warm, much
warmer than the cold sea in Maine where I used to splash
as a child. After all, Chu Lap Kok was just another island
like Newagen, happy with children's chatter and bird
songs in the newly planted trees.

The committee of welcoming farmers and their families
on the island pier looked exactly like a painting on a Chinese fan, with their big hats and black pajamas, with milling children and frantic chickens clucking and getting in
everyone's way. There were sixteen refugee families on
the island who had dug wells and planted gardens, trees,
and grass on the denuded hills now greening into beauty,
and had been given fertilizer and pigs to raise. I had to
admire every hair on the big boar, the sows, and precious
piglets. I glanced from the pigpen full of healthy, grunting
animals down to the beach below, where a small boy was

scrubbing the face of a baby so hard with sea water that she was yelling blue murder.

"Is Yiu Yee-tak, making fine his small sister, Yee-tai, for your inspection," S. Y. told me. "With his mother in Hong Kong working on roads and his father in TB hospital, Yee-tak is head of family."

"How old is he?"

"Twelve, but he is only eight big. It is because he has never had enough to eat."

"With all these gardens around here?" I asked skeptically.

"They must sell, cannot eat. Must have cash to dig more wells. Only today is special celebration lunch for you." When I looked alarmed, he said soothingly, "Rice in *congee* is cooked four hours. Even you can eat safely."

Luncheon was clearly a feast. Ten of us gathered around the big table which was covered with a plastic tablecloth decorated with large red cabbage roses. The only empty seat was beside mine. The rice in the *congee* was indeed soupy, but I had to pick my way around bits of dried fish, onions, peanuts, seaweed, and other odds and ends probably better not identified. In the center of the table was a vast bowl of cut-up chicken, cooked so recently from the hens that had clucked upon the pier that the bones were still red with blood. The plastic tablecloth was convenient, for one grabbed a leg, spat out the bone, and then belched in deep content. Seeing who could belch loudest was an exciting game, but I don't think I won.

"Come and sit down by Mrs. Fletcher, Yee-tak," S. Y. called to the boy lingering outside the screen door.

Yee-tak came in very slowly. His face had been scrubbed almost raw, his dark hair slicked back, and as he slid gingerly in beside me, he sat very still, his eyes on the red plastic roses. "Eat up, boy. There is plenty for all," S. Y. urged.

But Yee-tak just sat there, frozen, his hand clenched

into a tight fist. A man must not cry. Yet suppose I did not choose him for my friend? A lump rose in my own throat so that I could not swallow either. Who was I to play God to a small boy so scared he couldn't even chew? Unable to stand this any longer, I said, "It's all right, Yee-tak. Tell him, S. Y., I choose him!" I put my warm hand on his small clenched fist. "It's all *right,* my dear!"

His eyes were full of unbelievable joy as he snatched his bowl of *congee.* Now he could eat.

Yee-tak proved as brilliant as S. Y. had promised, and he was also right about the boy's not having had enough to eat, for when next I saw Yee-tak in Hong Kong he was six feet tall, in his last year of secondary school, ready to go on to college if his sponsors approved. The first thing I always do when I get to town is to invite to dinner all the childen at St. Simon's who belong to me and to my friends, chaperoned by the head of the school and his thin, sensitive wife. This time we were thirteen at the dinner table, including a couple of stray Koreans whose names I never did discover but who were hungry. Yee-tak had brought his small sister, Yee-tai, who was now grown big enough so that her head came up over the tablecloth if she sat on a telephone book. Suet Fah, as usual, sat next to me, every now and then sliding her hand into mine under the tablecloth. At seventeen she wore the uniform of the older girls, white blouse and dark-blue trousers, but both were rumpled as if she didn't much care how she looked and her formerly merry eyes were older and sad. What was wrong with her? I wondered anxiously. But I could hardly ask amid such a gang, and right after dinner the headmaster sent the children back to school in their bus.

"What's the matter with Suet Fah? Is she ill?" I burst out anxiously. "She looks worried."

"I did not want to speak before, to embarrass her," the school head explained. "We are having trouble keeping her in school. Oh, she loves it there, but her father wants her to go back into the flower factory. He wants to collect her wages."

"Oh, no!"

He nodded. "In old China, a child, especially a girl, is the property of her parents until she is twenty-one. When she went back to Siu Lam for her Christmas vacation, we had to send first a social worker, then a policeman to get Suet Fah back to school. I explained to her father that if he waited till she became a teacher, she would earn much more money. But she is torn two ways—what she owes her family and what she wants to do, to study—most unhappy." He shrugged philosophically. "Most adolescents are unhappy over something."

But I was worried. "I've been planning that when she got through at St. Simon's she could come to the States to live with me for a few years, go to our Sudbury High School. They say they'll be glad to have her. If she becomes really fluent in English, she can get a much better teacher's job back here in Hong Kong."

He nodded. "Don't worry. I think it will be all right."

But of course I did worry. The next year I delayed starting my book on the newly independent women in the East until after I had stopped in Hong Kong to see how things were going with Suet Fah. The head of St. Simon's came to my hotel room to tell me the bad news. "Suet Fah is married. Her father sold her to a man forty years old, with four children, for the bride price of about forty dollars. We suspect he has gone back to chasing the dragon!"

"Sold her!" I gasped, my mouth dry with fear. "Like a piece of furniture? But she's only eighteen. This is horrible!"

He said slowly, "I was afraid you'd feel this way. It is unfortunate, yes. But she is Chinese, remember."

"But she wrote she was looking forward so to coming to the States to study!" I promised wildly, "I'll go to the authorities, British, American, Chinese. Surely something can be done..." Such a marriage seemed to me more like a funeral. Suet Fah, who had cried and begged to be a teacher, who'd knelt in my arms to pray, "Our Father . . ."

"She's married and that's that. There is nothing you can do," the school head assured me gently.

"What's her husband's name? Can I go to see her?"

"Better not just now. It might make her lose face."

"I just want to tell her that whatever happens, I still love her!"

"She knows that already."

All I could do for her, it seemed, was to write out a check for her wedding present and give it to the head of St. Simon's to deliver. He took it gladly and then he said the last thing I would have expected at such a time when I was so despairing. "Why don't you adopt another child? Perhaps the small Yee-tai, who is in the first-year class?"

I stared at him. "And have my heart torn again? No, thank you."

"Have you been doing this charity, then, for your own sake or for the child?"

I flushed. But he was right. "Remember, all is not wasted. Suet Fah now has four children to teach what she knows." That was true also, but I was too sore in my loss to admit it. Yee-tai . . . Her small round face peeping up over the tablecloth as she sat on the telephone book had been still baby-sweet, and her parents were Christian. They'd never prevent her learning, getting ahead. "Very well," I snapped. "But don't expect me to love her as I do Suet Fah."

I found a brief note back home, sent through St. Simon's, from Suet Fah, thanking me for the wedding gift, but she said nothing more except, "Please don't worry about me." She had been swallowed up among the four million Hong Kong Chinese refugees whose ideas and customs were so different from my Western ones. I should have realized I could never buck the Chinese, not even to save a child; but if that were so, what real good could any Westerner do?

The regular letters from small Yee-tai were beguilingly fresh and gay. Right from the beginning her Chinese characters were more elegantly finished than Suet Fah's, but this made me miss my lost daughter more than ever. Yee-tai wrote:

> I am now in Primary Two. I passed all my exams. I got 90 in Chinese dictation and all other subjects were over 80%. And just think . . . I won the sack race yesterday!

She was so bright she might even surpass her brilliant big brother, but I didn't think he would mind, for she was especially his baby. But I missed Suet Fah's tear-blotted letters. Last Christmas I sent the school two gift checks, one to be given to Yee-tai and the other to be sent to Suet Fah, wherever she was. It was a gala day for me when I opened the cheap blue envelope, expecting a thank-you letter from Yee-tai, and found instead the uneven characters that could be only from Suet Fah!

She wrote:

> Thank you very much for your lovely Christmas card and for the five dollars. Please worry no more about me. My family life is very happy for I have a little daughter of my very own who is a delight. She is lovely. But I wish you would send me a photograph of yourself so that I can have you forever.

I put Suet Fah's letter into my jewel box after I'd mailed her the picture, in care of the school. I don't even know where in Hong Kong my older daughter lives or the name of my delightful Chinese granddaughter. But I love them both, forever.

CHAPTER 10

# In Pleasant Places

*The lines are fallen unto me in pleasant places;*
*yes, I have a goodly heritage.*

The only bonus a peripatetic merry widow does not have
to report on her income tax is the richness of making new
friends. Old friends are the roots lying deep for our vital
sustenance, but new friends are the spring verdure on
bare limbs which proves we are still alive.

During the past eight years when I have been wander-
ing the world, I have walked the teeming streets of Old
Delhi, the ghetto section of the Indian capital, holding
hands tightly with my friend, a Sikh taxi driver, and the
day before had gone to tea in the gardens of the President's home, which is so like Buckingham Palace, even to
the impassive palace guards who wear turbans instead of
bearskins, but who do not blink an eyelash as you pass
them by, that you wonder if you have been transported to
London. I wanted to stick a pin in their backsides to see
if they would squeak, "God save the President!" or "God
save our gracious Queen!"

As we entered the palace front door, a huge black-and-white sketch of the truly humble Gandhi struck the eye like a blow, but there was certainly nothing humble about the palace furnishings or the rigidly handsome, vast gardens into which we were ushered. Since the President was ill, the great Hindu philosopher, Dr. Sarvepalli Radhakrishnan, Vice-President of India, murmured a few friendly words to each of the hundreds of members of the World Council of Churches, "How are you? It is good to see you here!" and passed us on to the long tables laden with too sweet cakes and too weak tea, and to a sense of sadness that Indians had to prove they were as sophisticated as the long-gone British, that they still did not dare to be themselves. The quiet shade of Gandhi with his dhoti and prayers was as alien here as would be the Indian multitudes swarming the streets outside the palace, who were fighting daily not only for food for their skinny bodies but for the peace of mind that comes only from tall self-respect. As Gandhi knew and had, alas, died for.

The following day I wanted to explore Old Delhi to find a special addition to Rick's international weapons collection, the sharp knife which is given to every Sikh boy when he is seven and becomes a man, in a ceremony somewhat like the Jewish boy's Bar Mitzvah. But when I showed the desk clerk at the hotel the address of the shop I wanted to visit, he cried, "But you cannot go down there alone, madame! It is not safe! Best to give up such a crazy idea." I was no budding, daisy-fresh girl but a merry widow who did as she pleased. I sauntered outside to where the doorman, an imposing Sikh loaded down with gold braid, stood at the top of the steps. I asked him quietly, holding out my piece of paper, "Do you know a taxi driver whom you can trust to take me to this address in Old Delhi? Who will translate for me?"

"Certainly, memsahib."

He blew his whistle but by-passed three taxis and finally

opened the door of the fourth for me with a flourish. He and my turbaned taxi driver at the wheel of the car, so ancient that Detroit would have put it with awe into a museum, had a few words in Hindi. As we drove off, my driver smiled at me in the mirror. Like that of all the Sikh taxi drivers in New Delhi, his uncut beard was rolled around an elastic caught behind his ears, and his dark eyes were bright and curious.

"You are married, memsahib?" he demanded.

"Yes." I knew better than to admit I was now a lowly widow.

"You have a son?"

"Yes. It is for him I need the knife."

"Ah. We will find one then, never fear."

The streets of Old Delhi are so narrow, so cluttered with assorted traffic, both Old World and New, that progress is slow. Sleek modern limousines carrying either VIPs or lovely, smooth-haired ladies in bright diaphanous saris fought for passage with a lumbering team of placid oxen whose horns had been painted with gold and hung with wreaths of flowers by the family seated together on the hard, bare wooden floor of their native cart. Our rickety taxi, thank heaven, had good brakes, for we constantly stopped with neck-jerking suddenness when a pedestrian, taking his life in his hands, wove his dangerous way to the opposite side of the street. The worst jaywalkers were the sacred cattle ambling from one food shop to another as carelessly as if they knew that if we killed one of them, the driver and probably I myself might be torn limb from limb by the pious Hindu throng.

But we finally arrived. The taxi driver carefully locked the creaking, uneven doors, testing each one in turn, then held out his hand to me. I clutched it tightly as the curious bystanders swarmed closer and jostled us on the crowded sidewalk. Suddenly my new friend, dragging me after him, dodged down some cellar stairs to a dark small shop where the merchant and the taxi man assaulted each other in furious Hindi. Eventually the shopkeeper shrugged, opened a drawer, and took out a red velvet horror with gold tassels dangling from the scabbard. This was obviously tourist bait.

"No, no," I said firmly to my Sikh friend. "Tell him I want the real thing. A knife such as you yourself might buy for your own son!"

Reluctantly the shopkeeper opened another drawer and handed the driver a plain-handled knife with a steel blade so sharp that just drawing his finger along it to show us how keen it was cut the shopkeeper's dirty finger. I offered him my clean handkerchief to stop the bleeding, but he reached hastily for a filthy rag on the counter; anything touched by a Westerner, probably a Christian and certainly a woman, was unclean. The sooner we got out of his shop, the happier he would be. To this end I paid what he asked without bargaining, which startled him, and we escaped, with the knife wrapped in a piece of newspaper, to the upper air.

Fortunately my taxi-driver friend did not find me unclean, or perhaps he planned purifying ceremonies later on, but he still held my hand firmly as we sauntered together among the cluttered sidewalk shops, buying strings of sandalwood beads, queer-looking brass objects for which I had no possible use but which would fit into the odd corners of a suitcase, and finally a leopard-skin cap for me to tilt over one gay eyebrow. The smell of the streets was strangely exhilarating, compounded of incense, cooking food, cow dung, sandalwood, and sweaty bodies that jostled ours, but nobody seemed to find anything unusual in a turbaned Sikh and an American woman walking hand in hand. It was our business. This was the tolerant, lusty India which I had known existed outside hotels, palaces, and embassies but with which I had never before rubbed elbows. Suddenly a great affection for these people who could smile and savor life, even if many did not know where their next meal was coming from, flooded my mind.

I tipped my taxi driver well, of course, but I could not possibly pay him in cash for the genuine interest he had shown in finding the ceremonial knife or for his sharing of my pleasure in Old Delhi as a friend and equal. When we parted, we simply smiled at each other.

"Thank you," I said, and he bowed.

This was the real India, proud to be able to give, which I could love and to which I was to return frequently after this first visit.

The Thais, however, had been my familiar friends for many years. I had not then been to the many-templed Bangkok, but I had visited it often in my mind, for when Chula was homesick he used to tell me about the klongs where the lotus bloomed and the swift-flowing Chao Phraya River, down which the King was borne in a golden barge. Siam, as we called it in those days, was Chula's home and had for me the quality of a golden dream during that winter when I was seventeen, when Dad had the big church in Worcester and we all lived in the rambling Victorian parsonage with colored glass in the front door and the ugly Tiffany table lamp of assorted colors in the front parlor.

Chula and Izzy, the two Siamese boys, were classmates of my brother Ike's at Wilbraham Academy whom he brought home unexpectedly to spend the Thanksgiving vacation. Mother said mildly, "You might at least have let me know, Ike." But when he explained, "They were lonesome. They had no place to go," she smiled and welcomed the boys cordially. Izzy's real name was Privat Izrankura; I remember, because the syllables rolled pleasantly on the tongue rather like Peter Piper with his peck of pickled peppers. Ike wasn't sure what the rest of Chula's name was. "Anyway, he was born in the palace so he must be some kind of minor royalty," Ike said carelessly.

"Maybe he's the son of a concubine!" I was still a romantic.

Certainly the boys were both used to being waited upon. Every morning they would toss yesterday's underwear upon the rush-seated stool Ike had made in "shop" at school, to be washed and ironed, which, since we couldn't afford a maid, Mother had to do. But otherwise the boys were perfect guests; they ate what was put before them, admired the turkey, and whatever went wrong, they smiled as calmly as two small Buddhas. The only queer thing was that they treated me as if I were invisible. They never looked me in the face, and even when I asked Chula to pass the butter at breakfast one morning, he pretended not to hear me. I flushed. Certainly I was no Helen of Troy, but really . . . Finally Dad spoke out.

"Susie won't bite you, Chula."

"I cannot marry her," Chula explained. He drew out a little black notebook of rules he had agreed to before he came to this strange country. He had promised to always remain a good Buddhist and not to marry an American girl. . . .

"Good grief, Susie doesn't want to marry *you!*"

When Dad assured him of that, Chula beamed happily and passed me the butter.

For the rest of the vacation the four of us went everywhere together, even slyly into Boston to paint the town red by dancing the rumba on the roof of the old Brunswick Hotel. We were still at an age when outwitting the Establishment was fun. Yes, Virginia, we did our own thing, too, in those prehistoric days, and Chula and Izzy with their apparently bottomless pocketbooks—at least it seemed so to two parsonage mice—were our Santa Clauses. We'd pick up two of Ike's endless string of girlfriends, and the six of us would dine and dance on the starlit roof then popular with Boston and Cambridge students. We were drunk on the frantic drums of the orchestra, our own frenetic rhythm, and the happy belief that we were thumbing our noses at the Methodist Discipline. With Chula's arm around me as we waltzed to "Goodnight, Ladies," I was living dangerously.

Mother, however, was horrified when Chula, delighted that he did not have to marry me, bought me an expensive gold bracelet which made my mouth water.

"American girls do not accept jewelry from men—nothing except, well, flowers, books, and candy," Mother explained.

"Oh? Sorry," Chula apologized, and proceeded to shower me with five-pound boxes of candy, expensive spring flowers, and a pillow that was marked in big letters WILBRAHAM ACADEMY.

After their first visit the two Siamese boys no longer waited to be invited but would appear, beaming, at the parsonage door each school vacation, announcing royally, "I come!" Mother would sigh and make up the guest beds while they handed her a dozen long-stemmed red roses the like of which she hadn't seen since she had been voted "the prettiest girl in Ft. Worth, Texas." It was all very pleasant, international, and ecumenical, but after Ike went on to Ohio Wesleyan and the Siamese boys to Harvard, we grew apart, our interests changed. Ike met Lillian and got engaged, I fell in love with Jock, and we seemed to have no time for anyone else.

Years later, in 1961 to be exact, when I was up in the attic getting a suitcase to pack to fly across the Pacific with Polly, I came across Chula's old pillow marked WILBRAHAM ACADEMY. Now I was actually going to see the lotus flowers and the King's golden barge. Was it possible Chula was still living in Bangkok? But when I wrote to the alumni secretary for his address and Izzy's, the school wrote back that Privat Izrankura was dead and that they had no recent address for Chulalongkorn. So that was

Chula's real name. Probably we'd have no time to look him up and he might not remember me anyway after nearly half a century. I put the letter into my huge handbag that held everything from my passport to spare Kleenex and forgot about it. Thus, the strange thing that happened to Polly and me in the Oriental Hotel on the bank of the fabled Chao Phraya River, "Mother of Noble Waters," came out of the blue.

Polly had been to Bangkok before and had so many favorite shops to show me that we were busy all day riding about on those little bicycle affairs where the boy pedals in front and you hold on frantically to the slippery seat behind. The city was a shopper's paradise; we reveled in the rainbow colors of the beautifully handwoven Thai silk, of which I had a party suit made, and pored over precious jewels so modestly priced that I bought a jade ring which I'd always wanted but had never been able to afford, while Polly settled for two lustrous star sapphires. In between times Polly and I visited the gorgeous mosaic-walled temples, with bells under their gilded eaves swinging softly in the breeze, devil dogs as guardians, and pointed soaring spires. The most interesting temple housed the Emerald Buddha, hanging some forty feet up in the air, who, we were told, was so holy that he was dressed in summer or winter garb by the King himself.

"How does the King get up there," I wondered, "to dress the Buddha? Or do they let him down on his string?"

The trip upriver to see the royal barge was rather an anticlimax, for Polly and I were accompanied by a magpie flock of chattering tourists. But as we looked up at the tall golden prow, I could picture the young King in this gorgeous hundred-foot barge riding in ceremonial Oriental splendor, much as Queen Elizabeth of England does in her golden coach on special occasions, looking rather like I had imagined Cinderella in the fairy coach before it turned into a pumpkin. Yet we shall all be the poorer when fairy tales give way to computers and wonder dies. But the King's barge inevitably made me think of Chula. The note from Wilbraham was still in my handbag, so when we got back to the Oriental, I tossed it onto the hotel clerk's desk, asking, "Do you know how I could find out the address of Chulalongkorn?" The clerk read the letter and went white. "He lives at the palace! He's the King's uncle!"

"Oh? He used to go to school with my brother in the States. Maybe there are several Chulalongkorns and this is not *my* Chula I used to dance with! In any case, forget it. We're leaving in a couple of days." Besides, I added to myself, it's better to have the memory of a long-ago handsome young prince than to see a possibly potbellied one now.

But the excited clerk used his own judgment. I had barely gotten well curled up for my afternoon nap before the phone rang to announce, "There are two officers down here in the lobby who wish to speak to you! I think maybe they are sent by the palace."

"I'm resting. Did you say 'officers'? Oh, well, tell them to wait, please."

Polly and I had separate rooms because I liked air conditioning in this humid heat but she preferred the gently swaying ceiling fans, so I phoned her to ask, "You want to meet a couple of Thai Army brass?"

"Why not? Let's take a look at them, anyway."

The two khaki-clad gentlemen with imposing epaulettes on their shoulders, who jumped up when we arrived, were about our own age, very erect and good-looking. But they were both toothless, which didn't improve our understanding of their rusty English. We managed to make out that Chula was ill, away in London for medical treatment, but that they had been sent to act as our hosts to show us their city. Through the open hotel doorway we glimpsed a uniformed chauffeur standing stiffly beside a large black limousine. Would we please get inside, the officers begged politely, and let them begin?

"This is so sudden," Polly murmured coyly, but when I lifted my eyebrow she nodded, so I agreed. "We have engagements for today. Tomorrow, perhaps?"

Certainly, tomorrow. They would return at nine in the morning, would conduct us to their homes and arrange a lunch at the Golden Dragon, which had the best food in the city. As they marched out, Polly said it would be a good chance to see how the upper crust lived, but what rank were they, anyway? We never did find out, but we called them affectionately "our pet generals."

Breakfast at our hotel would have tempted a fasting anchorite, very hot, strong coffee, toast with English marmalade made with bitter oranges, and a young mountain of pomolos (grapefruit), iced oranges, papayas, and tiny bananas from which to choose. Our "pet generals" arrived soon after breakfast, accompanied by the pretty daughter of one of them, who was on her way to the Buddhist Ladies' Society meeting but who wished to meet us in case, when she visited the States next spring, she could drop by Polly's home in Las Cruces and mine in Boston; that these were two thousand miles apart we didn't mention. After leaving the pretty Thai girl at her meeting, our big car honked its imperious way through an enormous, crowded market where our hosts bought us a couple of fruit stands of pears and exotic fruits whose names we could not pronounce and which we did not want or need, but couldn't say so. One of our hosts suggested we stop to see his house. It turned out to be a huge wooden building with wide verandas looking out over a klong (canal) where the lotuses were indeed in bloom. We parked by five shiny big cars, which must have cost a fortune, gleaming in the walled back yard.

"Each of my sons and grandsons likes to have his own car," the grandfather explained. "That smaller house over there is my studio where I go when I can't stand the family racket. Sometimes I paint, sometimes I just sit."

"I know exactly how you feel," I said. "Love 'em and leave 'em."

He smiled. "There's a picture I want to show you, Mrs. Fletcher, in my living room."

It proved to be a faded photograph of a group of boys in knickerbockers, looking as bored as kids do for an official photograph. "Why, there's Ike!" I cried. "And Chula and Izzy!"

"And me," amended our beaming host, pointing out a plump lad with Oriental eyes. "Our Wilbraham class picture."

Imagine coming all the way to Bangkok to a strange, rambling house on a klong and finding on the wall my own brother!

"Now you should see a more modern Thai house," the friend from Wilbraham announced. "I will take you to visit my daughter and her husband. Both were educated in the States, she at Sarah Lawrence and he at Harvard."

The new house was also on a klong, but it had ceiling-to-floor screens to ward off the inevitable battalions of mosquitoes. The daughter was the most beautiful girl I have ever met in any country; exquisite, not only in her face and body, but in her graceful hospitality. She and her husband offered us cold drinks which the servant girl, dressed in black pajama bottoms and a bright blouse, brought in. Polly was staring over her glass at the husband, tall for a Thai.

"Aren't you the man at the bank who okayed cashing my check yesterday?" she demanded. "I was surprised you let me have so much money with only my passport for reference."

"Anyone who could afford to come here from New Mexico must have some assets." He smiled. "Besides, you look honest."

"Thank you, sir, for them kind words."

A child's sleepy wail came from the next room. I begged, "Could we see your baby?"

The small, rosy girl in the crib had already gone back to sleep, so we didn't disturb her. Her father's eyes caressed her proudly as he pulled up the blanket over plump, dimpled knees and smiled up at his lovely wife. "We call her 'Pim,' which means 'Duplicate,' because she's so exactly like her mother." When husband and wife looked that way at each other, I was suddenly lonely for Jock.

As we tiptoed back into the big, screened living room, I asked, "How shall you educate little Pim? Here or in America?"

"That is the big question." He frowned, taking a refill of his iced drink. "Proper lower-form schools are in short supply here, not nearly enough to go round. To get in a really good one, we had to register Pim the day she was born." He shot us an inquiring glance. Surely we were mature enough to take criticism without starting a student riot? He ventured, "Your government makes a big mistake by sending us cash for roads and military material, much of which sticks to the hands of the contractors and distributors."

I remarked that the same stickiness occurred in Massachusetts.

"Often our people don't even know where your gifts come from," he persisted. "They're stamped 'Gift of the United States of America,' but the Russians frequently manage to label the bags of rice, also. Most of our people can't read English, but they do know the Star and Sickle. What you should do is to send over architects to build schools, who will themselves pay the bills as they occur. Cut deep into the stone arch over each school doorway should be the words, 'Gift of the Children of America to the Children of Thailand.' Then, as they go in and out, our children will realize who our good friends really are."

He grimaced. "Nowadays you may have to pay a bribe to get your child into even a missionary school!"

"Surely not!"

"Well, I don't know what else you'd call it. Down payment? The day after Pim's registration was accepted, I got a request to contribute to their 'new building fund.' I sent them five hundred dollars. That ought to do it."

"Cynical, but practical," Polly agreed.

Pim's grandfather, brushing aside international peculiarities, said hastily that perhaps we ought to be moving along to the Golden Dragon; he'd ordered luncheon for one o'clock. We left the nice young Thai family reluctantly, but the lunch did prove sumptuous. I hadn't the slightest idea what we were eating, but it certainly tasted different from what they served at the hotel. I ate so heartily that I could hardly stagger into the hotel lobby. Polly, of course, was all vigor and in radiant health, ready to drag me downstream the next day to see the early morning river market. "Meet you at seven A.M.," she said firmly.

"Crack of dawn. I'll never make it," I wailed.

Polly took off her white gloves and put them into her handbag. She observed smugly, "Well, I may be the one who always gets skin trouble, but you can't seem to stomach the Orient."

The crisp air at 7 A.M., however, was reviving, and as our small motorboat pushed its way along the narrow winding branches of the river, its banks edged with small wooden houses open to the view, I decided life might be worth living for a few more hours. Each house at Thornburi had its own small landing, with usually a swarm of children playing with a pet monkey or parakeet. The captain of our expedition had given us bananas and peeled pomolos to munch on, but just as I was about to take a bite, I noticed the body of a dead dog floating downstream and hastily tossed my fruit to the nearest monkey. We were by now in the thick of the market, canoes filled with bright, newly washed fruit and vegetables, kitchenwares, and what-have-you, including masses of blooms in glorious colors. When I tossed the Thai girl paddling beside us an American quarter, she handed up her entire canoeful of flowers! "She's as generous as our 'pet generals,'" I told Polly. "I wonder if they'll be at the airport to see us off."

"I shouldn't think so. Saying good-by twice would be an anticlimax."

A huge pile of letters from home was waiting for us back at the hotel and we fell upon them avidly. Everyone was wishing us "A Merry Christmas," for December twenty-fifth was only a few days away. As soon as I was sure Rick and Sylvia were all right, I drew a deep breath of relief. "Funny, isn't it? No matter where you travel or how much you like it, you go right on being at home. More American?"

"If you're born an azalea you can hardly be a radish," Polly pointed out reasonably. "But you might be a bigger and better azalea."

Our "pet generals" did not come to the plane to see us off the next evening, but all Bangkok lay like a crown of glittering jewels below us as our plane soared aloft. I murmured to Polly, "It was a perfect visit, except I wish I could have seen Chula. I hope he isn't seriously ill in London. Do you think I ought to send him a get-well card?"

"Using what for an address?"

"Maybe we'll meet again in our next life. I can't decide what I want to be, the first violin in the Boston Symphony, a ballet dancer, or a lady astronaut."

Polly observed that hobnobbing with Buddhist high society seemed to have given me big ideas.

The next time I visited Bangkok I was alone, the Vietnam war was on, and everything was changed. The stifling-hot, humid Don Muang airport even had an air-con-

ditioned restaurant where I went to wait for my friends,
since my plane had gotten in early. The big room with a
bar at one end was alive with GIs and officers of all ranks,
ribbons, and ages, for Bangkok was a favorite city for R
and R (rest and recreation leave). I myself had just returned from a hectic week in Saigon, where I was scared
every moment but tried not to show it as I interviewed
bombed-out refugees for my new book. Even my hotel
room was not a safe refuge, for it had no lock on the door
and I had been advised to close my wooden shutters
before I put on my two-watt bulb in my room evenings,
for fear of snipers from across the river. Since I had a
smattering of French, I was frequently asked by the hotel
clerk to come down to interpret to him what the American
guests wanted. Most of them were young GIs who hun-
gered to chat with "someone from home." Thus I discovered in our common homesickness that the generation
gap did not matter. So when I saw in the airport restaurant
a big round table of six GIs with tall brown bottles in front
of them, I went over and asked if I might join them. I
explained that I had recently been in Saigon myself.

That was the password. The boys all rose politely, and
one pulled out my chair.

"What were you doing there, ma'am?" The young marine didn't say "an old-timer like you." "What's Saigon
like? I never could get a pass to stay over."

"A city holding its breath, expecting the worst and usually getting it," I said soberly. "With some of the prettiest
girls in the world who ride around on bicycles with their
gauzy *ao-dais* floating out behind them like wings. But
down at Cai Be, the farmers wore black shorts and the
girls black pajamas, as you doubtless know."

"But Cai Be's way down on the Delta! Route Four is
dangerous!"

"I was riding down with a doctor and his wife from the
Asian Relief who were planning to start a hospital and day

nursery," I explained. "On the way, we stopped to interview refugees living in their new homes that the government and USAID had built beside the road which the VC mined every night and we unmined each morning. Some of the houses looked quite festive where the new owner had trained morning glories across the front door, and each home had an all-purpose ditch dug around it, full of ducks and their precious pigs."

"They drink that muddy gunk!" exclaimed the GI with the scars from jungle rot on his face and neck. "When I was stationed near Tuy Hoa, we dug them poor ginks deep wells. But try to make 'em drink there. I guess they're immune to bugs."

I chuckled. "When the doctor wanted to take the picture of one mother and her baby, she was all smiles. But of course, none of the babies wear diapers. This one let go while the doctor was focusing his camera, but the mother just reached down and dunked his rear end in the drinking water!"

The roar of laughter from our table made all heads turn. "Those kids are the cutest little buggers," the marine said eagerly. "Our outfit adopted one who had his leg blown off; we bought him an artificial leg. Cripes, can that kid get around!"

Another boy broke in. "We gave the orphanage near us a Christmas party. We decorated a palm tree with a big tin star cut out of a can and gave each kid a pencil and an orange."

They were all interrupting now to tell what their outfits had done, from swiping lumber to build shelters for women who were having their babies right out in the open on the seashore, to the medic who, after his hospital duty, had helped to run a clinic to inoculate for the black plague. Not without reason have these young pragmatists, who face today's facts and make the best of them, been called "the most compassionate army in history."

The Green Beret hadn't said anything up to now, but as he leaned forward across the table, the brass bracelet made from an old shell casing which the mountain people give only to those they choose as their blood brothers slid down his wrist.

"I was stationed up on the Laotian border, adviser to a regiment of South Vietnamese and Montagnards," he said slowly. "Those mountaineers are grand people. They have nothing, really, but they're sharp to learn. I wished I'd studied agriculture or medicine in college so I could be a real help. The two years I was a student I protested right and left against everything, but was never *for* anything. Now I know what I want to do. If I don't get buzzed off in the next three months, I'm going back to a good cow college to learn the things these Montagnards need. And then I'm coming back . . ."

The tinny voice of the airport announcer warning that the military transport was now leaving for Saigon interrupted us, and, shouting good-bys as warmly as if I'd been from their own hometown, the six GIs grabbed their baggage and took off, leaving behind them the brown, half-empty bottles. It was only then I noticed that they'd all been drinking Cokes. As I stared at the childish drinks, a man's voice spoke from across the aisle.

"That's because they are going *back,*" the grizzled, middle-aged sergeant called across from his table where he was guzzling from a big brown pitcher. Of ice and bourbon? "A lot of the weak brothers get so soused they have to be poured aboard the plane for Saigon, but the smart ones drink Cokes." He lifted his glass and assured me, "Just tea. I'm going back, too, on the next flight."

After what I'd seen in Vietnam, these kids could drink an ocean of champagne if they liked. They were a sturdy breed of young Americans who had not taken well-publicized refuge in any church but whose sanctuary was their own quiet conscience where no TV cameras lurked or newspapermen clamored. Why assume that the only ones who hate war are those who bravely burn their draft cards? These boys at my table had bet their lives to obey the draft law; many were reluctant warriors doing their job with guns and bombs, but in their own time building shelters for women in labor or making a Christmas tree out of a dusty palm for kids who had never owned a toy in their lives. Of such GIs it might well be said:

> Unbounded courage and compassion join'd
> Tempering each other . . .
> . . . make hero and the man complete . . .

The Vietnam war was probably the greatest blunder in foreign policy the United States had ever made which had cost us over 36,000 lives. Yet perhaps this mess wasn't a total loss if half a million young Americans had come to know for themselves that the small shopkeepers who were bombed out, the rice farmers with burned fields and homes, their wives and children, yes, even the enemy, were people too. Perhaps those GIs who make it back home may even insist upon our developing a foreign policy that makes sense, upon our using our billions to give the developing countries, instead of handouts, tools to help themselves so that they may no longer be beggars but may stand proudly erect, helping to build their own future.

My friends had found me in the cool restaurant, so I hastily tipped the waiter gathering up the empty Coke bottles enough for all six boys, and left once more for the Oriental Hotel, which used also to be a favorite of Somerset Maugham. It had changed from the quiet place Polly and I had known; an orchestra was playing what passed for American jazz in a neon-lighted bar and there were no more gentle ceiling fans; Polly wouldn't have liked the raucous gewgaw glitter, rather pathetic really, like a wrinkled light-o'-love pretending to be young. But my room looked out on the swift-flowing river, where the same old, thin lady was still paddling her pirogue ferry across to the other side for a few bahts, and the monkeys were still chained up in the trees beside the swimming pool for the GIs and the children to feed. But my room was so empty without Polly that I took the elevator up to the rooftop restaurant where its glass walls showed all Bangkok down below. At least there would be lights, people.

"Good evening, Mrs. Fletcher!" The maitre d' came up to me and bowed low, remarking with a welcoming smile that they hadn't seen me for a long time. It had been two years. How could he possibly have remembered me? He said briskly, pulling out my chair, "The prawns that you like are good this evening and . . . what year Beaujolais did you prefer, madame?"

Cosseted and comforted, I was home again, with a friend.

But it was in Africa that I made my most unexpected friends—lions, cheetahs, baboons, and the long-lashed, long-necked giraffes nibbling the tops of trees, then, alarmed, loping like badly wound-up toys against the vast horizon. Seeing these great beasts in their own habitat instead of moping in a zoo, I came to realize for the first time that they were individuals who had as much right to their own place in the world as we human animals. More right, perhaps, for were they not created before man? Both Genesis and modern scientists seem to agree on the order of precedence, and what does it matter whether the sixth day of creation was twenty-four hours or billions of years long?

In Nairobi, men and beasts live so near together that when a lion wandered from the nearby National Park Reserve onto the airfield, it was routine that he merely be shooed back home before the airplanes could land. The wild-animal reserve was only three miles from my hotel and, as often as I could, I joined Jay, my friend from Nepal and Sudbury, and several of her children—her tiny Volkswagen was too small to accommodate all seven—and took a run over to visit a pride of lions or to hunt for the big crocodile, which recently had his picture taken by a newspaper as he pulled a wildebeest slowly but inevitably into his pool for supper.

"I'll give a shilling to the first one to spot a cheetah," I offered one afternoon to the kids, who were all agog in the back seat. Tara, the three-year-old whose name is Nepalese for Star, since she was born in Kathmandu, was the first to yell, "I spy him! Give me the shilling!"

"Where?" I asked. "I don't see him . . ."

"Under that bush!" Tara yelled.

The shadows of the flickering leaves had blended in with his spots to make the cheetah almost invisible. But he was there all right, panting in the heat. I gave Tara her shilling and we drove on to watch a papa and three mama lions taking an afternoon siesta under a tree while the cubs crawled over their inert bodies and spat with each other like any siblings. The big male lion could have batted our little red car over easily, but we were safe enough so long as we stayed inside and obeyed the street signs which read: PLEASE DO NOT DISTURB THE ANIMALS. DRIVE LEFT FOR LIONS. DO NOT HOOT. The zebras and impalas flowed by in the hundreds, slipping over the low tawny hills like water, as we drove by. It was like living in a dream of felicity between man and beast which couldn't be true but was; the Nairobi children were so used to this that they yawned and begged to go home to spend Tara's shilling.

Perhaps I caught too much of the children's nonchalance and forgot that, while these fascinating animals might be neighbors, they were still wild, responding to their instincts to select their own menus and to protect their young. When Jay and I drove up—minus the children—to spend the night in Treetops Hotel in the Aberdares, where Princess Elizabeth had been staying when her father died and, while up a tree, she suddenly found herself a queen, I refused to be unduly impressed. Hunters with rifles met us at the gate of the game reserve to escort us the few hundred yards to the hotel steps by which you mounted into a clump of sturdy trees supporting a three-story building.

"What are those little baskets for, around those tree trunks?" I asked the hunter.

"Blinds to hide in, in case an elephant charges."

Those little, light things? Tourists might not pay the Treetops' steep prices unless they were properly scared? When Jay and I were ushered into our room and found comfortable beds with light-blue sheets, with a proper toilet just down the corridor, although you did have to leap over a few tree limbs to get there, I was even surer that this was a tourist trap, however world-known. The hostess put her head inside our door to invite, "Tea is being served on the roof. Be sure to shut your windows to keep out the baboons." Our windows were already shut, fortunately, for I certainly would not have bothered.

The baboons really did come to tea, some fifty of them, mothers with intriguing babies clinging to their undersides, big baboons and little ones, all grabbing for the slices of pineapple which the hotel had provided for us to feed them as we drank our tea and guzzled little frosted cakes. Sitting down on the ground below us was one enormous old baboon, watching for danger with a careful eye. I shouldn't like to argue with that tough old guy, I was telling Jay, when we heard shrieks from down inside the hotel and a woman rushed up on the roof to gasp, "Help me! The baboons are in my bedroom scattering face powder all over everything. They've torn up my traveling bag!"

The hotel help didn't even say, "I told you so"; they sighed and went to her rescue. Later we were served a six-course dinner. I murmured to Jay, "I thought a safari was roughing it! Pale-blue sheets and filet mignon!"

Jay looked a bit disappointed too.

But there was nothing phony about the animals which we watched, fascinated, from a wide veranda, whispering so we would not scare them away as they ambled about or stood knee-deep in mud in the great water hole in front of Treetops or licked avidly at the salt. When it grew dark, great spotlights were turned on the water hole so we could see the newcomers. The hunter named them off for us: bongos, other species of antelopes, wildebeest, forest and wart hogs with their tails straight up over their backs like a handle, and many more whose names I can't recall. The elephants came so softly we didn't realize they were there until a huge male came almost up to our veranda, flapped his great ears, and raised his trunk so close we could have fed him peanuts, if we'd had any. Being so near and yet so far was uncanny. We were so enthralled we didn't go to bed until long after midnight; half an hour later the hostess woke us, whispering, "A rhino fight!" The two great awkward beasts threatening each other with their ugly horns seemed suddenly to come to some agreement, for they finally ambled off to drink separately at the water hole while we yawned our way back to bed.

"I wouldn't have missed Treetops for anything," I admitted to Jay on our way home next morning. "Especially the rhinos and the velvet-shod elephants. But I thought the guards-with-guns bit was rather too much."

How wrong I was! A few weeks after I left Nairobi, Jay sent me a clipping from the newspaper *The Nation:*

## ELEPHANT SHOT AS IT CHARGES

A large cow elephant was shot and killed at Treetops on Tuesday afternoon as it charged an elderly Australian woman who was visiting this game lodge in the Aberdares.

The elephant dropped dead less than 15 feet from where

Mrs. Rae Hedley of Melbourne, Victoria, cowered in fright . . .

Hunter Kenneth Levett, who was escorting the tourists to the lodge, killed the enraged elephant with a single shot as it broke away from a herd of about 60 animals who were on the salt lick below the lodge when the visitors arrived.

"As we approached the lodge from our vehicles we could see that a calf had got stuck in the mud," said Mr. Levett yesterday. "Its mother was quite naturally rather anxious.

"We waited in the blinds as the cow tried to push its youngster free. But she only succeeded in pushing the calf further into the mud."

Mr. Levett waited for nearly an hour for the mother to rescue its baby. As it got later and the elephant was nowhere nearer to pulling out the youngster he decided to escort the few tourists in the party across the last 50 yards to the tree house steps.

"He took us across two by two," explained Mrs. Hedley.... "Suddenly this elephant left its baby and careered towards me with its ears flapping madly. I didn't think it would really attack me but it kept on charging and I realized it was going to kill me.

"It came so close that I actually felt its breath. Then Mr. Levett with one shot killed the elephant. Blood gushed out of its head and the animal just dropped in a heap less than 15 feet from me."

Both hunter and elephant had been merely doing their jobs. What mother would not have rushed, trumpeting, to protect her child? Pity she had to die for it. What right had we, anyway, to turn the private life of the animals into a circus with spotlights? To me they *were* Africa and man the admiring alien. I can hardly wait to save enough cash to go on a real dust-and-sun safari with tents, campfires, and cameras, not to kill, but to get better acquainted.

# CHAPTER 11

# What Your Travel Agent Doesn't Tell You

"Lucky you!" caroled the blue-coated airline agent as he stamped my round-the-world ticket last year for the morning flight from Honolulu to Los Angeles. "You're going to see *Ten Little Indians!*"

"But Agatha Christie killed them off years ago! *And Then There Were None,*" I protested, dismayed. I'd saved those precious hours of flight to figure out just what I was going to ask the VIPs I was to interview the next morning. I said bitterly, "I just want to get there as quickly and quietly as possible. Is that too much to ask?"

What idiot advertising agency sold the airlines on going into the circus business? Hot dogs for kiddies, Laurel and Hardy perennially throwing pies, blaring music to spotlight your entrance as star performers, hostesses in beautiful kimonos, saris, or mini-miniskirts offering you, instead of peaceful passage from here to there, leg shows, fans, slippers, king-size pillows, and your choice of comic books. The first time I flew to Tokyo, before I got wary, I was showered with so many gadgets made in Japan, I could barely stagger off the plane! Who pays for all these gewgaws? You and I, of course—just as the bill for green stamp "giveaways" in supermarkets is added onto the price of a head of lettuce. So far they haven't figured out a way to get a performing elephant onto a plane, but I daresay some enterprising public relations man will manage it soon and the crunch of peanuts will be added to the general din.

"But you don't have to look at the movies, and the earphones protect your privacy," protest the airlines virtuously.

To me, sitting in a modern jet going five hundred miles an hour with antediluvian listening devices that go back to the days of crystal radio sets sprouting out of my ears is an anachronism. Besides, they *hurt* my ears.

As to ignoring sixteen little boxes flickering yellowly over your head whenever you inadvertently glance up—try to do it; sooner or later you have to go to the john or eat lunch, and then the little people who live in late late TV programs take over. Willy-nilly, I watched ten little Indians being axed on the head, poisoned, shot, and pushed over cliffs. If the airlines must offer movies, why not feature the country toward which you are rushing at approximately the speed of sound? I consider it an insult for them to imply that I am so empty-headed, have so few inner resources, that I have to be constantly titivated.

Another prescribed procedure which always seems to me slightly ridiculous in an aircraft streaking along at an altitude of 40,000 feet is for the hostess, looking very pretty in her orange life jacket, to warn that, in case of emergency, you should not pull those little hanging squiggles that inflate the jacket until you are out of the plane and into the drink. I suspect that if I fell 40,000 feet into the ocean I would be in no condition to pull little squiggles.

Airlines, like householders who save little pieces of string, have queer ways of economizing, I have found.

Another time I had taken the 10 A.M. flight from New York to London because I hate night travel when someone in the seat in front of you is always flashing his little reading light in your eye when you want to sleep; but this way I could get a good night's rest at my hotel and go, refreshed, about my next-morning business in London. As we approached that great city, it was already dark and after ten at night, London time. Maybe it was only afternoon in New York, but my mouth began to water for that nicest meal in England, hot, strong tea with buttered scones, bitter marmalade, and biscuits.

"When do they serve tea?" I asked the tweedy English businessman in the seat beside mine.

"They don't. This is an *Amurrican* plane," he accused me. "It'll be midnight before we get into the city. That's why I give this flight a miss whenever I can."

My tweedy Englishman was optimistic. One does not gallop through customs in leisurely, polite England. After a long wait for my suitcase, which I could not lift when it arrived, and the hunt in my overstuffed handbag for the tiny key I could not find, I joined the weary line of "aliens" (a nomenclature which always subdues me like a spanked child) who were shuffling along while another official in gold braid was always popping up to demand, "Your passport, please, madame." Naturally, out came my Kleenex, traveler's checks, and a couple of soda mints. Why doesn't the first official to inspect your passport pass the word along to his mates that you are not a crook fleeing justice or smuggling in diamonds? No, indeed; they wouldn't consider speaking to each other; each customs, immigration, and health official wants his own peek at the leering little picture you hope doesn't look like you.

After surviving all this, I had to stand in line again to change my dollars into pounds and shillings to pay the porter and the taxi, so that when I finally staggered, exhausted, into the lobby of my hotel, it was one in the morning and I would gladly have swapped all the biscuits in the United Kingdom for a hot dog.

Night flights over international boundaries in the Orient can be even more unnerving than daylight travel. The last thing the crew want the weary traveler to do is to sleep.

"We have the best pilots and the prettiest hostesses in the air!" boasted the ad for the German airline in which I flew one night from Cairo to Bangkok. The pilots certainly were tops as hog callers. I had just tucked the pillow donated by the prettiest hostess under my cheek and was contentedly dozing off, when suddenly the bright lights all flashed on and the loudspeaker bellowed, *"O sole mio!"*

"Welcome to Teheran, folks! This is your captain speaking. It is now twelve o'clock midnight, local time. All passengers will please proceed by bus into the air terminal."

We sleepwalked down the ramp, were herded into a rattletrap bus, and debouched at the terminal, where they enclosed us with bars and attendant policemen in what appeared to be a dentist's office with white tile walls. As a consolation prize, we were given lukewarm "limonade" and offered "folk art" at ridiculously high prices for dolls you could have bought back home in the five-and-dime. As far as seeing what Teheran looked like, we might as well have been in El Paso, Texas. Slightly sick at my stomach from the "limonade," I scuttled back to my plane seat, crouched thankfully under my blanket, and was again dozing off when . . .

*"O sole mio!* Welcome to Karachi, folks! It is now two A.M., local time. All intransit passengers will please . . ."

"Oh, no, you don't. This is my bedtime. I'm not going anywhere in any bus," I told the handsome German steward. My merry widow blood was up as I yanked out the two armrests in my row of three empty seats, lay down and wrapped my blanket firmly around me, mummy style.

I told the steward, who was fairly dancing in the aisle over the antics of the crazy American, "Strap me in so I won't fall off the seat when we take off."

What can a big strong man do when a woman passenger takes the bit into her teeth, short of throwing her into the local hoosegow? The steward did what I asked and so, at long last, I slept. Did I say "long"? It seemed only a few eyewinks before . . .

"*O sole mío!* Welcome to Calcutta . . ."

The sun was up and so, alas, was I. It was 4 A.M. Fortunately there had been a cholera outbreak here so we were not allowed off the plane, were merely sprayed with loud-smelling disinfectant and more soulful welcoming in Italian of the incoming Indian passengers.

"The first thing I'll do when I get off at Bangkok will be to buy that fool record," I promised myself grimly, "and jump up and down on it! I'll send the pieces to the airline at Cologne! Or it might be more to the point to buy them a Brahms lullaby."

The most callous exhibitionism I have ever seen, however, was when our Japanese jet flew over Vietnam on our way to Tokyo and the captain announced jovially, as if he were offering us free tickets for *Hello, Dolly!,* "Down below, on our left, is a fine view of Danang!"

"Didn't anyone ever tell you there's a war on?" I asked the little hostess in her pale-blue kimono, gay with cherry blossoms as the travel posters had promised.

"We used to fly around the combat area, but it took too long," she explained. "We use an assigned corridor."

"What about Migs?"

"We're flying way above anything they can throw at us. [But Migs had wings, too, didn't they?] We're perfectly safe."

Perhaps we were. But forty thousand feet down below in that white blob of an airfield, in those blurred green jungles, our American sons were not safe; men, women, and children were screaming with pain, being blown to bloody fragments. Suddenly it seemed more frightening to me than any Mig that we middle-aged travelers, sipping cold drinks, could fly on comfortable cushioned seats over a battlefield where the bright youth of two countries were sweating and dying.

When I flew into Saigon a few months later, I discovered an even harder to understand phenomenon; I didn't have to have a visa on my passport to enter Vietnam because I was American. When I told my editor this later, he commented grimly, "What a hell of a war. Welcome, tourists!" Our civilian plane had to land in daylight so that the snipers could be cleared out safely for us valuable assets for the war effort. There were no taxis allowed in the airport since so many VC had tossed bombs out cab windows; even the Asian Christian Relief people, who were my hosts, had to show a pass for their bus. As I climbed up the steep step to the front seat, I couldn't help wondering if the war wouldn't have been over much sooner if we'd put some regiments made up of commentators like me (I don't know one end of a gun from another, but I know some barbed words), together with visiting senators, congressmen, and other VIPs, into the front lines as GIs.

Another annoyance about which travel agents seldom warn unwary travelers is the airport "head tax" or exit fee that some countries demand today. The traveler has carefully used up all his bahts, rupees, or what have you, knowing they will be of no use in the country to which he is flying, when suddenly an official hand reaches out for "Ten piasters, please." "Just to get out of Egypt?" you inquire incredulously. It is embarrassing to have to sponge on your friends at the moment of farewell, to ask them to empty their coin purses for you. Trains do not hold you up this way—why airports? Of course, if you happen to have an American dollar handy it is good in any country, but equally of course, the exit officials never have any change.

It's a racket some of our American airports are now considering adopting.

Equally harassing are the loving friends taking leave of overburdened travelers who offer at the last moment charmingly painted toy elephants or a handbag for Aunt Emma, or they may even hang a loud-smelling Hawaiian lei around your already sweaty neck. When you've figured to the ounce how much you can carry aboard the plane, even an orchid may be too much. In Hong Kong I was lugging a typewriter—the lightest weighs at least eight pounds—a hatbox of heavy shoes, and my handbag stuffed with a twelve-transistor radio that I bought so cheaply in Hong Kong I couldn't resist the bargain, but which made the bag so heavy I could barely lift it off the floor. Imagine my dismay when a young Chinese friend at the airport thrust into my arms a huge bouquet of red roses! Going up the ramp, I had to steady the blossoms with my desperate chin.

"Aren't those roses gorgeous!" gushed the air hostess.

"Here!" I handed them over thankfully. "Keep 'em."

Another warning for the international traveler is to read the fine print on the travel folders you are given, as well as to look at the pretty pictures. Every time I had missed a connection and had had to stay overnight due to the late arrival of my flight, the airplane company had paid for my bed and board at an excellent hotel. But one night after my plane from Rhodes had been delayed for hours by a storm, I arrived, buffeted and airsick, in Athens after midnight with no reservations. After an expensive two-hour ride around the city looking for a pillow upon which to lay my head, I found a room in the city's most expensive hostelry. But what did that matter since my stay-over was due to the airplane company to which I had paid $1600 for my round-the-world ticket? Next morning I was presented with an astronomical bill. It seemed that since Rhodes to Athens was an intra-Grecian rather than an international flight, I had to pay. "Read the fine print, lady."

But merry widows must be watched over by a special guardian angel. At 2 A.M. one morning I was dumped at the New Delhi airport, with not a taxi in sight, not even, in fact, a bicycle. As I stood on the platform looking around desperately for transport, a big black limousine with a liveried chauffeur drew up in front of me. A perfectly strange gentleman leaned out the back window to ask, "Would you like a lift uptown? May I drop you at your hotel? I'm Cyril Jones from London."

"Never speak to strange men, Susie!" Dear Mother . . . "Thank you very much, Cyril Jones. I'm Grace Fletcher from Boston."

As I climbed gratefully into the cushioned back seat, I reflected that not only modern youth but even the "Establishment" merry widows had learned that in a world of atom bombs and spacecraft, outworn mores are ridiculous. Imagine an astronaut saying to the man in the moon, "Sorry. We haven't been introduced, I think?"

Cyril Jones and I arranged to meet again in Singapore, where we had a magic evening together, dining under enormous stars in the dreamlike open-air restaurant in the Raffles Hotel garden, where the sentinel trees are trimmed into fairy shapes, candles flicker in the flower-scented air, and the moon silvers the bows of the softly playing violins. In this enchanted garden time does not exist, and, if you glance up quickly, you may see the shade of Rudyard Kipling flitting into the friendly shadows.

Having lamented, however, the vagaries of the airlines, it is only fair to add that the airplane companies may also act as *pater familias* and admit the lonely traveler into the family. The only place where you get acquainted with a total stranger quicker than in a plane is in a hospital ward after the lights are out. I do not suffer gladly the gushy female who settles down beside me and gabbles her life history, but even seatmates with whom I struggle politely for a place to rest my elbow are often kind for no reason at all except that I am traveling alone.

Jets have indeed made this a small world, as the cliché insists. I had just boarded a plane in Hong Kong one morning when a voice cried, "Why, Susie Fletcher, what are you doing here?" She was a close friend from New Jersey.

Then there are the friends that a traveling merry widow author collects like postage stamps, because they recognize her from TV programs or newspaper pictures. I have argued for years with my editors over their putting my picture on the jacket of my books which, I insist, can only disenchant the reader; but the photograph must resemble me in some manner, for flying into Manila one morning I sat down beside a man with a clerical collar who was reading one of my books. He glanced up, looked puzzled, and then stared at his book jacket, then back at me. "It *is* you! You wrote this book I'm enjoying, about what's right with our young people!" When I nodded and smiled, he explained that he was an archdeacon from New York State and would I please come and talk to his churches? This was the first time I had picked up a priest.

"Hey, I just saw you on TV!" another stranger blurted when he bumped into me as we were both hurrying across a busy airport. "Yes, yes," I murmured and started off, but he stepped in front of me, pleading, "The MC said you were from Boston. I come from Medford, Massachusetts, myself. How about us neighbors having lunch together?" I agreed if we could go Dutch. We really did have several mutual friends. His plane left before mine, and when I asked for my bill, it was already paid. It's economical being a merry widow who knows the world's a chancy place, and so what?

One airplane played cupid for the lovely young daughter of a friend of mine, although the girl wasn't even aboard. Her mother had enjoyed the red-headed college boy who sat down beside her so much that they chatted all the way to Boston, where the daughter met her at the airport. The girl and the redhead took one look at each other and became a modern Romeo and Juliet. Six weeks later the young people startled their respective families by announcing they had eloped! The marriage has turned out to be an unusually happy one with a small son as proof. But they call him Tod instead of TWA.

I myself have belonged to the Pan American family for fifteen years and they have rescued me from some strange predicaments. On our last trip to Spain when Jock was ill, we flew to Barcelona without hotel reservations, a bad mistake, for we drove for hours around the crowded city, looking for a room. Jock's face was so white with fatigue it frightened me, so I asked the cab driver in desperation, "Don't you have a friend, perhaps, where we could at least rent a room for what's left of the night? My husband is ill."

"Si, si, señora." He drove us down a dark little alley which blossomed into a blaze over a front door. The sign in electric lights enthused, "Welcome to the Sixth Fleet." The lobby was full of nice young sailors joking rather loudly with their girlfriends, and yes, we could have a room with breakfast. I didn't become vaguely uneasy until I followed the bellhop into the strangest setup I had ever seen, an enormous bell-shaped roof arching over stairways —ladders really—which led up to three floors, and each corridor had rows and rows of closed doors. When we reached our bedroom, Jock fell onto the big double bed, utterly exhausted, and I went to the window to draw down the shade. I looked down into a well of lighted windows . . .

"Jock, come here quickly!" I gasped.

He came and glanced down. "It's a cathouse, darling. Sorry, but I can't go a step farther. There's a lock on our door. We'll put our raincoats over the pillows and lie on top of the spread until morning."

Which we did. When we revived enough to go downstairs next morning, carrying our own bags to the front door, the clerk called after us, "But, señor, you paid for breakfast!"

"Get us a cab for Pan American, please," Jock ordered the doorman.

When we told the Spanish clerk at the airline what had happened, he murmured, "Most unfortunate . . ." and then burst out laughing. Jock and I laughed, too, until the three of us were breathless. Our friend the clerk not only found us a room in a more circumspect hotel, but he discovered that we had been overcharged a hundred dollars by his own airline, since our tickets called for first class and we had flown economy. He gave us a refund slip and happily —for a hundred dollars is not hay—we left for an enormous breakfast, since we had had nothing to eat since noon the day before.

It was the height of the tourist season. No seats for home were available except two on the Lisbon-to-Boston flight a week later, so we decided to wait it out at the Estoril, the ritzy Portuguese seashore resort where there are more ex-kings, impecunious barons, and assorted titles than there is sand. But as I went the round of travel agencies, they insisted that the only rooms available during "the Estoril Casino season" cost forty dollars a night. The kings must have raided the treasury before they skipped the country. So again I consulted Pan American.

This time the Lisbon clerk was a cute little Chinese girl with a shy smile. I sputtered, "Don't tell me you pay such exorbitant prices when your crews stay over between flights. We can't afford them either."

"Nobody could." She reached for her telephone; all I could understand of her Portuguese was "Pan American." She got us a room in a boardinghouse full of retired British colonels and air hostesses, only a block from the sea, where for a twin-bedded room plus four excellent meals we paid two and a half dollars a day apiece.

Every good airline looks out for its own, which is more than I can say of American trains, though I admit I haven't ridden on one since I reached the age of consent. But when I hear a jet soaring above me in the sky, my heart flies aloft with it. I guess I belong to the jet set.

The human touch is, I suppose, what the airlines are groping for with their hot dogs, movies, and steaks cooked aloft; but I, for one, will be glad when they skip the circus and go back into just the transportation business; when they select a hostess not because she has good knees for a mini-miniskirt but because she is what the British call "homely," a friendly hostess who doesn't bother me until I press her button for help. Only thus will even the ghost of privacy be possible when we swish over to London in a couple of hours in the Concorde or the Russian TU-144, where passengers will be four hundred peas in a pod. Where in our crowded airports are these monsters to land? How can such lemming hordes get through customs before daybreak? Get uptown? A fleet of whirlybirds might help, but where are *they* to land? On the steps of St. Paul's Cathedral or in the court of Buckingham Palace? Fortunately these are not my problems to solve. But one thing I am sure of: when I take off in my first spacecraft for the moon, if they show *Ten Little Indians*, I shall firmly demand to be transferred from Gumdrop to Spider.

# CHAPTER 12

# New Women of the East

"People are music, Susie," Dad told me dreamily one lovely June morning as we sat on the gray-and-yellow cliff at Newagen, listening to the rhythmic rote alongshore. "Each man in his time strikes his own note, dissonant or harmonious to the whole, but peculiarly his own."

Shanti Solomon (Shanti is the Indian word for "peace") was like a soft note blown from a silver flute when she came toward me across the hotel lobby in New Delhi, India, with her pale-blue silk sari flowing about her slender body and her face alight with welcome. I knew very little about her except that she must be a woman of the New East to come down alone on the train from the village of Etawah, for high-caste Indian ladies do not travel alone normally, not even to the marketplace. I knew also that she was the founder of the Fellowship of the Least Coin, which she had sparked in Manila ten years before and which now had supporting groups in forty-eight countries. I wanted to find out how, in a country where widows had so recently thrown themselves upon their husbands' funeral pyres, in suttee, this woman called

"Peace" had become what she was. From what roots sprang this new woman of the East whose soft fluting had been heard around the world?

"Was your family Christian or Hindu?" I asked Shanti as we settled comfortably into a couple of armchairs in my hotel bedroom.

Shanti drew a deep breath. "Both. My own father was murdered by his Hindu family because he and his family became Christian; they did not want such a reprobate to inherit any of their estate. He was poisoned only six weeks after I was born, the youngest of his twelve children. Only three of us lived, however, for my mother was only four- teen when she was married and knew nothing of how to care for a sick baby. Just before he died, my father asked my mother to put me in his arms. My mother has told me many times what he said. 'I am leaving you fatherless, poor little girl, child of my love. Shanti, my peace . . . But you will not want for anything for you belong to God's family. He will look after you.'* And He did," Shanti said in her soft Indian voice. "He gave me Reuben, my hus- band. After he died, in spite of what had happened, his oldest brother offered to take me into his home."

She shivered. "Being a Hindu widow in India is almost to die yourself," Shanti explained to me. She looked very small, almost lost in the big armchair, but her dark eyes were steady. "You become a vegetable with no voice of your own. All you have is passed over to your nearest male kinsman, who, by custom, must offer you a roof over your head. You may sit in your dark corner waiting to be thrown a crust of all that has been your husband's and yours. Do not look so horrified! You must remember that pride of caste dies hard in India; also the concept of abso- lute obedience to your husband is thousands of years old.

"But Reuben had always wanted me to be a *person* in my own right; he let me go on working with the village

*In Quest of the Least Coin.* William Morrow & Co., New York, N.Y., 1968.

women even after we were married, though he would not let me take any pay. In fact, it was he who pushed me into my great adventure when I first flew across the Pacific."

After World War II, when bitterness still lingered between people who had suffered and fought on both sides, Shanti had been asked to join a Presbyterian Reconciliation Team of six women from the United States, Japan, and India, "to try to knit together the raveled sleeve of forgiveness. We were to visit Alaska, Hong Kong, Japan, Korea, and the Philippines. I could understand how the underdogs in the countries where wives had seen their husbands starved, even beaten to death before their eyes, could still feel bitter, but I also thought that the overdogs, the Americans who had lost faraway sons, had much to forgive. But . . . to fly in my first airplane across the dark, hungry waters to the land of the bitter cold and the polar bears was too dangerous! I was terrified. 'Besides,' I begged Reuben, 'how can I leave you for three months? It is impossible.'*

" 'Of course you must go,' Reuben insisted. 'You will come back a bigger person. Who knows what you can teach me? And India?' Me teach my husband anything, he who was so wise and strong? But of course I went."

Reuben came down to Delhi to see her off, to help her pick out new saris for her trip. (Saris are those six-foot-long pieces of gorgeously embroidered cloth you wind around your middle and then toss the loose end over your shoulder. By some Indian magic, the sari does not fall off as mine did once when I wore it to a dance.) Indians do not kiss or cry in public, but as they stood near the great winged monster that was to carry his small wife away from him, Reuben's dark eyes said to her, "Take care, my love. God go with you."

Shanti's first shock came when the Korean government would not allow her or the Japanese member of the team

*Ibid.*

to cross its borders. She could understand how they might not welcome a Japanese so soon after the occupation, but "Why reject me?" Near daybreak she found an answer. "We Indians have drawn our skirts aside from the terrible suffering of the war-torn mothers and children on both sides and have done nothing to help them. We are like the priest in the story of the Good Samaritan, who passed by on the other side!" She wondered, *"What can I do now* to bring together these Christian women who have been so badly bent by war hatred?"

While she was waiting for the rest of her Reconciliation Team to come back from Korea, Shanti joined a group of Manila women who were studying the Book of Mark. They came from all walks of life, a high-school teacher, the wife of a prominent businessman who was herself a lawyer, the wives of bankers, the head of a great training school for teachers, the supervisor of the public schools in a large province of the Philippines, all trained, competent women who were asking themselves, as Shanti was, "What now?"

Suddenly one morning when the story of the widow's mite was being read aloud, where Jesus had commented that in giving her two infinitesimal coins the widow had given more than all the rest, Shanti dreamed a dream.

"That's it! The way to peace and understanding between East and West!" Shanti cried to her startled friends. "Don't you see? The widow's mite means more than giving money; it means giving yourself, your prayers, to help other women in trouble. If Indian women like me give their tiny paisas, worth only an eighth of the penny the Americans could give, and you Filipinos give your centavos . . . You can't see an atom or a prayer, but they are mighty for all that. The money may not amount to much, but it will be a token of our concern. A step toward peace! Any mother can teach her children tolerance in her home, and every teacher in her school . . ."

"Rich and poor, college graduate and the woman who cannot read, can all give their least coins on the same level, proudly!" Felicidad Catli, the head of the school for teachers in Manila, burst in excitedly. "Creeds do not matter. When we Protestants hear the Roman Catholic Angelus every night at six, wherever we are, in the fields, in the kitchen or in a jitney, we will remember ... We can teach our children that people are not monsters because they have ideas other than our own. Where is peace to begin if not in our homes?"

"We mothers have *got* to stand together," cried the wife of a Chinese banker who had ten children, "for when our sons die on the battlefield, a little of us dies, too."*

But one American in the Reconciliation Team, when they got back to Manila, protested, "Only twelve cents a year? Our women at home are too busy to bother with saving pennies!"

"You miss the whole point!" Shanti cried. "That's what's wrong with people who have everything. You don't understand how humiliating it is to be always on the receiving end as we Asians are. *We need to give if only for our own self-respect!* Your great American money has divided us. Let's see if our Least Coins cannot draw us together."

This "drawing together" has had fantastic results. During the past ten years, the Fellowship of the Least Coin has spread into fifty-two countries, not only all over Asia but in Europe, Africa, and North and South America, and has even penetrated behind the Iron Curtain into Yugoslavia and Czechoslovakia. How much any one country gives is never told. The first year the tiny coins amounted to only $4000, the second year to $11,000, but ten years later the total amount collected was over half a million dollars. This from tiny coins which often have so little value that, if they are dropped, bystanders do not bother to pick them up! It is significant that the final decision

*Ibid.

upon where this help goes to six continents still remains in Asia, with the women of the Asian Church Women's Conference, with headquarters in Bangkok.

"It comes from the world, it goes quietly back to the world," Shanti explained. "We do not initiate any project, but where a lift is needed over a bad hump in the road, we offer it. Sometimes it is buying an old army truck so the farmers of Mindanao can get their crops to market; or perhaps training an Indian scholar to help his own people, the Nagas; or perhaps"—she shot a glance at me—"teaching an underprivileged child to read in Harlem, New York City."

I gasped, "You give to rich America?"

She nodded. "For adolescent drug addicts in Harlem, for poor farmers on the Mississippi Delta, for children of migrants in California. Last year we bought Braille Bibles for your blind children.

"Least Coins are saved up in strange containers." She grinned impishly. " 'Down on the Cape' in Massachusetts, the ladies save in clam shells! In Malaysia, the coins are hidden in the hollow joints of bamboo sticks, and in match boxes in Yugoslavia . . . It would be easy to spend more on the containers than what you give. So we have fun!"

"When I was in Vietnam, I saw some of the maternity kits you women sent for the mothers having babies without any medical help," I told her. "Have you ever seen 'The Happy Place' the Least Coin helps in Ceylon?"

She shook her head, no.

"Prithipuri, 'The Happy Place,' was the most horrible, the most fantastic, the most wonderful setup I ever saw!" I burst out. "Imagine a home for retarded children run by a Buddhist monk and a defrocked Presbyterian minister who is now a Roman Catholic layman! The buildings run along a river where they wash four hundred diapers a day."

Shanti said, "I know we helped build them a rest house

for the volunteer workers. The monk, Reverend Bikku Sumanu, wrote us, 'It is fitting that Least Coins should care for the Least Wanted Children.' "

"They're that, all right." I shivered, remembering the long ward for Mongoloid and spastic children, little more than vegetables, who had been picked up by the police, after they had been wrapped in newspapers and dropped into trash cans, or who had been abandoned by families or hospitals who could no longer care for them. I had stared at them lying in their cribs in rows of horror . . .

"I know what you are thinking . . . euthanasia," Dr. DeKretser, who is in charge of them, had said to me gently. "But these are God's children, too; when He wants them He will take them."

This was the same man who had taught comparative theology in Northwestern University near Chicago. Now he was practicing what he had taught, that Moslems, Hindus, Buddhists, Christians went by different paths to the same place. I looked at the boy lying there with his legs so twisted they were wrapped around his neck. I asked Dr. DeKretser flatly, "Do you really find this more satisfying than teaching theology in Evanston?"

He hesitated an instant, then said quietly, "For me, yes."

When I had finished my outburst, Shanti observed, "I have always thought the Good Samaritan received more than he gave. After two thousand years, his name is still spoken in many languages."

"As yours is." But I did not say the words aloud to embarrass her. It was not herself but her husband, Reuben, of whom she was thinking.

She confessed, "When he died, I was so tired, so empty, I wanted to rest a hundred years! Then I remembered what Reuben had wanted for me. 'Go, Shanti . . . Who knows what you can teach all India?' "

As I stared at this little Indian widow whose flutelike

call to tolerance and understanding had touched chords in the hearts of women around the world, I could have kissed the hem of her sari.

"We have talked too long. You are dry," she said briskly. "Will you come with me for a cup of tea?"

The restaurant to which Shanti took me on that cold day in Delhi was dank, full of strange fragrances, as we stumbled up the dark stairway, but Shanti was radiant as she ordered a special brand of tea and little cakes. She explained, "Reuben and I used to come here together whenever we visited Delhi. I want you to know it too."

"Jock was English, so we had tea every afternoon."

Were Reuben and Jock, whose taste in tea was still remembered, perhaps laughing together wherever they were? Or maybe, as Maeterlinck had said, the dead come to life only when those who love them remember. Remembering was only a deeper note in the vibrant music of still being alive. Being a merry widow was a state of mind, choosing to belong to a bigger family than her own whose surname, like Shanti's, was spelled "peace."

Maki Vories Hitotsuyanagi, the Japanese widow in whose hospitable home I stayed for many weeks, lived in Omi-Hachiman on the shore of Lake Biwa, the lovely shimmering lake which you could watch change with sun and shadow from the top of the small mountain where the Fox God's temple stood. Maki was as different from Shanti as it was possible to be, yet they had both been wives who had been greatly loved and who, after their husbands died, had chosen to stretch their horizons rather than to shrink them to the compass of their personal grief. Shanti was in her forties, but Maki was eighty-two, a tiny woman lively as a cricket, who rose at dawn and wore out my much younger legs as I tried to follow her through her busy day of teaching, lecturing, presiding over an important business meeting, or welcoming the Buddhist priest who brought his children to her Christian school "because here they learn history as it truly happened."

Maki was an aristocrat, born and bred in the home of nobility (her father had been a daimyo, a count), and she had once been a member of the Royal Household. She still was; as far as the citizens of Omi-Hachiman were concerned, she wore an invisible crown upon her head. Had she not been decorated by the Emperor himself? And yet she greeted the humblest Eta from the town slum with dignity.

Maki accepted the obeisance of her neighbors as naturally as the rain that fell continuously while I was in Japan that spring. Her age alone would have entitled her to reverence in country Japan that, unlike Tokyo, still held to the old ways. In her own household there was certainly no appeal from her decision: this included her guests. I remember one evening when I was speaking about the United States to a large group of Japanese men and she was interpreting for me. I would speak for about five minutes in English, then wait for her to catch up, which she did in a couple of short sentences. Finally I got up enough courage to ask, "Maki, are you sure you're telling them all that I say?"

"I am telling them all that is necessary for them to know," Maki said. And that was that.

But just as all roads lead to Rome, so did all conversations lead back to Merrell, her husband, to whom Maki had been happily married for over forty years, but who had been dead two years. But not to Maki.

We had just finished my first meal in her home when Maki laid down her napkin, stood up, and invited me, "I want you to meet my husband."

"But . . . but I thought . . . I mean . . ."

"Come."

I followed her up the dark wooden stairs to her bedroom, wondering wildly how on earth I could be introduced to a man already in his grave.

Their bedroom still had twin beds, his and hers, which I could just barely make out in the twilight that filled the room, but upon Maki's dresser something shone. It was a little wooden cross covered with luminous paint which shed a gentle light upon a square box wrapped in a white table napkin.

"The ashes of my husband," Maki introduced us.

What could I say? "Glad to meet you"? I just stood, speechless. I had heard that the Japanese Buddhists often kept their family's ashes for forty days until the spirit had gone to its final rest, but Maki was Christian. . . . But she was also very Japanese; at her age it was natural for her to go back to her childhood in a Buddhist daimyo's home. But she still kept the cross . . .

"I waited until you came to put Merrell into his family's mausoleum, up on the mountain. I knew you would not want to miss the ceremony," Maki said.*

I hate funerals; to me they are relics of barbarism, for the body is merely a castoff garment which should not be left around to harrow the family, but should be given to a teaching hospital for students to learn from, or, at the very least, be put back into the earth from which it came, as quickly as possible. But I was a guest in a strange land; if I could be of any possible comfort to Maki, I was glad.

"I will wear my ceremonial robes with the Hitot-suyanagi crest," Maki told me. "Tomorrow at the services there will be several hundred people, I expect. You will sit up front with me as my family."

"A great honor," I agreed. "But my suit and coat are bright red, hardly suitable. I do have a white Thai silk raincoat . . ."

"Wear it over your suit," Maki advised. "You will need warmth up in the shadow of the mountain."

Maki looked queenly in her ceremonial robes of heavy black silk with the curled willow leaf of her family crest

* *The Bridge of Love.* E. P. Dutton & Co., New York, N.Y., 1967.

embroidered here and there, even a few on her obi. Her tabi and sandals were white, as was the scarf folded at her throat, and her thick gray hair made a proud crown. I pattered behind her meekly in my raincoat which fortunately was long enough to hide everything else. We drove in a big black car to a place where more than two hundred Japanese were sitting under a canopy. Maki and I were enthroned in two big armchairs in the front row. I could not understand a word of the service in Japanese, but I got up when the mourners did and sat down with them, while my thoughts went back over the fantastic love story of Maki and Merrell Vories Hitotsuyanagi.

The Japanese princess and the country boy from Flagstaff, Arizona, U.S.A.! How different could two backgrounds be? They had spent over thirty years looking for each other, but when they finally met, each had known at once that they belonged together. They had crossed by the fragile bridge of love to find each other.

Maki had been a maverick in her father's household from the time she was a small girl.

"I hated my father for what he did to my mother," she told me with a cold, quiet passion, more impressive than shouting. "He brought concubines into our home and flaunted them to my mother who had to care for them and their ill-born children. She loved them, educated them as her own, but she never explained to me why she had become a Christian, a silent one who never told her heart but kept it all inside herself. In a daimyo's household the husband could do no wrong; even when he came home roaring drunk, she did not protest but endured her humiliation in patience as a good Japanese wife. I said to myself, 'I will never marry! I will have no concubines in my house and no drunkards. I would rather die an old maid.' "*

She kept stubbornly to her decision until she was thirty-

*Ibid.*

five. She had inherited her father's strong will, which enabled her to stand up to him when he brought her the names of rich and noble young men from whom to choose. She turned them all down until, at twenty-five, she was such a "disgrace" to her family that they sent her to the United States to study and to keep people from saying, "What an odd girl! Why doesn't her father crack down on her, make her marry?" But they both had the Hitot-suyanagi stubbornness. Maki enjoyed her studies at Bryn Mawr, but illness forced her into the home of a friend; she would much have preferred to stay there for the rest of her life, but the friend died and her elder brother, Keizo, sent her a cable that she must come back to Tokyo, for her father was dying.

Keizo had a palatial home in Tokyo where he often entertained royally, and the evening when Maki came home he was to have as his guest of honor the American ambassador. He told Maki casually, "There will also be an American architect who is to build me a couple of banks, here and in Osaka. I would like you to see his plans, as you are familiar with Western architecture."

The architect was Merrell Vories, who had taken up architecture to pay for his social and community projects in Omi-Hachiman. Maki came to the dinner table with properly downcast eyes, but when she looked up . . . she caught her breath. As Merrell's blue eyes smiled into her brown ones, she knew at once this was her man and that he knew it too.

Merrell proposed marriage to her at once and she agreed. Let the family thunder and roar as it would. A member of the Royal Household marry an impecunious American do-gooder? It was impossible. Maki told them flatly, "If you do not let me marry Merrell, I shall become a nun!" She meant what she said, but to make it easier for her family, she suggested that she ask for permission to resign from the Royal Household so that she could marry

an American commoner. When her request was granted
for the first time in Japanese history, the family threw up
their hands in resignation. "I will give you the biggest and
best wedding Tokyo society has ever seen so they will
know we approve," announced the proud Keizo, trying to
put the best face on this unfortunate alliance.

And so they were married in pomp and circumstance,
the princess and her lover, who found he had only sixty-
seven cents in his pocket and their two tickets when they
got on the train for Karuizawa. The family summer home
there was only a small unpainted wooden house among
the trees, but to both of them it was heaven.

"When we walked in the woods together, they were
burning bright with azaleas," Maki told me nostalgically.
"Burning bright like our love in unconsuming beauty."*

From the very beginning she saw him as ten feet tall.
His belief that even laborers were human beings, not ro-
bots, iconoclastic for Japan, excited her. "I allow my workmen to build only eight hours a day instead of from sunrise
to sunset, as is usual," he told her. "The strange thing is
that, when they come to work rested, they can beat the
time of those who work twelve hours! They get the same
pay." When this proved to be true, it eventually changed
the building codes of all Japan. Merrell also insisted to
Maki that labor and executives were equal parts of the
same business, so should get the same pay; to show this
really worked, he started the Omi Brotherhood, which ran
factories successfully and used what they earned to help
the community. They built and equipped the first modern
hospital for tubercular patients in Japan near the mountain where Merrell was to be buried.

As a bride, Maki threw herself into their joint projects.
She, who had seldom even dressed herself in her father's
home, washed the filthy walls of their first home, papered
them with newspaper. She sold the jade necklace her

*Ibid.*

father had given her as a wedding present to equip a kindergarten which would draw the street urchins off the narrow Omi-Hachiman streets, dangerous with traffic and open sewers. The door of their home was always open to any neighbor, even to the Etas, the untouchables whom the rest of the village despised because they worked with leather, who were often dirty and always ignorant. But through all this tumult Maki and Merrell, enclosed in the tight circle of their love, were alone but together.

Yet Merrell, she finally realized with the sensitive antennae that wives have, was "troubled in his mind." One day he said to her, "Darling, there is something we must talk over. I have always criticized immigrants who took all that America had to give and yet did not become citizens. I have worked here and lived here in Japan longer than in my own country . . . thirty years. It is my home, especially now that you and I are married. Should I not become a Japanese citizen?"

"If you like, dear," Maki agreed. "We will ask your friend, the Shinto priest, Oka-san, how this can be accomplished."

"But I must still remain a Christian," Merrell told his Shintoist friend.

"Of course," Oka-san agreed. "Shinto and Christianity both believe that the spirit is more important than material things; that is why we have no idols or saintly images in our temples. Besides, these are two different things, the Shinto religion of ancestor worship and State Shinto. To become a Japanese you will have to pledge allegiance to the Emperor (who, as you already know, is a marine scientist and does not consider himself divine) and to Japan. These are civil ceremonies."

"In the United States new citizens do the same thing," Maki interpolated. "They pledge allegiance to the flag and to the republic for which it stands."

"Ah, so?" said Oka-san. (Japanese really do say that, not just in the movies. Another saying that used to amuse me was their answering the telephone, "Mushi, mushi!")

Merrell also found he must choose a Japanese name, and what could be more appropriate than Hitotsuyanagi? "We Japanese often adopt sons when we have none of our own and I will adopt you." Maki smiled.

Thus her American became a Japanese citizen. Mr. and Mrs. Merrell Vories Hitotsuyanagi. . . . How could they possibly know that it would be only a few months to Pearl Harbor?

What was Maki saying to me? I came back to 1967 Japan at the foot of a greening spring mountain as she murmured in my ear, "Come, Sue, we must climb the sixty-seven steps up to the mausoleum."

Unfortunately, I have no head for heights and the stone steps were small and uneven. As I swayed dizzily behind Maki, who in her eighties mounted easily, a friendly Omi brother put his arm around my waist and steadied me so that we arrived safely at the open door. Inside, the mausoleum was piled high with flowers; they put Merrell's ashes into what looked like a steel filing cabinet, next to that of his father. For the first time Maki would be alone in their room tonight.

A reception followed the interment. Maki was magnificent. She stood in her ceremonial robes beside the long table burdened with the too sweet cakes and tea, while she shook the hand of each guest, smiling. "Baby Keicho has a new tooth? Wonderful!" She beamed. "How did Nuchi make out in his college exams?" Not a word about the desolation in her own heart at this final wrench. She would not lay the burden of her grief upon another's shoulders. Even when we got back home, she came into my room to be sure I had everything I needed before she went into her own bedroom after a hard day that might well have floored a woman of twenty. At last she could be alone with her bitter sorrow; she still had the little luminous cross, but it shone on an empty place.

I lay on my own bed, thinking how queer it was that *things* survived so long when people were gone. I remembered how, when I was cleaning out Jock's dresser after he went, I had found a box of medals he had won during the First World War. I called Rick to show them to him, and he said casually, "Oh, yes, Dad showed them to me once; he said they were to be mine some day." My two men whom I thought I had known so well, and yet Jock had never told me about his medals. Was keeping them in a box in my desk any different from Maki's keeping her box of ashes wrapped in a napkin?

But it still puzzled me why Merrell, who was so patriotic an American, could have given up his country at this particular time to become a Japanese citizen. Many missionaries from the States had been shocked, too; one had even written that Merrell was a traitor. The next morning I must ask Maki exactly how this had come about.

"Pearl Harbor was Gethsemane for Merrell and me," she told me. Her eyes looked heavy, as if she had not slept. "For we loved both countries.

"We had a bad time during the war. People called us spies, grabbed our house, our hospital for military purposes. We had to retreat to Karuizawa, where there was no heat in winter and very little food. Our rice ration was cut to a handful and our C ration was a cabbage leaf every other day. Merrell was so undernourished that he had a heart attack, and I could walk only short distances, I had so little strength. We even ate roots but could do nothing about heat; the fallen tree branches had long ago been gathered by the freezing villagers. But my husband was never bitter. He wrote:

"Let me not hate . . .
The man who hates me . . .
But let me count him as a brother still."*

I must have looked still unconvinced, for she added, "Come, I will take you to Oka-san, the priest, our friend. Perhaps he can convince you that going to a Shinto shrine does not make you a Shintoist any more than having an audience with the Pope makes you a Roman Catholic."

The little maid helped us put on our shoes and we walked down the narrow paved road past the tightly crowded-together little houses, all a weathered gray and innocent of paint, each so exactly alike that one had to count from the street corner to discover which door was his. But behind this unprepossessing exterior were, I knew, gorgeous painted screens and scrolls that might have been in the family for hundreds of years, and, still further back, fantastically beautiful small gardens that were the joy of their owners; so did the Japanese mind disclose itself to a Westerner, bit by bit, as it came to trust you.

The streets seemed unusually crowded that morning with people rushing busily here and there. "What are those tall straw mushroom-like things they are putting up?" I asked Maki. "That one must be forty feet high!"

"They are towers to be burned tonight at the festival to honor the Emperor Ojin. Six hundred years ago he went across Lake Biwa—it is the biggest lake in Japan and can be terribly dangerous, with enormous waves—to fetch his royal mother from a village on the opposite shore. But a terrible storm blew up, so bad that he could not even see our shore. The townspeople built great bonfires to guide him so he came safely to shore with his mother."

Six hundred years ago, when the United States was only a mote in the eye of God! Small wonder a brash, adoles-

* *Ibid.*

cent nation like ours found it difficult to penetrate into the inner garden of ancient Japanese culture.

Oka-san, the Shinto priest, was a round-stomached, rosy-cheeked man in a long white robe, sitting cross-legged upon the tatami of his living-room floor, who welcomed us cordially. His wife, bowing low, brought us the ceremonial tea and little cakes while Maki and I, nibbling politely, sat opposite the priest. She would chat with him in Japanese and then translate for me.

"Oka-san says that Merrell used to boast to his neighbors, 'I am more Japanese than you, for I *chose* this for my country and you were only born here!'" When the little priest laughed, his whole body shook. He pointed to a long scroll with Japanese characters that hung on his wall in the place of honor.

"It speaks of Merrell," Maki explained. "I will read it to you.

"'William Merrell Vories ... has done many good works personally and socially *by teaching Christianity* and has made many friends; he has settled here as his permanent home ... He is making his pledge in the language of this nation to be a loyal subject [of Japan]. Hear him in peace, O God, and bless him forever....'"*

Certainly this was clear enough, I was thinking, when the priest's little wife came into the room speaking in low, apologetic tones. "She reminds him there is to be a wedding and he is due at the shrine. We must go," Maki said, rising gracefully from the tatami. I got up more like a camel, awkwardly.

"A Shinto wedding! Oh, please, ask him if we may go to watch!" I begged eagerly.

"We will be most welcome," Maki translated.

But the priest, his wife, and his two daughters were already hurrying away toward the gray stone shrine down the road. We followed discreetly behind them, past the

*Ibid.*

two ugly temple dogs that frightened away bad spirits, but they let Maki and me by. "Since the war, the government does not pay the salaries of the Shinto priests, so the whole family must help out. Most of the weddings are Shinto, but for the funerals the Buddhists collect," Maki explained. The priest had disappeared into the inner shrine too holy for anyone but himself to enter, but we joined the wedding party already assembled in the outer shrine and tiptoed toward the back seats. Oka-san's wife, in a bright green overdress, was tuning the *koto*, a great harp so heavy it rested on the floor, and arranging drums in one corner of the open pavilion while the two daughters, dressed in full bright red skirts and white blouses, were putting the *sake*, the sacred wine, up on the altar. The altar was also piled high with *sakaki*, the evergreens that symbolized eternal life because the leaves had survived the death of winter.

Oka-san, emerging from the inner shrine, wore over his white robe another gorgeous robe of royal purple, then a third robe of gold whose wide sleeves were lined with orange; on his head the priestly headgear made him seem twice as tall as before. He reminded me of the Japanese print of a warrior I had at home on my living-room wall. He carried in his hand a wand from which hung *gohei*, white papers folded in a special way to make them into prayers. "The wand is because the god is too holy to be approached directly," Maki whispered. "The prayers are for the good life of the bride and groom."

Amid all this Oriental splendor, the bride wore a Western white wedding dress and veil, while the groom also was all dressed up in striped pants and a morning coat, rented for the occasion. But the parents of the wedding couple and the go-betweens wore rich dark kimonos. The *koto* wailed, the drum boomed, and one of the daughters whirled around the altar in the ceremonial dance, while the other daughter brought to the groom first (naturally), and then to the bride, tiny flat cups of the sacred wine from the altar.

"Three times three they drink. This is the most important part of the ceremony," Maki murmured. "Now they are married as when the minister says, 'I pronounce you husband and wife.'"

A strange thing happened then. The bride, in turning to accept the congratulations of her family, saw Maki, in her simple dark-blue dress that brought out the silver in her proud gray head, sitting in the back seat of the shrine. With a little cry of joy the bride came running down the aisle to bow low to her, murmuring in Japanese. Her new husband followed, then the whole wedding party, all bowing to Maki.

"What's the matter? What do they say?" I demanded.

"They say I do them honor, coming to their wedding." Maki was bowing back, the color warm in her cheeks. "She used to be one of my girls I taught in my school. They . . . they want me to be with them in their wedding picture."

This was the woman whom not only the Emperor Hirohito had decorated for her excellence in education, but also the wise, beloved citizen whom the whole city delighted to honor. As I watched them all clustering around her, I understood why Maki, the Japanese princess who had renounced her noble blood to marry the commoner she loved, would never be a humble democrat; her very genes forbade that. From a family trained for centuries in *noblesse oblige,* she understood that those to whom much had been given must also give much. She, from her wealthy father's noble household, had found new riches in the American democrat from Flagstaff, Arizona, who gave in his different way. But the same little luminous cross had taught them both how to love.

# CHAPTER 13

# "I Always Thought I'd Write a Book"

The helicopters roar over my head, ripping apart the peace of the serene countryside where the little thatched farmhouse stands placidly in the rice field. Suddenly there are bombs falling, guns, soldiers; the thatched roof goes up in flames, a woman screams, and there is appalling thunder.... The thunder is my Vietnamese room boy pounding on my hotel room door. "Madame! Is O.K.?" I come back from hell and call shakily, "Fine. I was just having a nightmare!" But that afternoon down on the Mekong Delta, as I sat helplessly watching, the nightmare had been real.

For hours, it seems, our plane has been circling round and round in the thick black cloud of the monsoon, waiting for a safe moment to land at Hong Kong's one airstrip for jets. The jagged peaks that guard the harbor are invisible, but thus all the more menacing. "We are going in!" The captain's Japanese voice on the intercom sounds tinny, muffled. "Our fuel is getting low. Please be sure your seat belts are tight. Take off all glasses and put a pillow before your face." And hold your breath, praying silently, "O God . . ."

Drifting off to well-earned sleep with the fragrance of the daphne you weeded this morning coming in your open bedroom window . . . The laborer is worthy of his hire of dreams.

The bare hospital room is very still except for Jock's heavy breathing. His shoulder is bare, thrusting out from the white sheet, so close I can reach out, touch the dear freckles still golden from the Spanish sun; but I cannot help him. Suddenly his breath stops altogether and so does mine. This, then, is the end? There is a tearing sound; he is breathing again! "It is the Cheyne-Stokes syndrome," the doctor says gently, his hand on my rigid shoulder. "It could go on for hours. Will you not come and rest a while?" How can I leave my beloved alone with the shadow of death crouching in the corner?

These are some of the scales I have had to practice long and painfully before I could play the terrible, beautiful, triumphant symphony of just going on living. Being born again is like the first birth, a lonesome solo. But always I have gone on writing, purging myself of joy and sorrow by putting them into words.

So when the inevitable lady in the flower hat comes up to me after I have finished speaking to an audience and gushes coyly, "I've always thought that when I had time . . . when the children are grown up and I'm not so busy . . . I'd write a book!" I just stare at her. Then I advise, "Sit right down and begin. If you can wait, you are not a writer." Laughter and tears, failure and triumph, diapers and the beard of the adolescent anxiously sprouting independence are equally grist for the writer who has a devil or an angel upon his shoulder, commanding, "Write!" The result may not be happy any more than intercourse always produces a healthy baby, but gestation of a book, once begun, is as inevitable as a nine-months pregnancy.

Writing, for me, has always been as necessary as breathing; I cannot live without it. My first verses (certainly not poetry) were published in the *Springfield Republican* when I was only eight (longer ago than I care to remember). I had been paddled out in a canoe on the river at night and had seen the moon upside down in the black water. I realized with wonder that the universe was not set in an immovable frame but that what I saw depended upon the angle from which I looked at it.

> Two men looked through prison bars,
> One saw mud but the other saw stars.

By the time I was a freshman at Boston University, I had had stories printed in several magazines and thought I was an author.

Dallas Lore Sharp, professor of freshman English, himself a backyard naturalist and author of note, soon cut me down to size.

English One was conducted in what was formerly the huge dissecting amphitheater of a medical school, and Sharp used to operate on the liver and lungs of our puny themes on the same spot where the aspiring medics formerly cut up their cadavers. Was he a surgeon! If even the skeleton of a plot survived the scalpel of his wit, the author was lucky; he plucked out flowery adjectives as if they were incipient cancers. "Verbs are alive and healthy," he used to insist. "If you want your narrative to have real guts, stick with nouns and verbs."

Like most teen-agers, I knew more than the Establishment, and to prove it, instead of taking my pen in hand, I turned in as my weekly theme a story which had already been printed in a magazine. When Sharp picked it up from the dissecting desk, I knew smugly that he was about to announce, "One of our class has had a story published!" Instead he slammed the magazine down upon the desk, lamenting, "Alas, this unhappy student has committed the crime in print so it will always be held against her!" He selected and read a paragraph that sounded treacly even to me.

" 'The Maiden's Prayer,' " Sharp commented acidly. "This story has more clichés than I knew existed. Why doesn't the author skip the pretty valentines and write about something earthy? Sunrise, poverty, rats?"

By this time I was shaking all over, I was so angry; I would have rushed from the amphitheater, but that would identify me as the perpetrator of this crime. When finally that terrible hour had crept by, I went out with the rest of the class, not even daring to pick up the magazine from the wastepaper basket where Sharp had tossed it. If my story was ripped into unrecognizable bits and pieces, so was I. For I had begun to suspect that what he had said was true, that this story was a clutch of clichés and I was no author.

"But I can write!" something cried inside me. "I must write. I'll show that butcher!"

I sat down in my splinter of a room at the YWCA—Boston University then had no dormitories for women—and grimly wrote the silent conversation between me and the cockroach that bustled out from under my radiator to stare hungrily at me. I told how he (or was it she?) and I felt, as comrades, low-down and dejected, until I offered my cockroach friend a crumb of cake, which he gobbled up and went happily back under his radiator. In my enclosing letter I said, "Thank you for showing me as I am. But couldn't you at least have offered me a crumb of comfort?" I mailed this cockroach masterpiece to Dallas Lore Sharp, and by return mail his answering letter came:

I know how Livingstone felt when Stanley discovered him in darkest Africa! Being a teacher is not easy. Do you think I would have treated you so ruthlessly unless I thought you could take it? That you were worth saving? Now both of us can get on with our jobs.

We became fast friends. Often when I was discouraged about a piece I couldn't quite get written as I wanted to, Sharp would pick up a pad of yellow paper and a pencil, hand them to me, and demand, "What exactly do you want to say? Say it and shut up." How many times I have repeated to myself that advice! I know no better rule of thumb for clean-cut writing.

What I want to say here on my yellow pad is simply this: a writer's life is gay, exciting, and very hard work. Nor is there much monetary reward unless one is a genius or, through a fluke of publishing, his book is the right one at the right moment and becomes a best seller. But if, when the book is finished, even one reader can say, surprised, "Why, that's true! It happened to me!" or can burst into a refreshing gale of laughter, the author has his reward. The nicest thing about being a merry widow writer is that you have already accepted the fact that life is unjust, insecure under the Damocles sword of atomic missiles, ghettos, and student riots. But you can still smile, if wryly. "If a nation stops laughing at its own infirmities, there is nothing left."

Even a funeral can have its humorous side. One rather ghoulish member of Dad's first country parish enjoyed attending funerals so much that she never missed one in our town whether she knew the deceased or not; whether he was Protestant, Jewish, or Catholic, she would sit on the front pew, swathed in black veils and weeping copiously. When she lost her own husband, she finally got the chance to manage her own family obsequies. She told the undertaker firmly, "Get lost. I'll take care of everything." She was so busy getting the relatives into the proper limousines, according to their closeness of kin, to ride to the cemetery, that she forgot the corpse. Dad had to help the undertaker heave the casket into the hearse, and the three of them—the undertaker, minister, and corpse— tagged along at the tail end of the procession.

Except for a bit of luck, Polly and I ourselves could have easily ended our earthly careers on that morning in Calcutta when we ventured to dispute the right of way with a Hindu sacred bull.

When I ran short of cash in New Delhi, Charles, who was one of the directors of the First National City Bank of New York, said, "That's easy. I'll just cable the manager of our Calcutta branch to let you cash a check on my account." But things do not move as fast in India as in the States; the cable company informed him, "There will be a small delay of three days in sending your wire."

"You can get there yourself before that," Charles told me, disgusted. "Hop the plane, Susie, and I'll go on trying to get in touch with Calcutta."

I had only ten dollars left in my purse when I met Polly in Calcutta, so early the following morning she and I hied ourselves down to the financial district. The bank was located in an imposing building, but we couldn't get up to the front door because an enormous white sacred bull was lying on the bottom step enjoying the morning sun, with his big wet nose at one end and his tail at the other end. In India one does not dispute the whims of a sacred bull lest he stir up the ire of Hindu fanatics, so at first we tried cajolery.

"Nice bull, good bull," Polly urged. "Please, move over!"

The bull merely glared haughtily at us. If we tried to by-pass his great horns, he shook them at us, and if we tried to step over his tail, he humped his huge rump. I wailed, "But I've got to get some cash! I'm practically penniless!"

"I'm certainly not going to be stymied by a cow, especially a Hindu one," Polly snapped. "You pull his tail while I push his nose a little. If he gives an inch, run like h . . . heck."

She did and I did and the bull was so startled that anyone dared disturb his imperial majesty that he actually did move down a little so we could leap by, make the safety of the bank's revolving door, which debouched us, gasping, onto the black-and-white marble floor. It seemed a strange way to cash a check. When we asked for the manager, he proved almost as uncooperative as the bull, for Charles's cable had still not arrived and how could a couple of middle-aged ladies just barge in to demand five hundred dollars?

"Listen," I pled, "I've known Charles and Miriam for twenty years. He's a director of your bank and he promised me . . ." No soap. I was just wondering how long I'd have to wash dishes to pay for my hotel when a messenger laid a flimsy paper on the manager's desk. "It's Charles's cable!" I surmised.

"Cash this lady's check immediately for her," the manager ordered the messenger. He excused himself. "If you ladies only knew how much grief that bull has caused us! When we first opened up, he used to walk right inside here and we couldn't manhandle him for fear of offending our Hindu customers. That's why we put in the revolving door."

"He probably just wanted to make a deposit," Polly surmised.

Amid roars of laughter we departed. The bull moved over of his own accord when he saw us coming.

But the tragic hunger on the streets of Calcutta soon dried the laughter on our lips. Not too long before we had arrived there, four million Hindu refugees had been catapulted into the city by the bloody battle between Hindus and Moslems which had resulted in the birth of Pakistan.

In spite of frantic efforts by the government and private agencies, it had proved impossible to feed and house this horde, so many were still starving upon the sidewalks as we passed by. Wrapped in their rags, apathetic and dirty, they did not even look up when we stepped over their bodies to get to the front door of our hotel where there were four doormen, each to let in his own kind, Brahman, Moslem, Buddhist, or Christian. Thus four men would eat that night.

Polly and I had been invited for dinner at the home of a pediatrician, trained at Harvard Medical School, who headed the Children's Hospital in Calcutta. They were a delightful family, the young doctor, the wife in her lovely, elaborately embroidered wedding sari, the two small children allowed to stay up to see what Americans looked like. The wife had learned at Cambridge not to put too sharp spices into the curry, so we ate hugely, and chatted about The Yard and Widener Library with its lavish million books. Our host drove us back to the hotel in his car. Looking at the voiceless, starving bodies lying there on the pavement, I felt suddenly like throwing up.

"I left enough of your good curry on my plate this evening to feed a family of four," I recalled bitterly. "I wish I had brought the scraps along."

He shrugged, this good man who spent his days and nights combating malnutrition and disease in sick children. He said, "If you had tried to give it away, they would have torn you to bits. A starving man has no manners."

I said bitterly to Polly as we went to our room, "I shall never come back to this terrible city again! Because I can't bear not doing anything! Why should we have everything and they nothing?"

Talk about prison bars and mud . . . where were the stars? Yet soon I was to discover an India reborn to dignity. Do you believe in miracles? When you've been caught up in one, as I was, you have to believe.

The miracle in New Delhi started out unhappily. A year later, on the afternoon of the day before I, alone, was to take the plane for Kathmandu, I went down to the hotel bar to get a cup of tea (India has "dry days" when even a glass of sherry may not be sold), slipped on a rug thrown carelessly over a low step down, and found I could not stand up again on my feet. So I phoned to Bishop Mondel, the head of the Methodist Church in Delhi, whom I had met on my former trip to the city, asking him to recommend a doctor. He sent me his own orthopedic surgeon.

"He's a Sikh!" As he stood there in my bedroom doorway, he was so tall his turban nearly touched the top of the door, but otherwise he was dressed like a Harley Street specialist, striped pants and a morning coat. "I wonder if he really knows his stuff?" I thought anxiously.

He examined my ankle and said briskly, "We need an x-ray for this. I think it's broken." He smiled at my grimace of dismay. "Don't worry. I studied at Tulane University."

"The hotel doesn't have a wheelchair . . ."

"Put your arm around my neck and hop," he ordered.

As I hopped down the corridor on my good leg, my arm around the neck of the tall Sikh, the people we met in the corridor looked startled, but we made it to the elevator. As I hopped by the desk in the marble-floored lobby, the clerk held out a telephone receiver.

"Mrs. Fletcher, the American Embassy is calling."

"Bishop Mondel says you're in trouble," a pleasant voice said. "Is there anything we can do to help?"

"Not right now," I said gratefully. "But if my ankle turns out to be broken, I'll probably need some crutches."

"We have them in all sizes. Just give us a ring and a Marine will bring a pair over. How tall are you?"

I told her and rang off, and the doctor's little car tore down the busy street, dodging pedestrians and cows as we roared off to X-ray. The ankle had a bad crack and a ligament was torn off the bone.

"Thank heaven, I won't have to clump in a cast all over the Himalayas," I said hopefully. "I'm taking the plane for Kathmandu tomorrow."

"Indeed? Who said you wouldn't need a cast?" demanded the doctor. "These torn ligaments can be the devil if they're not protected. I am driving you to my hospital."

"I'm taking up an awful lot of your time," I protested uneasily. "I know you have a big clinic."

"That's what I'm here for."

It took another half-hour to get to the hospital, and as we drove, the doctor told me he had just been married to the pediatrician there and she wanted to meet me. By the time we got to the hospital lobby, my ankle hurt so badly that I heaved a sigh of relief as the doctor lifted me onto the waiting stretcher. "I'll give you a pain shot," he promised. Through the haze of my relief I watched him prepare the sticky pile of plaster and water so deftly that he didn't get a speck of white on his immaculate striped pants. He invited his wife in to talk with me and she proved so amusing that I forgot to groan.

Finally the doctor stood back, satisfied.

"I've given you an especially sturdy walking cast, since you have to travel."

"How soon will it dry? So I can walk?"

"About twenty-four hours. You'll need crutches at first."

"Then call the American Embassy, please. A Marine is standing by to bring me some."

"It will not be necessary to call out the Marines!" The Sikh doctor drew himself up to his full height. "I am taking care of you!"

"Oh, thank you," I murmured weakly as he handed me my crutches.

The doctor further announced that he and his wife would drive me back to my hotel. When I protested that I could take a taxi, he explained, "We've been married only six weeks. The only time we have together is what we snatch from the clinic." Who was I to come between bride and groom? As we neared my hotel, I wanted desperately to tumble into bed and rest, but the least I could do was to offer them hospitality. So I asked if they'd like to come up to my room for a cup of tea.

They would, thank you; only it would have to be fruit juice. Oh dear, I'd forgotten they were Hindus. Was it skipping a point for them to eat with me, a Christian? I was sure of this when I saw the wife quietly take apart a sandwich to be sure it was orthodox before she ate it with her lemonade. The friendly tea party went on and on till I could have screamed with pain and fatigue, so finally I asked briskly, "You must tell me, Doctor . . . how much do I owe you?"

"Since you are an American, there will be no charge."

"But . . . but . . . that isn't right! You've spent nearly all day with me and you're a busy man with a clinic, a big hospital . . ."

He drew himself up until he looked as tall as India. "America has been so good to me and to my country I am glad to be able to repay a little. It is my pleasure."

They were grateful to the United States! They truly liked us! The shock was so great they were gone before I recovered, and, in any case, what more was there to say except thank you? I could have sung "The Star-Spangled Banner," even the high part where I usually squeak. This doctor and his wife were, of course, only two straws in the great haystack that is India, but straws can show the way the wind blows. Maybe it's worth a billion or two to discover that, more often than we read in the news media, the warm wind of friendship from the developing countries blows the way of the richest nation in the world as it tries to share its resources in a bumbling, awkward, adolescent way. The miracle that happened to me in New Delhi was that I learned for the first time how blessed it is to accept as well as to give.

The invisible friends a writer makes through his "fan mail" are frequently more real than those he meets in the flesh, for the letter more often reveals the writer's inner self than casual conversation does. Some spark in what the author has written must have exploded upon contact to make a stranger take pen in hand. Whether the message comes printed in pencil on lined paper by a grade-school pupil who has enjoyed *Preacher's Kids,* or on the sophisticated expensive notepaper of a famous psychiatrist in Beverly Hills, California, discussing my "kid book," *What's Right With Our Young People,* or in an aerogram from Bangkok or New Zealand, I always answer personally. Whether the letter writer approves or disapproves makes small difference; or perhaps he only covets the stamps from my overseas mail, or has traced his family tree to prove we are related through Adam. The significant fact is that we have made contact over the miles that separate us. Strangely, there is no generation gap. Many thoughtful teen-agers write to discuss an idea, pro and con, and one fifteen-year-old reviewed "the kid book" for an international wire service.

The most poignant letter came to me from a preacher's wife who was sitting beside her very ill husband while she read aloud to him *In My Father's House,* the story of my dad and mother loving and laughing together in a parsonage similar to their own.* She wrote:

> I am sitting beside my husband's hospital bed reading, with him saying, "Why, that's just like us! Remember . . ." Your book gives my husband so many chuckles and tears that he forgets his bitter pain. We have six sons, also in the ministry, to each of whom my husband wants to give a copy of this book. Your American publisher says his edition is exhausted and we do not have much time left. Is there anywhere

*In My Father's House.* McGraw-Hill, New York, N. Y., 1955.

else we could buy six copies? I would appreciate this so much . . .

I wrote at once, airmail, asking my publisher in London to rush her six copies of the English edition and to send me the bill. She thanked me when they arrived. At the end of the year when my accounting came, my publisher had not charged me for the books either. Thus does the world salute the brave who step confidently from this life to the next.

I shall never be a millionaire in anything but memories, and this pleases me. Thank heaven, I still have to write to eat so have no time to "enjoy ill health." Nor will I grow old for fear the TV master of ceremonies will call me something worse than a schoolteacher! As a matter of fact, many merry widows have never been married. I met one such gay spinster widow at Phnom Penh airport in Cambodia recently. For years I have wanted to visit the magnificent Khmer ruins there, the gems of a lost civilization. Each time I call up my travel agent to route me to the Orient, I always say, "This time I *am* going to Angkor Wat!" Once I even had reservations but found the Cambodian border closed when I arrived. On another occasion some friends, caught in the war emergency, had to charter a plane for $600 to fly them out of Siem Reap and had arrived at my hotel in India so bedraggled and exhausted it did not seem a good time to pay even a temple a visit. Usually I was traveling under pressure of a due date for the printer and could not spare the time. This last trip, I had to interview in nine countries in six weeks and was exasperated when my plane stopped for an hour at Phnom Penh, but I could not get off.

It was a fiercely hot July day; even the plane panted, waiting. A middle-aged lady got on, dropped, breathless and dripping with perspiration, into the seat beside mine, and kicked off her dusty shoes. She gasped, "I've waited for thirty years to see Angkor Wat, the temple I've been teaching my classes about from the *National Geographic.* Well, I've seen its thousand stone elephants, snakes a mile long, and Buddhas hacked out of the jungle but still smiling . . . I wouldn't go back into that furnace for a million dollars! But I wouldn't have missed seeing this if it costs me ten years in a nursing home!" She wriggled her aching toes in her stockings with runs in them and grinned at me. "Old age is a pest. You got to treat it with DDT . . . disdain, drollery, and thumb your nose at it!"

If this spinster schoolteacher wasn't a merry widow, I never met one. The spirit of adventure, the savoring of life . . .

I felt a similar identification with a Chinese girl in a patched red jacket when I went with S. Y. Lee to a country church near Hong Kong one cloudy Easter morning. He had phoned to say that he was preaching the sermon in a chapel in the New Territories and that Michael and Sylvia were driving up with him. Didn't I want to go along? Easter was no day to spend alone. Thunder was rolling among the dark hills, and soon long silver spears of rain began to fall as we whizzed over the slippery, wet roads. The racket on the tin roof of the little church with no glass in the windows, where S. Y. deposited his children and me while he went to get on his Anglican robe, was so loud it all but drowned out the cries of small children running up and down the aisles, yelling till their parents reached out to yank them into chairs and comparative quiet.

"What a big congregation, every seat taken!" I marveled to Michael. "Just like Easter at home, where some people go to church only once a year. Or maybe at Christmas."

"It's not piety," Michael whispered back. He pointed to large baskets of colored Easter eggs at the doorway.

"Everyone gets an egg after the service."

"That's nice."

"You don't understand. It isn't just fun. *Today everyone is sure to eat.*"*

This was hungry China. Would they take in enough in the collection plates to pay for the eggs? But there weren't any spears stacked by the church door as there had been last Easter at the Masai tin chapel in Kenya where they had prayed for my "grand safari." Still they were singing the same hymns there, and back home in our little chapel in Sudbury, and here in China, where the foot-pumped little organ gasped and squeaked.

The Anglican church processional with S. Y., the local Chinese minister, and the choir boys and girls in their blue robes was familiar enough, as was indeed the hymn we all rose to sing. "Christ the Lord is risen today, Allelujah!" I twisted my hymn book this way and that. Did one read Chinese from left to right, up or down, or both? I compromised by keeping silent while they sang the verse in Chinese, but came in strong on *Allelujah!* I have a high, strong voice and I must have sung with an American accent, for heads turned to stare at me; I was attracting attention, I'd better shut up. So the next verse around I didn't sing. But Michael dug into my ribs with his elbow, insisting, "Allelujah!" He didn't want me left out of Easter. So I bellowed away obediently, punctuating all the endless verses.

Since I couldn't understand a word of S. Y.'s sermon, which he had told me concerned the prodigal son, I made up a sermon of my own. "The prodigal son went to a far country . . ." Who would ever have dreamed a few years ago I would be spending Easter in China? . . . "But when he came to himself, he said, I will go unto my Father . . ." But I was already there, I thought, looking around at the intent, high-boned Chinese faces. Christ had also been an

*"Easter Shopping in Hong Kong," *Christian Herald*, April 1965.

Oriental. I remembered a painting I had seen in a Hong Kong shopwindow of "The Flight Into Egypt" which had pictured Mary, Joseph, and the Baby setting out from the shore in a sampan to paddle to Egypt. Well, why not? It made as much sense as the American baby doll lying in a plastic manger under a German Christmas tree in my Methodist parsonage childhood.

"Amen and amen," chanted the choir. Both S. Y.'s and my silent sermon were ended. As the recessional disappeared, with one accord the congregation rushed for the egg baskets. One small boy was so greedy he dropped the shell on the church floor, stuffed the egg whole into his mouth, choked, and had to be pounded on the back. Fortunately the baskets were empty by the time I got there, for I had noticed that the eggs seemed to be dyed pink all the way through.

"The minister has asked us to take tea at his home," Michael announced, so I followed the children down the long, low concrete apartment building to the proper entrance. There were windows only at each end of the long room, crowded with the minister and his family as well as with all the church officials, but there was light enough to see that every face was anxious, turned toward the treasurer counting the cash in the collection plate.

"Is something wrong?" I asked S. Y., but he was counting, too, and made no answer. Next to him stood the minister's little girl, a shy child with fine dark hair like Suet Fah's, with a yellow patch on the elbow of her best red jacket. I remembered how embarrassed I had been when I was rushed to the hospital for an emergency appendectomy—I was eight—and the nurse had looked at my ragged underwear and sniffed, "Your mother must have dressed you in a hurry!" Mother never had time to darn our clothes; perhaps she didn't want to. Dad, who had loved Mother since she was six, had explained, "Your mother mends other people's lives instead of underwear." This atmosphere of gloom was getting me down. I insisted again, "Is anything the matter?"

"No," the little minister answered me too loudly, almost defiantly. "Allelujah!"

S. Y. told me finally, under his breath, that every Easter until now the Anglican churches of Hong Kong, large and small, had pooled their offerings so that each church received the same amount. But the larger churches had protested helping to support the smaller country chapels, so that this year the local minister got only whatever his congregation put into the plate. The treasurer made an announcement in Chinese, the minister's little girl whimpered, and her father reproved her sharply.

"How much did they get? Less than last year?" I demanded. "What is the little girl saying?"

"Thirty dollars. Last year it was a hundred. The preacher's daughter asked, 'How, then, shall we eat?' but her father told her, 'Peace, child, can you not trust the Lord to provide?'"

How many times I had heard those same words from my dad . . . I reached into my handbag for my traveler's checks, signed a couple, and handed them to the treasurer. His face lighted up . . . Who says Orientals are inscrutable? . . . He cried, "It is a miracle! She has made up the difference from last year!" He rushed for his record book, his pen poised, and asked excitedly, "What name shall I write for this wonderful gift?"

"From another preacher's kid," I murmured.*

The money did not matter, but maybe this was a miracle after all; the little Chinese minister's prayer had been answered before it was uttered. Who could know that a strange "rich" American would be in that country congregation that morning? Certainly not I, nor the minister, for S. Y.'s invitation had been a last-minute one. How could an ugly Tiffany lamp in a parsonage in Worcester, Massachu-

*Ibid.*

setts, light up a dark little rectory in far-off China? Perhaps there *were* more things in heaven and earth than this world dreams of.

After four trips around the world, exploring and writing about the Orient, discovering everywhere friends of like heart and mind, I do not find it hard to believe in six impossible things before breakfast, in a viable warm understanding between nations, East and West. I do not take much stock in people who shout, "Believe as I do or you'll go to hell!" Like modern youth, I question all creeds except that of kindness. Hell might prove a lot more ecumenical than an exclusive heaven, whether Moslem, Buddhist, or Christian. Dr. Albert Einstein also drew up his own creed, as simple and majestic as he was—is. He explained, "It is enough for me to contemplate the mystery of conscious life perpetuating itself through all eternity."

I want merely freedom to be myself and to allow the other fellow to be himself; then perhaps we can talk to each other over the back fences that separate us. Is this too much to ask? Of course it is. But reaching for the unattainable stretches the muscles of both mind and spirit, may yet take us to the stars. Meanwhile, I shall go on being "a chile amang ye, takin' notes."

There are five-talent authors, two-talent writers, and scribblers like me who have not buried my one talent in a napkin through lack of humility, but because I cannot; writing is as much a part of me as my two eyes and feet. As Elizabeth Barrett Browning, a five-talent poet, wrote to her beloved before they were married, "Like to write? Of course I do. I seem to live while I write ... it is life, for me. Why, what is to live? Not to eat, drink and breathe ... but to feel the life in you down all the fibres of being, passionately and joyfully."*

*\* The Love Letters of Robert Browning and Elizabeth Barrett.* Selected by V. E. Stack. William Heinemann Ltd., London, Eng., 1969.

It is proof of the divine spark within us that while each man and woman, black, white, yellow, or cream-colored, has within himself his own heaven and hell, he may at least choose his own attitude toward the genes or the circumstances into which he has, willy-nilly, been born. At any age he can decide to be born again, knowing that growth is possible until death. Perhaps afterward?

Jock and I had as usher in our wedding party in 1924 a Harvard Medical School graduate who was later convicted of murder and, being of unsound mind, was given a life sentence in a hospital for the criminally insane. Here, after treatment, he recovered his mental health and did such competent research in tuberculosis among the other inmates that he was pardoned by the governor of the state and his council. Later his doctor's license to practice medicine was restored to him. This brave man voluntarily gave the rest of his life to treating other prisoners in the hospital jail—as he said, "The most pitiful wretches in the world, drug addicts, hopeless alcoholics, rejects from a smug society, my friends"—where he had been confined for twenty-five years. When he died, the entire staff, doctors, administrators, and prisoners, contributed to having his portrait painted and hung over the hospital entrance as a memorial because they had loved him.

A lack of citizens concerned for such rejects from society is one of today's most dangerous threats to our national stability, for, in a democracy, unless each man accepts his own responsibility for his neighbor, the result is more crime and panic. Similarly, each individual must decide for himself whether old age shall be a swamp of self-pity or a takeoff pad to new adventure.

The jewel that many years can give is awareness—*you know when you are happy.* When you are a child, happiness is a red balloon, a lollipop, a tinsel Santa on the Christmas tree. Later it is being one of the gang, whether

it's the groovy generation wearing girl's hair and twang-
ing a monotonous guitar or, as I did, dancing the Charles-
ton on the old Brunswick Hotel roof with Chula from
Bangkok. This is the first bright young "gimme" self. In
the second life of marriage and motherhood, passion
grows into something bigger; like the Tibetan god on my
*tonka,* this love is so holy it has no name, yet is compassionate. A child is born, a twig on the family tree which
has become, at last, rooted in reality. But sunset is as sure
as dawning; the second day dies too.

In the third life you discover the dreadful ache of loneli-
ness that must be filled. Children leave home and your
beloved goes behind the last curtain; you're alone, bewildered, sick, walking on one leg. But not finished. The sun
still shines to warm your back, the rosy daphne in your
garden still smells sweet. You are free to follow the call to
a new world, whether discovered in your own backyard
or on the back side of the moon. Then, as you walk down
a strange street, a child, black, white, or yellow, calls,
frightened, "Where are you? I need you!" and slides his
hand into yours and is safe. In the lilt of his laughter,
suddenly you *know* that you are needed and happy for
this moment, this tiny instant. But it is enough, for time is
not measured by the tick of a clock but in heartbeats.

You collect, like many-colored jade cool in your hand,
the lovely places you have seen—sunset flaming on the
high snows in Kathmandu in the Himalayas; sea water
warm against your fingers trailing from the tiny sampan,
a chip in the vast South China Sea; a garden in Singapore
where the air smells of jasmine; a slow fan swaying in
Penang in a room full of dreams and the lisp of a silver sea;
night in the bright, jeweled harbor in Hong Kong under
the dark shadow of Red China's barren, brooding hills; an
emerald Buddha in a Bangkok temple full of peace and
the slipping orange shadows of priests; the opalescent
glory of the setting sun seen through the smoke of a thou-

sand cow-dung supper fires in New Delhi. You rediscover the Garden of Eden on a hot, golden afternoon in Africa when, from your car, you watch a tawny lioness lick her cubs beneath a thorn tree and giraffes with movie-star eyelashes nibble the tops of acacias. Here even the silence has velvet feet—suddenly an impossible elephant is standing there, raising his curious trunk and flapping his ears like the great wings of an archangel. Such days I have known! A homesick night when a great airship lands, with the Stars and Stripes emblazoned on its side, so that I am home again and comforted. A Chinese child kneeling within the circle of my arm while we pray together, "For Thine is the kingdom and the power and the glory . . ."

Welcome to my world!

**DATE DUE**